D0939964

STATE LEGITIMACY
AND DEVELOPMENT
IN AFRICA

STATE LEGITIMACY AND DEVELOPMENT IN AFRICA

Pierre Englebert

LYNNE
RIENNER
PUBLISHERS

BOULDER
LONDON

Paperback edition published in the United States of America in 2002 by
Lynne Rienner Publishers, Inc.
1800 30th Street, Boulder, Colorado 80301
www.rienner.com

and in the United Kingdom by
Lynne Rienner Publishers, Inc.
3 Henrietta Street, Covent Garden, London WC2E 8LU

Published in hardcover in 2000.

© 2000 by Lynne Rienner Publishers, Inc. All rights reserved

ISBN 1-58826-131-X (pbk. : alk. paper)

Printed and bound in the United States of America

The paper used in this publication meets the requirements
of the American National Standard for Permanence of
Paper for Printed Library Materials Z39.48-1984.

5   4   3   2

À ma mère, Hélène Van Campenhoudt,
pour m'avoir donné le goût de l'étude

À ma tante, Marie-Thérèse Van Campenhoudt,
pour avoir apporté le Tiers-Monde dans notre maison

Contents

Tables and Figures

TABLES

FIGURES

Acknowledgments

This book began as dissertation research in the Political Economy and Public Policy Program at the University of Southern California. It benefited from the knowledge, insights, and interest of what I can only call the dream team of Ph.D. committees: Jeffrey Nugent (chair), Laurie Brand, C. R. D. Halisi, William Rideout, and James Robinson. I am very grateful to them and to Faride Motamedi, who has kept together over the years a remarkable interdisciplinary graduate program in political economy. They helped make my time at USC a most intellectually stimulating and rewarding period.

Along the way I received insightful feedback and helpful suggestions from many other persons whom I also wish to thank, while simultaneously exonerating their responsibility; these include Hayward Alker, Paule Bouvier, Deborah Brautigam, Robin Brooks, Nauro Campos, Steve Conroy, Francis Deng, Carol Graham, Jon Isham, Saori Katada, Michael Kevane, Peter Lewis, Terrence Lyons, Mike Mochizuki, Sandra Morales, John Odell, Mancur Olson, Meghan O'Sullivan, James Ron, Samira Salem, Michael Schatzberg, Howard Shatz, Alice Sindzingre, Richard Sklar, Thierry van Bastelaer, Nicolas van de Walle, Quang Vuong, Michel Welmond, Stephanie Wolters, Crawford Young, and August Zajonc.

I am also grateful for the opportunities I have had to present and discuss portions of this book at the Department of Economics at the University of Southern California; the Department of Political Science at Georgia State University; the Department of Politics and the International Relations Colloquium at Pomona College; the Institutional Reform and Informal Sector Center at the University of Maryland at College Park; the Foreign Policy Studies Program and Center for Social and Economic Dynamics at the Brookings

Institution; the School of Politics and Economics at the Claremont Graduate University; and meetings of the African Studies Association, American Economic Association, American Political Science Association, International Studies Association, Western Economic Association International, and the Western Political Science Association.

Despite all the intellectual support I received, there would be no book without funding for my research. For this I am grateful to the Graduate School at the University of Southern California, the John Randolph Haynes and Dora Haynes Foundation, Phi Beta Kappa of Southern California, the USC Center for International Studies, and the Brookings Institution. While at Brookings, I received kind and efficient help from the library personnel under the direction of Susan McGrath.

I have been in the Department of Politics at Pomona College since the fall of 1998, where I have found a congenial, supportive, and enriching environment in which to teach and do research. I thank my colleagues in the department as well as my students. Among the latter, I owe a special debt to Jerry Yang, my research assistant, for his diligence and problem-solving skills, and to Christina Guerrero, who artfully drew the maps for Chapter 5. Patrick Brilliant, Mahvish Jaffri, Peter Neva, and Keeley Wynne helped with proofreading the manuscript.

I dedicate this book to my mother, Hélène Van Campenhoudt, who relentlessly promoted to us the value of education at the expense of her time and income, and to my aunt, Marie-Thérèse Van Campenhoudt, who, with her Parisian hostel for immigrant women, gave me a first window into the developing world. Finally, I thank my wife, Beth Bodnar, for her advice, support, loving companionship, and for the sheer joy of our life together; and our sons, Luke and Tom, for bringing dinosaurs and candy back into my life.

—*Pierre Englebert*

I

Introduction

For anyone who cares about development, Africa is a painfully enduring puzzle. Since 1960, Africans have seen their income rise by less than one-half of a percent per year, leaving the continent with the worst development record and the highest concentration of countries with negative growth of all regions in the world (Figure 1.1).[1] As a result, many Africans are worse off now, after some spent forty years of independent rule, than they were in the 1960s, after about seventy years of colonization. External shocks and the international economic environment certainly have not spared Africa, but that alone cannot explain its lack of performance. Other countries and regions of the world have faced similar external constraints at one time or another, and neither droughts, civil wars, nor volatile terms of trade are unique to Africa. In fact, there is now a broad consensus that what has most distinguished Africa from the rest of the world over the last three-and-a-half decades is the weak *capacity* of its states to respond to environmental, external, and other supply shocks and to design appropriate policies and institutions for growth.[2] Surprisingly, however, as well documented as Africa's propensity for bad policies and poor governance may be, there is as yet no consensus as to what intrinsic quality makes African countries inimical to developmental capacity.[3]

There are, however, increasingly frequent claims that Africa's poor policies and weak institutions derive from a purported lack of norms of trust and civic participation that elsewhere are believed to improve prospects for development by making states more accountable to societies. The weight of African traditions, some argue, stifles the emergence of associative life, and its parochial lifestyles prevent the spread of trust in society.[4] In a word, Africa is allegedly short of

Figure 1.1   Per Capita Real GDP Growth by Region, 1960 (or independence if later) to 1992 (or most recent estimate)

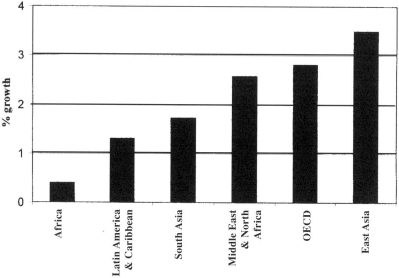

Source: Heston and Summers (1991).
Note: OECD, Organization for Economic Cooperation and Development.

"social capital."[5] In a somewhat germane argument, others suggest that the problem with Africa lies in its ethnic heterogeneity. They reason that ethnically heterogeneous societies display polarized political systems. In such systems, ethnic leaders play the game of national politics with little else in mind than the interests of their own ethnic group. Their ethnic bias leads them to adopt inefficient policies aimed at redistributing the resources of the state to their constituent group and to neglect growth-promoting policies based on a rational economic calculus. In other words, the politicians' emphasis on the size of their ethnic slice leads to a shrinking of the national pie.[6]

As useful as these two new approaches have been, their relevance has been hampered by their failure to account for an often overlooked empirical feature of Africa. Africa's average development performance may have been dismal, but some of its countries have actually achieved significant and sustained takeoff, growing in some cases at rates more often associated (until recently) with the economies of East Asia (Figure 1.2). In fact, Botswana had the fastest rate of economic growth of all the countries in the world

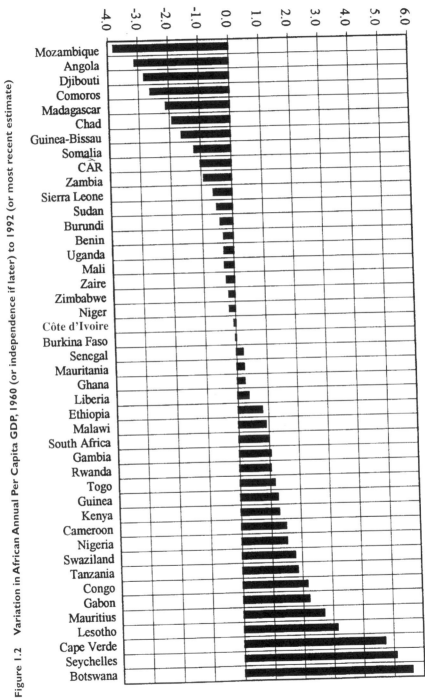

Figure 1.2   Variation in African Annual Per Capita GDP, 1960 (or independence if later) to 1992 (or most recent estimate)

Source: Heston and Summers (1991).
Note: CAR, Central African Repbulic.

between 1960 and 1985 (World Bank 1993). It is not obvious at first what distinguishes these African success stories from the rest of the continent—some are islands and some are not; some have resources and some do not; some have embraced state-centered approaches to development and some have not. They do not appear, however, to be significantly different from their counterparts in terms of either civic culture or ethnic heterogeneity.[7] Africa's broad range of economic performance therefore casts a shadow of doubt over the prevailing explanations of its average stagnation. If there is something about being an African country that is inimical to growth, the fast-growing African countries suggest that it is either not generalized or it can be overcome. It behooves us to identify what truly differentiates these African success stories from the rest of the continent, in order to shed light on what differentiates Africa in general from the rest of the world.

Bearing in mind that each specific country faces a set of numerous conditions that affect its economic performance, in this book I hope to single out one factor and provide a joint—but still partial—explanation of both stagnation and growth in Africa. The essence of my argument relates the developmental capacity of states to their degree of historical legitimacy. Because I will use the terms *developmental capacity, state,* and *legitimacy* on many occasions, I clarify my usage of them immediately.

1. *Developmental capacity* refers to the capacity of governments to design and implement policies for growth and to provide good governance to their societies and markets. Good governance, in turn, involves the creation and maintenance of accountable and efficient institutions. Taking some liberties, I will often refer to good governance and institutional quality interchangeably.

2. *State* is a broader concept than *government* or *regime* and also includes the territory, laws, the bureaucratic and military apparatus, and some ideological justification of the state's existence.

3. In this book, a state is *legitimate* when its structures have evolved endogenously to its own society and there is some level of historical continuity to its institutions. State legitimacy is thus a historical, structural condition of the entire state apparatus. As used here, the concept of legitimacy does not imply a normative judgment about the moral righteousness of states. Nor does it matter whether a government is just, democratic, inclusive, popular, or otherwise accountable to its citizens. In fact, I use the phrase *state legitimacy*

rather than legitimacy alone to convey these differences from the usual concept of political legitimacy.

I begin my argument by highlighting the "imported" origins of many African states, instruments of colonization abandoned by their creators and often appropriated by new domestic political elites upon independence. I show how this genesis has tended to create structures that conflict with preexisting political institutions, underlying norms of political behavior, and customary sources of political authority. These new African states are not the endogenous creations of local history. They are not embedded in domestic power relations. They lack legitimacy.

Leaders of these states face a peculiar challenge and are also limited in the options available to them to address it. Their challenge is to acquire sufficient hegemony over their society in order to stabilize and routinize their power. But they find it difficult to use developmental policies and institutions to generate support for themselves, as these require a level of bureaucratic loyalty and a degree of supply response from private agents, which their states lack to begin with. Hence, these leaders are more likely to resort to patronage, nepotism, corruption, and other patterns of political behavior that are occasionally subsumed under the category of *neopatrimonialism*.[8] These policies knit the fabric of an instrumental legitimacy for the state by substituting patron-client links for its lack of moral foundations. In the process, the modern state is reduced to a merely instrumental role, a set of resources that rulers use to foster their power: fiscal revenues are distributed to create networks of political support as rulers personally appropriate public funds to finance political allegiance; employment at the service of the state is used as a means of patronage; public investments follow political rather than economic rationales; and trade and pricing distortions are introduced to create rents and vested interests. The state's capacity to provide robust institutions and to design and implement policies that favor growth suffers as a result. Bureaucracies turn into ghostly institutions. Eventually, the rule of law vacillates, as does the trust of citizens in their institutions. As respect for institutions diminishes, corruption spreads. Private agents, domestic and foreign, stay away from such volatile economic environments. Investments dry up, and both households and firms seek refuge in informal activities. Altogether, the economy stagnates while the very logic of the system makes it resistant to reform.

This, in a nutshell, is the political dimension of economic stagnation in Africa.[9] Certainly, low-legitimacy states are not unique to Africa, but their concentration in the continent is unique among all regions of the world and accounts in part for the differential in economic performance between Africa and the rest of the world. Within Africa, however, there have been variations in the extent to which the imported state has conflicted with preexisting institutions or has been historically endogenized by local elites. Some countries were either never truly colonized or they witnessed a co-option of the postcolonial state by the remnants of precolonial institutions—modernized offspring of customary systems, some of which escaped the colonial era less scathed than others. These conditions reduced the potential for conflicts of allegiance between postcolonial and precolonial institutions. In some island-states, there were no precolonial human settlements and therefore no preexisting institutions to conflict with the postcolonial state. In all these cases and a few others, politicians had less need to use the state as an instrument for building political hegemony. Free from the constraint of acting as a resource to fledgling political elites, these states have therefore been able to play a developmental role, to provide better governance to markets, and to show greater capacity to shape economic outcomes in a growth-oriented fashion. Hence, while the low average level of state legitimacy in Africa contributes to its weak average performance, the variations in the extent to which the postcolonial state does violence to precolonial relations of authority within Africa have led to different strategies of power that, in turn, have significantly contributed to variations in economic performance among African countries.

My central argument, therefore, is one of power, with elites choosing policies as a function of their respective power payoffs. These payoffs, in turn, depend on the degree of legitimacy of the state. When there is minimal conflict between precolonial and postcolonial political structures, leaders find greater power payoffs from choosing policies and forging institutions that foster development. Freer from the immediate imperatives of coercing support for building hegemony, they are able to "deliver the goods," and their existing legitimacy is further enhanced by the efficiency of their policies. But under conditions of weak initial state legitimacy, bureaucrats are insufficiently loyal to the state and private agents distrust its institutions. This raises the relative returns, for the elites, of neopatrimonialism over developmental statehood. In my analysis, neopatrimonialism is not an African cultural feature but rather the equilibrium outcome of a set of historical conditions, which I characterize as state illegitimacy. My approach to Africa's development crisis is neither culturally deterministic, nor predicated upon a diagnosis of leadership failure.[10] Rather, it is a structural theory in which political actors respond rationally to the historical constraints they have inherited. As J. Samuel and Arturo Valenzuela argued some twenty years ago about the assumptions of dependency theory with respect to political elites in "core" and "periphery" countries: "What varies is not the degree of rationality, but the structural foundations of the incentive systems which, in turn, produce different forms of behavior given the same process of rational calculus" (1978:266).

By differentiating levels of state legitimacy between Africa and the rest of the world and also within Africa, I offer a theory that is relevant both to Africa's average stagnation and to variations in economic performance and developmental capacity within Africa. This theory also demonstrates there is nothing intrinsically African about the region's overall performance. As such, it has potential explanatory power in other parts of the world as well. This is, therefore, more than a book about Africa. It uses Africa to better understand how the nature of the state affects policy choices and development prospects worldwide.

Others before me have highlighted the transplanted nature of the African state, and my work owes much to them.[11] The distinguishing feature of my theory is its explicit consideration of the match between precolonial and postcolonial institutions as the determinant of the power conundrum of postcolonial elites and its consequent capacity to account for variations in performance within Africa (and to some extent, within other regions). Another dimension of my work is that, unlike other discussions of the legacy of colonialism, it provides a formal quantitative treatment of the available evidence. Quantifying state legitimacy may seem unreasonable to some. Yet by looking at the specific history of each country of the world, one can decide whether its state represents the outcome of an endogenous process of institutional evolution or is more akin to an institutional transplant. On this simple basis, I have created a measure of state legitimacy, capturing the degree to which contemporary state institutions evolved endogenously to society or were imported and, in the latter case, the extent to which such imported institutions clash with preexisting relations of authority. The resulting variable captures what Kalevi Holsti has called *vertical legitimacy,* an estimate of the strength of the relationship "between society and political institutions" (1996:97). Although this approach will sometimes fail to capture the idiosyncracies of some episodes of state formation, this is a cost that is practically inherent to the process of aggregation involved in quantitative analysis. This cost must be weighted against the ability of quantitative analysis to measure an average trend for the whole world, something that country case studies alone would miss. It is also alleviated by frequent additions to my discussion of country-specific qualitative evidence.

Vertical legitimacy, or the quality of the relation between society and political institutions, is a crucial dimension of overall state legitimacy. Another one, no less important, is the level of agreement on what constitutes the polity—the politically defined community that underlies the state. Borders, which delineate and differentiate polities, provide another critical measure of the legitimacy of states. Of course, to a certain extent borders are everywhere arbitrary. Yet they are particularly so in Africa, where they often were drawn by colonial powers as a function of colonial imperatives rather than with respect to the political and social realities on the ground.[12] Based on these peculiar historical origins, it is possible to measure the extent to which the boundaries of contemporary African states clash with those of preexisting political institutions and, thereby, to further differentiate levels of state legitimacy across Africa. I did this by creating a variable that measures the percentage of an African country's population belonging to an ethnic group partitioned by colonial borders. The greater this proportion, the more arbitrary the postcolonial state vis-à-vis precolonial institutions, and the weaker its legitimacy.

Ethnicity is of course itself a fluid concept and an unreliable source of identity or institutional affiliation. The reliability of ethnic identity is, however, of relatively little importance to my work to the extent that I use it only as a proxy for precolonial institutions to assess the arbitrariness of the borders of contemporary states. If an ethnic group exists on both sides of a contemporary border, then no matter how intense the ethnic identity, the border cuts across a preexisting area of common political culture. Calling again upon Holsti's (1996) useful terminology, I refer to this as *horizontal legitimacy,* or the extent to which there is agreement about what constitutes the polity or the community that comprises the state. In other words, whereas vertical legitimacy may refer to the presence of a consensus on the content of the social contract, horizontal legitimacy implies an agreement about who participates in the contract negotiations. It establishes a link between the population and the territory of a state.

I use these two variables, together with many other ones usually associated with growth, policy choices, and institutional quality, in a set of cross-sectional regressions and other statistical procedures, in order to assess their developmental effects worldwide and within

Africa. My data set covers more than one hundred countries from 1960 (or the year of independence, whichever comes later) up to 1992. The results indicate that state legitimacy favors developmental capacity and growth, and that policy choices and the quality of governance and institutions are the main variables mediating these effects. Altogether, the economies of historically legitimate states grow more than 2 percent faster than those of their nonlegitimate counterparts, as measured by annual changes in their per capita gross domestic product (GDP). This amounts to about 40 percent of the growth differential between Africa and the fastest growing economies of East Asia over the same period. Furthermore, controlling for state legitimacy eliminates the commonly identified negative effect on growth of being an African country, suggesting therefore that the model fully captures what differentiates Africa's growth performance from that of the rest of the world.

Within Africa, vertical legitimacy accounts for about 4 percent growth per year (more than six times Africa's average rate of growth since 1960) and represents up to half the variation in economic performance across the continent. Horizontal legitimacy's effects are less pronounced. Yet with an annual growth impact of about 1.7 percent, these effects remain highly significant and account for about 20 percent of the variation in economic performance across Africa. Differences in legitimacy among African states "explain" from one-fifth to one-half of the variance in their developmental fortunes. The direct effects of legitimacy on the quality of governance are even stronger. In fact, horizontal state legitimacy alone has more power to explain governance than do social heterogeneity, political culture, or colonial background. And in other regions too, when the data permit, state legitimacy appears to differentiate countries with respect to state capacity and GDP growth.

These findings force us to think once again about the nature of the state in Africa and about our intellectual and policy commitments to its stability. If the legitimacy deficit of the African state bears such responsibility for the dismal poverty of so many Africans, for their lack of economic opportunities, and for the predation of their governments, are we well inspired to dismiss altogether any notion that at least some African states may need to be redefined, whether in terms of their institutions or even—sometimes—of their boundaries? Certainly, it is challenging to imagine the shape, configuration, and design of hypothetical successors to the current states of Africa. And we would probably be misguided to make a sweeping recommendation for systematic change across the whole region. But African and

non-African intellectuals and policymakers who refuse to consider
state reconfiguration as one among several options for reform use-
lessly limit the range of the possible.

There will no doubt be resistance to this idea. For one, the principle of territorial integrity, potent in international law and enshrined
in the Charter of the Organization of African Unity (OAU), constrains the policy debate by defining the boundaries of what is nego-
tiable and by largely excluding from it discussions of the state's very
existence. This obstacle is compounded by the fact that the main are-
nas of the development policy debate—international organizations
such as the World Bank or the United Nations—are themselves composed of states with their own rigidities and no intention of sinking
into oblivion. In addition, we are all somewhat socialized into sancti-
fying the state. When we observe conflicts between states and societies, we count upon the latter to shoulder the burden of an inevitable
adjustment. We conceptualize problems of development in terms of
societal shortcomings within an unquestioned state structure and
conclude, for example, that if African states are underperforming
compared to their counterparts elsewhere, it must be that African
societies are either too ethnically polarized or lack sufficient bonds
of social capital to hold their institutions accountable to themselves.
What I hope to show, however, is that the historically determined
structures of African states lead perfectly rational policymakers to
choose institutions and policies inimical to development. African
state structures may then be in greater need of change than Africans
themselves. Recent attempts to redefine state sovereignty as state
responsibility, rather than as freedom from foreign interference, suggest an evolution of attitudes that may be more propitious to a debate
on African statehood.[13]

In fact, institutional and territorial adjustments are already taking
place across Africa in the margins of formal policy structures. In several instances, parallel networks—whether self-help (as in Congo's
province of Eastern Kasai, where local religious authorities have
largely taken over public policy), criminal (as in Sierra Leone's
"shadow state"), or customary (as in Uganda, where the Buganda
kingdom has its own government and administrative structure)—are
taking over traditional responsibilities or prerogatives of the state.[14]
Meanwhile, attempts at redefining borders and polities are being
waged violently in many parts of the continent, as in Sudan, the
Great Lakes region of Central Africa, or among the Tuaregs of Mali
and Niger. In other words, African state reform is not waiting for the
green light from Washington institutions. If this ongoing reconfigura-

tion is to proceed with less human cost, Africa may need support to create a policy environment in which state reform can take place in a manner that minimizes violence.

At any rate, by illuminating the issues of predation, neopatrimonialism, rent seeking, urban bias, administrative decay, and state collapse as ultimate consequences of the legitimacy deficit of African states, I suggest that a reform of the state should claim a policy priority over existing approaches to Africa's crisis, such as structural adjustment, which attempts to correct policies without addressing the roots of policy choice; civil service reform, which assumes that training Africans into better bureaucrats and isolating some key government agencies from social pressures for redistribution will solve Africa's capacity crisis; or assistance conditional upon electoral democratization, which tends to privilege the letter of democratization over its spirit.[15]

State reform in Africa would certainly be a costly endeavor. This much is not controversial. Yet by providing the first estimates of the formidable costs of African statehood in terms of foregone development, my results suggest that state reform may well be cheaper in the long run than the costs of inaction. As disheartening as the scope of the needed changes may seem, the diagnosis of Africa's crisis as one of state legitimacy should still generate greater hope for Africa's future than either social capital theory or the ethnic heterogeneity hypothesis. For if Africa's crisis of development were truly one of lack of social capital or of excessive ethnic polarization, then there would be little room for any policy recommendation. Indeed, Robert Putnam's (1993a) work on Italy has shown that social capital builds up over centuries, and we know that ethnic identity cannot be suppressed overnight. If these were the real roots of Africa's predicament, Africans would be all but doomed to poverty and state failure for centuries to come. My results suggest that the relevance of social capital theory to Africa is unclear and that ethnic fragmentation per se is not the core problem of African underdevelopment. Furthermore, by bringing to light the conditions under which state structures constrain policy choices and governance quality, my findings single out the responsibility of a human creation—the state—that can be altered, whether in its laws, its component institutions, or even its borders.

*   *   *

This book has three parts: The first explains the theoretical and empirical links between policies and governance on the one hand, and economic growth on the other, provides comprehensive measures of the developmental capacity of states, and ranks countries of the world along these variables (Chapter 2). Chapter 3 looks at the performance of African countries on these different indicators. The picture that emerges is one of a region that systematically performs worse than any other region of the world with respect to about all the important development variables, but also of a continent whose average stagnation hides a wide range of performance on these variables, with a significant minority of success stories. In the second part, I present a theory to account for both Africa's average stagnation and the range of intra-African development performance, first discussing the failure of the social capital theory and of the ethnic heterogeneity hypothesis to address this double dimension of Africa's paradox (Chapter 4). Chapter 5 looks at the comparative origins of the state in Africa and at the widespread neopatrimonial nature of its policies and institutions, then articulates how the choice of policies and the quality of institutions are in fact a function of their power payoffs for elites—payoffs that are in turn predicated upon the legitimacy, or historical continuity, of the state. The third part provides empirical evidence, testing the theory both in the context of Africa's differentiation from the rest of the world (Chapter 6) and in the context of the variance in performance within the African continent itself (Chapter 7). In Chapter 6, I also revisit and challenge the empirical robustness of the social capital and ethnic heterogeneity theories. Finally, in the Conclusion I discuss the relevance of current lending programs by development agencies to Africa's realities and explore some implications of my findings in terms of the institutional and territorial stability of African states (Chapter 8).

NOTES

1. The picture is even bleaker according to the *World Bank Africa Database 1998/99* CD Rom, which cites an average per capita GDP for all of sub-Saharan Africa, including South Africa and Nigeria, of $499 in 1965 and $494 in 1995 (expressed in constant 1987 U.S.$).

2. See Ndulu and van de Walle (1996).

3. This theoretical paucity is partly because, until the 1990s, the argument that Africa's crisis was one of policies and institutions had not fully established itself against competing theories that stressed structural constraints to Africa's development, such as its unequal insertion into the world economy or its lack of regional integration, or ones that called for less state

intervention and greater use of market mechanisms in African development. The former approach is best illustrated by authors such as Walter Rodney (1972) and Samir Amin (1974), who provided an African-oriented version of dependency theory. A less radical version of this point of view was later taken up by the Organization of African Unity (1980) in its *Lagos Plan of Action* and by the United Nations Economic Commission for Africa. The latter approach was vocally defended by the World Bank until its change of heart in the late 1980s, especially in World Bank (1981), World Bank (1984), and World Bank (1986).

4. See Serageldin and Taboroff (1994), Dia (1996), and World Bank (1998a).

5. The concept of social capital, as I use it here, was developed by James Coleman (1990) and popularized by Robert Putnam (1993a).

6. William Easterly and Ross Levine (1997) presented the strongest version to date of this argument in an already seminal paper in the *Quarterly Journal of Economics*.

7. Jennifer Widner and Alexander Mundt (1998) have actually found more evidence of social capital in Uganda than in Botswana, although the latter has had a significantly better economy and more efficient state institutions over the long run. As for ethnicity, the homogeneity of Somalia has not prevented its political and economic failure. These anecdotal examples only mean to hint at the potential weaknesses of these two theories. In Chapter 4, I review them in greater depth.

8. The term *neopatrimonialism* derives from the concept of patrimonial rule originally developed by Max Weber (1958) to describe regimes where the distinction between private and public rule (and purse) is tenuous. It is commonly used nowadays to refer to regimes where the appearance of rational bureaucratic rule is but a veneer over personal power. Médard (1982) and Bratton and van de Walle (1994; 1997) provide excellent discussions of the concept and of its applications to the African setting.

9. Others have identified this dimension before me, including Sandbrook (1986) and Lewis (1996).

10. For such an approach, see Achebe (1983), Sachs (1996), or Ayittey (1998).

11. On the "imported" or "transplanted" state, see Hyden (1983a), Sandbrook (1985; 1986), Badie (1992), Davidson (1992), and Dia (1996).

12. For a systematic study of the origins of contemporary African boundaries, see Brownlie (1979). Sautter (1982) provides a compelling assessment of their arbitrariness.

13. See Deng et al. (1996).

14. On Eastern Kasai, see *The Economist* (1996) and French (1996). On Sierra Leone, and the rise of criminal activities by segments of the state, see Reno (1995; 1998), and Bayart et al. (1999). On Buganda, see Nsibambi (1994), Bertrand (1997), and Mukyala-Makiika (1998). For more encompassing discussions of state "reconfiguration" in Africa, see Villalon and Huxtable (1998) and Joseph (1999).

15. On structural adjustment in Africa, see World Bank (1994a). On civil service reform, see Dia (1993; 1996). On the policy to make development assistance conditional upon electoral democratization, see Lancaster (1993).

PART I

State Capacity and Development

2

The Developmental Capacity of States

DECONSTRUCTING DEVELOPMENTAL CAPACITY

The concept of state capacity has received some rather encompassing definitions in political science and development studies. One approach uses it to refer to the capacity of governments to achieve their stated objectives, whatever these may be, even when opposed by other groups in society (Skocpol 1985; Brautigam 1996). An even more inclusive definition deems capable those states that penetrate society, regulate social relationships, extract resources, and manage to appropriate them (Migdal 1988). I have adopted here a less ambitious and more focused approach, which I refer to as developmental capacity and define as the ability of governments to design and implement economic policies for growth and to provide good governance to their societies and markets. This approach captures some of Theda Skocpol and Deborah Brautigam's definition but limits itself to achieving growth-oriented goals either through specific policies or through providing the institutional foundations for efficient market operations (good governance). Nongrowth objectives, such as promoting income equality or environmental preservation, are kept aside because this study's emphasis is on explaining economic growth and stagnation. I also ignore the extractive capacity of states because extraction can take place in the context of regular taxation or accrue to predatory elites with no developmental capacity.

With its emphasis on developmental goals, my approach is not unlike earlier notions of "developmental statehood" (Johnson 1982; Wade 1990), but it places less emphasis on a state-versus-market conception of development. In fact, it promotes instead a state-cum-market understanding of development. It derives from recent research that argues development is a function of a certain set of economic policies (Rodrik 1996) and institutional conditions (Keefer and Knack 1995a; Ndulu and O'Connell 1999) and asks why some governments fail to adopt these policies and institutions, turning predatory instead, while others do adopt them and become developmental (Evans 1995; Robinson 1997a; Robinson 1997b). My definition of capacity really captures whether states are capable of "foregoing predatory urges in favor of long-term benefits that may not necessarily accrue to the specific individuals who inhabit the state's space of power" (Kevane and Englebert 1999:263).[1] Henceforth, I refer to this capability indistinctly as developmental capacity, state capacity, or simply, capacity.

What then are the policies that have long-run developmental benefits, and by which mechanisms are they conducive to growth? And what is it about the dimensions of good governance, such as the accountability of governments, the prevalence of the rule of law, and the quality of state institutions, that favors the productivity of economic systems? Over the last ten years, a flurry of studies on the determinants of growth has largely contributed to answering these questions. A brief review of their findings provides better understanding of the nature of state capacity and suggests guidelines for measuring it.

Developmental Policies

In conducting the business of running a country, governments adopt a wide range of economic policies. They raise revenue and spend it, regulate and control the activities of private agents, and allocate resources among sectors of their economies. In guiding their actions, they usually keep an eye on short-term considerations such as avoiding recessions or inflation, promoting a sector or a region, generating employment, or providing patronage. Some of these policies, however, have far-reaching implications for the long-run performance of their economies. For better or for worse, they will affect their countries' welfare long after the governments that chose them are gone.

Government decisions about the level and allocation of public investments make up one such policy area with momentous long-run implications. Surprisingly, however, many types of public investments appear to have no productive economic effects whatsoever, and as a result, there is little evidence of any growth benefit of public investments in general (Barro 1991; Easterly and Rebelo 1993). In part, governments are more likely to act as residual investors and to finance projects whose insufficient returns have discouraged private operators or to choose investments according to political rather than economic rationales. This no doubt leads them to allocate their resources to less productive outlets. There are, however, two categories of public investments that have sweeping developmental benefits: education and infrastructure.

Investments in education favor the formation of human capital. For any given stock of physical capital, output will be greater the higher the level of human capital of the workforce using it (Romer 1986; Lucas 1988). In other words, more educated people can extract more productivity from a similar stock of material productive forces. Therefore, the greater the proportion of children that governments can place in school, the more likely these children will become more productive citizens and lead their countries to faster growth in the future. Empirical studies have provided robust and consistent support for this hypothesis.[2] Robert Barro (1991), for example, found that the range of variation among countries in gross primary and secondary school enrollments in 1960 (the percentage of children in school from the appropriate age group) explained a range in variation in average per capita growth (over the period 1960 to 1985) of about 5 percent, or half the total variation in growth rates over that period.

Although education is occasionally privately supplied, it remains a matter of public policy in most countries, especially in less developed ones. The findings of growth theory suggest that policies that expand the availability and the quality of education lead to higher subsequent rates of economic growth. Therefore, governments able and willing to divert resources away from short-term consumption and toward investments in education lay the foundations of their country's future growth.

Investments in infrastructure have equally powerful effects on growth. Providing roads, bridges, railways, telecommunication networks, power, and the like facilitates economic activity by private agents and magnifies their productivity. It will do an economy little good if its farmers produce a surplus but are unable to deliver it to markets because the roads are beyond repair. Infrastructure allows the realization of economic gains by producers and the exploitation of economic opportunities by entrepreneurs, and it leads to greater development of markets and a more efficient division of labor. It is no wonder that of all the categories of public investments they reviewed (education excepted), William Easterly and Sergio Rebelo (1993) found sectoral investments in transport and communications (roads, rail, telecommunications, etc.) had the strongest positive effects on growth. Subsequent evidence confirmed that the number of telephones available per thousand workers (a measure of the extent of the telecommunication system), the percentage of a country's roads that are paved, and the efficiency of electricity transmission systems all correlate strongly with long-run growth (Easterly and Levine 1997).

Given the constraints of their budgets, governments allocating resources to education and infrastructure face a trade-off away from current expenditures, such as wages and salaries, military spending, or the purchase of goods and services for the daily functioning of the bureaucracy. This trade-off actually provides additional development benefits, as high current government expenditures appear to be by themselves inimical to growth. Of course, some level of day-to-day government expenditure is necessary for the simple provision of basic public goods such as laws, regulations, and their enforcement. This much has been clear since the days of Adam Smith.[3] But it is quite likely too that, beyond a certain level, an increase in the size of government and its expenditures will put more burden on the economy than it will bring benefits (Barro 1990). Government expenditures require the generation of revenues. If the government finances its excess consumption by borrowing on financial markets, it will put upward pressure on interest rates. This will in turn crowd private investors out of borrowing opportunities and reduce the share of private investments in the economy. As investments decrease, so will the rate of growth of the stock of productive capital in the economy and, eventually, the country's rate of economic growth. If the government decides instead to raise taxes, it will reduce the disposable income of its households. Part of this reduction will be compensated by a decrease in private consumption, but another part is likely to come from households' savings. Diminished savings will shrink the pool of resources available to finance investment and cause the interest rate to rise, with further damaging consequences for private investments.

If the government allocates its expenditures to productive investments, such as education and infrastructure, the evidence suggests that the payoffs will more than compensate for the costs. But if it chooses instead to hire more civil servants or increase the number of ministries and embassies, it will have created a liability for the country's future development. There is, therefore, a contradiction between the short-term and long-term effects of government spending. In the short run it is usually agreed that any spending by the government has positive effects on output. John Maynard Keynes after all suggested that "if the Treasury were to fill old bottles with bank notes, bury them at suitable depth in disused coal mines which are then filled up to the surface with town rubbish . . . there would be no more unemployment" (Keynes 1953). In the long run, however, it matters where the government allocates its resources (Barro 1991; Fischer 1993; Sachs and Warner 1997a). The sum of these findings suggests that the ways in which governments allocate their budgets have momentous implications for their future growth prospects. Investments in education and infrastructure favor growth. Large current expenditures, on the other hand, appear to crowd out private investments or reduce private saving rates and mortgage a country's developmental potential.

There is another set of policies with implications for long-run development. Many recent studies by economists have singled out the negative effects on growth of distorting market signals. The theoretical argument is slightly more controversial here, as others have contended that the "miracle" of rapid growth in East Asia was to a large extent the consequence of a fair amount of government-imposed distortions, not least in the financial and labor markets.[4] The aggregate quantitative evidence, however, is more supportive of the orthodox view of the beneficial effects of free markets. Indeed, distortions in the prices of goods, services, capital, or foreign exchange, or in the flows of imports and exports, introduce biases in the allocation of resources by private agents and blur their perception of actual scarcities and opportunities. In some cases, if the government is well informed, consistent, and disciplined in its implementation, these distortions may lead to developmental gains, as in some East Asian economies (Amsden 1985; Wade 1990; World Bank 1993). But in most cases, their consequences are likely to be detrimental (Krueger 1974; Bates 1981; World Bank 1981).

There is consistent evidence, for example, that distortions in foreign exchange markets are negatively associated with growth (Fischer 1993; Easterly and Levine 1997). When exchange rates are overvalued, exports are penalized, and domestic agricultural producers, faced with artificially fierce foreign competition, tend to retreat into subsistence farming or smuggling. There is also related evidence that the degree of openness of an economy to foreign trade, as measured by the ratio of its exports and imports to GDP, correlates positively with growth (Sachs and Warner 1997a; Easterly and Levine 1997). Imports of capital and intermediate goods are necessary to provide the foundations for manufacturing and industry. Exports, for their part, displace the market into the international arena, forcing producers to compete on a larger scale and to streamline the effectiveness of their production processes, which leads to increases in productivity that are beneficial for development. Although the volume of a country's trade results from a myriad of individual decisions among domestic and foreign producers and consumers, governments nevertheless influence their economy's degree of openness with their uses of import tariffs and quotas, export taxes, and exchange rate policies. Again, there is a trade-off for governments between fostering long-run growth by liberalizing international trade flows and extracting immediate resources from such flows by taxing trade and distorting exchange rates. Governments of fast-growing countries typically encourage exports, whereas those that restrict international trade preside over slower-growing economies.[5] Finally, distortions in financial systems also prompt misallocations of resources and reduce the rate of innovation by blurring functions of the financial system such as the evaluation of prospective entrepreneurs, the mobilization of savings, and the diversification of the risks of innovation (King and Levine 1993). William Easterly and Ross Levine (1997) have provided empirical evidence of the positive growth effects of a measure of financial depth—the liquid liabilities of the financial sector divided by GDP—that they found to proxy for the absence of financial sector distortions.

In summary, policies that have an impact on long-run growth can essentially be aggregated into two subgroups: those that involve a trade-off between current consumption and investment for the future and those that introduce distortions in the economy. In general, if current government consumption is sacrificed for investments in infrastructure and education and if fewer distortions are introduced by governments into the economy, then the rate of economic growth will be faster. However, not all states have the capacity to sustain these trade-offs and adopt these developmental policies. Indeed, government spending buys political support and so do distortions that create rents to reward backers and clients. Understanding what determines the propensity of governments to resist these trade-offs is a big step toward understanding the sources of developmental capacity and economic growth.

GOOD GOVERNANCE

There are other, more subtle ways in which governments can provide or withhold the foundations for economic growth. Guaranteeing the rule of law and the enforceability of contracts, establishing efficient institutions, bureaucracies, and judicial systems, avoiding corruption, and being otherwise accountable and responsible to their citizens— all have substantial development benefits too. Political scientists have subsumed this set of government actions into the concept of *good governance* (Brautigam 1991; Hyden and Bratton 1992). The assumption is that accountable and predictable regimes that submit themselves to the rule of law create an environment favorable to the development of economic activity and of individual autonomy. They need not be democracies in the electoral sense, as long as some mechanism exists by which rulers and institutions are held account-able.

The idea of good governance surfaced into the mainstream of development studies when the World Bank, in a 1989 study of Africa's "long-term perspectives," suggested that "underlying the litany of Africa's development problems," there was "a crisis of governance" (World Bank 1989:60). This apparently benign statement marked one of the first steps of a trend in the Bank's research and policies away from purely economic factors and toward an acknowl-edgment of the role of political and institutional variables in the process of development in Africa and elsewhere.[6]

To be sure, the World Bank's forays into the business of gover-nance—and by extension, the political economy of development and the nature of relations between state and society—have not been without their fair share of confusion and controversy. The Bank's use of the concept of governance (later adopted by bilateral and other multilateral donors who have stressed its "democratic" version and used it to impose political conditionality on development lending[7]) has led to criticisms from several academics. Statist thinkers have pointed out that governance still implies a reduction in the role of the state, from active economic leadership to institutional support for markets. They have contrasted this minimal role with the proactive involvement of the state among late developers (such as Germany and Japan) and the East Asian miracle economies and have conclud-ed that the World Bank's version of governance was but old promar-ket policies under a new guise (e.g., Leftwich 1994). Others have also highlighted that the purely managerial and rule-providing role of the state, as understood by the Bank's idea of governance, would pre-vent the governments of developing countries from creating political order for their societies and from advancing the process of state building, which calls for a certain amount of economic deviance to be effective (Moore 1993).

A different strand of critique has also called attention to the assumption, implied by the Bank's discourse on governance, of a modernizing civil society to which the state would be but a neutral appendage. If the state is to guarantee property rights, society is then supposed to have developed markets and a capitalist outlook. But many indigenous societies in developing countries do not currently provide such foundations to growth. Hence, there is an inherent contradiction in the governance approach to development, as it requires the state to be responsive to social forces and yet needs the state to shape these forces into vectors of modernization and development (Williams and Young 1994). Alice Sindzingre (1995) has made a similar point, to which she adds that the selection by the Bank of some state institutions for capacity-building projects leads to the fragmentation of the state apparatus and, eventually, to a contradictory decrease in accountability. Nevertheless, despite these enduring differences of perspective, the concessions of state-centered theorists to market mechanisms in the 1980s and the acknowledgment of the importance of the state by the World Bank in the 1990s have brought about a minimal consensus on the importance of governance in development that did not exist earlier.[8]

The recent empirical evidence strongly supports the idea that good governance, defined as the quality of state institutions, the accountability of governments, the stability of property rights, and the absence of corruption, has beneficial effects on growth. In 1995, Paolo Mauro was the first to bring quantitative measures of good governance into the empirical literature on growth. Specifically investigating the relationship between government corruption and growth, Mauro showed how the prevalence of corruption reduces the level of investments a government can attract. Other authors have since expanded this approach and confirmed that institutional and bureaucratic quality in general favor growth by securing property rights. Philip Keefer and Stephen Knack (1995a) found that government's guarantees for the enforceability of contracts and the protection of entrepreneurs from expropriation had a greater impact on growth than did political stability. Jeffrey Sachs and Andrew Warner (1997b) showed that an average index of institutional quality had substantial positive effects on growth over the 1965–1990 period, and Hélène Poirson (1998) suggested that improvements in a similar index were related to better economic performance over the last decade. Johannes Fedderke and Robert Klitgaard (1998) confirmed these earlier findings.

In addition, there is increased evidence that other dimensions of governance have developmental effects. Barro (1997) found a robust but nonlinear effect of political freedoms and civil liberties on growth that suggests, at early levels of transition from authoritarian to more liberal regimes, that "an increase in political rights tends to increase growth and investment because the benefit from limitations on governmental power is the key matter" (1997:59), whereas these effects vanish in more fully democratic systems. In addition, both Easterly and Levine (1997) and Dani Rodrik (1998) have observed that the percentage of a country's citizens who do not speak the official language is negatively correlated with economic growth. When the citizens of a country do not speak the language in which their government operates, they are more likely to be alienated and less capable of holding their government accountable for its actions. The realm of formal economic activity is diminished as a result, and opportunities for misuses of government power are maximized.

Not all governments are capable of accountability, predictability, and responsibility vis-à-vis their citizens. Just as with developmental policies, good governance implies trade-offs, and these have political implications. Circumventing the rule of law gives governing elites opportunities to adapt their policies to the political exigencies of the moment. Corruption allows for patronage, bureaucracies for nepotism. Understanding the sources of good governance is therefore also critical if we are to make sense of the roots of development.[9]

MEASURING DEVELOPMENTAL CAPACITY

So many elements of policy choices and good governance relate to growth that it would be unwieldy to continue the discussion at such a level of detail. In this section, I have created three summary measures of the indicators discussed so far. One evaluates the choice of policies governments make. The second estimates the quality of governance they provide, and the third summarizes both into an overall index of developmental capacity. Later, I will use these summary measures to investigate the effects of state legitimacy. Here, I briefly discuss the methodology behind these indices before ranking countries along them and turning to an assessment of their strength in predicting economic growth.

As stated previously, policies that positively affect growth fall into two categories: those that encourage accumulation of human and physical capital and those that reduce distortions and allow for more efficient allocation of resources. Drawing my data from the empirical studies mentioned earlier, I combined both types of policies into a general index of the developmental nature of policy choices, which averages six indicators: public investments in education, public investments in infrastructure, current government expenditure, distortions in the foreign exchange market, restrictions on free trade, and distortions in the financial sector.[10] A conventional arithmetic average, however, would make little sense for variables expressed in widely different units; thus I used what statisticians refer to as the "first principal component" of these six variables. This method produces a linear combination of variables that are jointly correlated. This combination has the desirable qualities of having a mean of 0 and a standard deviation of 1, and of maximizing the joint variance of its components. According to Robert Putnam, who uses the same technique in his landmark study of Italian democracy, this is "the most reliable and valid means of combining multiple indicators of a theoretical variable into a single index" (1993a:216). Because policies that relate to capital accumulation have a greater variance with each other than with those that express the amount of distortions in the economy, the index puts slightly more emphasis on the former than on the latter. This is consistent with the available evidence that links accumulation policies more robustly with growth. The specific scores of each country in the sample on the policy index are presented in Table 2.1. A score of 0 represents the average level of developmental policy choice across the world. A positive score means a tendency to adopt policies that are conducive to growth. A negative score suggests that a government cannot afford to trade off present consumption and the rents of distortions for future growth. Most OECD (Organization for Economic Cooperation and Development) countries and East Asian "dragons" score relatively high on this index, and most African countries relatively low.

I followed the same technique to create an index of good governance. In this case I generated the first principal component of seven different dimensions of governance: the enforceability of contracts and the risk of expropriation of investments (both of which measure the reliability of property rights and the rule of law); the prevalence of corruption; the quality of government institutions (including the level of citizens' trust in them); the quality of the bureaucracy (including an assessment of the prevalence of red tape); the extent of civil liberties; and the degree of linguistic alienation of citizens from their government. Data for the first five indicators are the same as

Table 2.1 Country Scores on the Developmental Policy Index

1. SINGAPORE	4.10	58. PERU	0.24
2. LUXEMBOURG	3.20	59. COSTA RICA	0.20
3. SWITZERLAND	2.50	60. HONDURAS	−0.04
4. JAPAN	2.24	61. INDONESIA	−0.09
5. FRANCE	2.20	62. TUNISIA	−0.16
6. GERMANY, WEST	2.12	63. GUYANA	−0.22
7. BELGIUM	2.05	**64. BOTSWANA**	**−0.23**
8. FINLAND	2.02	**65. SWAZILAND**	**−0.27**
9. MALTA	2.00	66. JORDAN	−0.29
10. NORWAY	1.96	67. SYRIA	−0.30
11. ITALY	1.87	68. SRI LANKA	−0.32
12. NETHERLANDS	1.86	69. GUATEMALA	−0.44
13. IRELAND	1.85	**70. TOGO**	**−0.53**
14. ICELAND	1.83	**71. CÔTE D'IVOIRE**	**−0.54**
15. CYPRUS	1.79	**72. ZIMBABWE**	**−0.56**
16. AUSTRALIA	1.78	73. ALGERIA	−0.62
17. SPAIN	1.75	**74. CAMEROON**	**−0.64**
18. AUSTRIA	1.70	**75. KENYA**	**−0.66**
19. YUGOSLAVIA	1.60	**76. LIBERIA**	**−0.69**
20. NEW ZEALAND	1.58	77. EL SALVADOR	−0.70
21. CANADA	1.58	78. MOROCCO	−0.79
22. MALAYSIA	1.48	79. NICARAGUA	−1.02
23. GREECE	1.43	80. HAITI	−1.07
24. KOREA, SOUTH	1.32	**81. CONGO**	**−1.08**
25. DENMARK	1.31	**82. ZAMBIA**	**−1.13**
26. UNITED STATES	1.31	83. INDIA	−1.20
27. JAMAICA	1.30	**84. MADAGASCAR**	**−1.22**
28. ROMANIA	1.29	85. PAKISTAN	−1.28
29. BARBADOS	1.26	86. PAPUA NEW GUINEA	−1.29
30. TAIWAN	1.16	**87. MAURITANIA**	**−1.42**
31. HUNGARY	1.01	**88. NIGERIA**	**−1.45**
32. POLAND	0.95	**89. BURUNDI**	**−1.48**
33. VENEZUELA	0.94	**90. BENIN**	**−1.49**
34. SWEDEN	0.90	**91. BURKINA FASO**	**−1.50**
35. BELIZE	0.85	**92. GAMBIA**	**−1.52**
36. BAHAMAS	0.82	**93. SENEGAL**	**−1.55**
37. MEXICO	0.73	**94. GUINEA-BISSAU**	**−1.56**
38. BRAZIL	0.71	**95. GUINEA**	**−1.60**
39. CHINA	0.71	**96. SOMALIA**	**−1.66**
40. THAILAND	0.69	**97. CENTRAL AFRICAN REPUBLIC**	**−1.69**
41. TRINIDAD and TOBAGO	0.68	**98. ZAIRE**	**−1.69**
42. FIJI	0.67	**99. RWANDA**	**−1.71**
43. URUGUAY	0.67	**100. MALI**	**−1.74**
44. MAURITIUS	**0.67**	101. EGYPT	−1.80
45. DOMINICAN REPUBLIC	0.63	**102. NIGER**	**−1.87**
46. ECUADOR	0.63	**103. GHANA**	**−1.93**
47. TURKEY	0.61	**104. SUDAN**	**−1.98**
48. ARGENTINA	0.60	**105. UGANDA**	**−2.18**
49. UNITED KINGDOM	0.60	**106. CHAD**	**−2.31**
50. PANAMA	0.58	**107. ETHIOPIA**	**−2.37**
51. LESOTHO	**0.56**	108. MYANMAR	−2.38
52. CHILE	0.55	**109. TANZANIA**	**−2.42**
53. PHILIPPINES	0.53	**110. SIERRA LEONE**	**−2.68**
54. SOUTH AFRICA	**0.50**	**111. MOZAMBIQUE**	**−2.88**
55. COLOMBIA	0.45	112. BANGLADESH	−2.93
56. PARAGUAY	0.44	113. NEPAL	−3.16
57. ISRAEL	0.40	**114. ANGOLA**	**−3.70**

Notes: Bold characters denote sub-Saharan African countries.
Figures rounded to two decimals.

those used by Mauro (1995), Keefer and Knack (1995a), Keefer and Knack (1997), Sachs and Warner (1997b), Barro (1997), and Fedderke and Klitgaard (1998). They derive from the *Inter-Country Risk Guide* (ICRG) published by Political Risk Service, a Syracuse-based consulting firm that sells country risk analyses to private investors.[11] These indicators are subjective rankings produced monthly by local experts and averaged on an annual basis. Although subjectivity is a potential problem, there are of course no direct ways to measure these variables. As Barro puts it, "the willingness of customers to pay substantial fees for this information is perhaps some testament to their validity" (1997:27). The measure of civil liberties is the well-known *Gastil* index as averaged in Ross Levine and David Renelt (1992). Finally, linguistic alienation is measured by the percentage of households who do not speak at home the official language of the state (Easterly and Levine 1997).[12]

The resulting index of good governance puts slightly more emphasis on the five ICRG variables because they correlate more strongly with each other than with the two other indicators, although the latter's influence in the index remains far from negligible. Again, the respective country scores in Table 2.2 indicate the relatively better governance of OECD and East Asian economies.

The general similarity of the country rankings on the policy index and the governance index is rather striking. Countries that choose the right policies for growth also tend to provide better governance to their societies and markets. In fact, both indices are strongly correlated ($r=0.82$), as Figure 2.1 makes clear. This correlation is in fact quite remarkable given that the two indices come from entirely different sources. The fact that they cannot therefore be tainted by some joint measurement bias leaves no doubt that the two indices capture two dimensions of the same reality and that the concept of developmental capacity as an amalgam of policy choice and governance quality is indeed a meaningful category.

On the strength of this finding, I created an overall measure of developmental capacity, averaging both the policy and the governance indices into yet another first principal component encompassing the six policies and seven dimensions of governance and providing a summary snapshot of each country's level of capacity. Table 2.3 presents the individual country scores. OECD and East Asian countries again monopolize the first quartile. The first Latin American country is twenty-ninth, and the first African one is thirty-fourth.

Table 2.2 Country Scores on the Good Governance Index

1. SWITZERLAND	4.25	55. JORDAN	−0.60
2. LUXEMBOURG	4.18	56. TUNISIA	−0.63
3. NETHERLANDS	4.13	**57. MAURITIUS**	**−0.70**
4. SWEDEN	4.07	**58. KENYA**	**−0.72**
5. DENMARK	4.07	59. NICARAGUA	−0.77
6. NEW ZEALAND	4.07	60. SRI LANKA	−0.93
7. ICELAND	4.07	61. ALGERIA	−0.93
8. CANADA	4.00	**62. GABON**	**−0.95**
9. NORWAY	3.97	**63. CAMEROON**	**−1.01**
10. BELGIUM	3.85	**64. ZIMBABWE**	**−1.19**
11. FINLAND	3.83	65. HONDURAS	−1.19
12. UNITED STATES	3.79	66. YEMEN	−1.23
13. AUSTRIA	3.78	**67. TANZANIA**	**−1.23**
14. GERMANY, WEST	3.76	**68. GHANA**	**−1.25**
15. UNITED KINGDOM	3.69	**69. MADAGASCAR**	**−1.27**
16. JAPAN	3.66	70. SYRIA	−1.39
17. AUSTRALIA	3.60	**71. SENEGAL**	**−1.40**
18. FRANCE	3.45	72. PERU	−1.48
19. IRELAND	3.23	**73. MOZAMBIQUE**	**−1.49**
20. ITALY	2.59	**74. BURKINA FASO**	**−1.49**
21. PORTUGAL	2.28	**75. MALAWI**	**−1.50**
22. SINGAPORE	2.27	76. INDONESIA	−1.51
23. SPAIN	2.06	**77. MAURITANIA**	**−1.55**
24. TAIWAN	1.97	**78. NIGER**	**−1.57**
25. HONG KONG	1.70	79. PARAGUAY	−1.58
26. ISRAEL	1.64	**80. BURUNDI**	**−1.60**
27. GREECE	1.44	81. PANAMA	−1.66
28. CYPRUS	1.35	82. GUYANA	−1.68
29. COSTA RICA	1.31	**83. RWANDA**	**−1.78**
30. BOTSWANA	**1.30**	84. EL SALVADOR	−1.79
31. KOREA, SOUTH	1.12	85. SURINAME	−1.82
32. BRAZIL	0.97	86. PAKISTAN	−1.86
33. THAILAND	0.84	**87. NIGERIA**	**−1.96**
34. LESOTHO	**0.84**	**88. TOGO**	**−2.03**
35. TRINIDAD and TOBAGO	0.68	89. GUATEMALA	−2.04
36. VENEZUELA	0.66	90. PHILIPPINES	−2.04
37. MALAYSIA	0.66	**91. ZAMBIA**	**−2.11**
38. SOUTH AFRICA	**0.48**	92. BOLIVIA	−2.13
39. CHILE	0.42	**93. SIERRA LEONE**	**−2.23**
40. PAPUA NEW GUINEA	0.28	**94. ETHIOPIA**	**−2.36**
41. COLOMBIA	0.17	95. BANGLADESH	−2.37
42. TURKEY	0.10	**96. ANGOLA**	**−2.41**
43. MEXICO	0.06	**97. CONGO**	**−2.51**
44. SWAZILAND	**0.04**	98. MYANMAR	−2.62
45. INDIA	0.02	**99. UGANDA**	**−2.86**
46. JAMAICA	−0.04	**100. SOMALIA**	**−2.88**
47. ARGENTINA	−0.10	**101. BENIN**	**−2.92**
48. URUGUAY	−0.19	**102. SUDAN**	**−2.97**
49. ECUADOR	−0.22	**103. GUINEA-BISSAU**	**−3.19**
50. GAMBIA	**−0.33**	104. HAITI	−3.33
51. MOROCCO	−0.39	**105. MALI**	**−3.42**
52. EGYPT	−0.39	**106. LIBERIA**	**−4.00**
53. CÔTE D'IVOIRE	**−0.41**	**107. ZAIRE**	**−4.10**
54. DOMINICAN REPUBLIC	−0.44		

Notes: Bold characters denote sub-Saharan African countries.
Figures rounded to two decimal places.

Figure 2.1   Correlation Between the Good Governance and Developmental Policy Indexes (r=0.82)

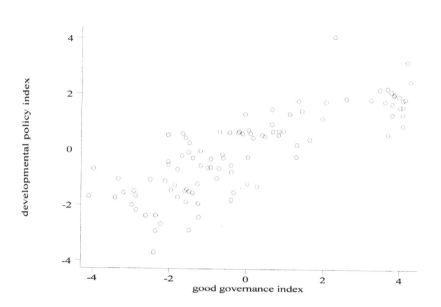

A SIMPLE MODEL OF CAPACITY AND GROWTH

How do these three indices relate to long-run economic growth? Do they appropriately capture the developmental effects of the variables they comprise? And if so, how much do policy choice, governance, and overall capacity actually contribute to the rate of growth of per capita GDP across nations, after controlling for other factors known to have an impact too?

A simple look at the correlations between the three indices and average per capita GDP growth over the 1960–1992 period leaves little doubt as to the strength of the associations. The correlation coefficient between the policy index and economic growth is 0.67. Figure 2.2 illustrates the strength of this relationship and reveals the extent to which the policy index captures dimensions of the origins of growth.

At 0.55, the good governance index correlates somewhat more weakly with the rate of economic growth (Figure 2.3). Yet this by no means implies that its relationship to growth is weaker. The correlation coefficient captures only *linear* relationships. Therefore, if two

Table 2.3 Country Scores on the Developmental Capacity Index

1.	LUXEMBOURG	1.85	51.	JORDAN	−0.21
2.	SINGAPORE	1.74	52.	PERU	−0.23
3.	SWITZERLAND	1.65	**53.**	**CÔTE D'IVOIRE**	**−0.25**
4.	JAPAN	1.45	54.	PHILIPPINES	−0.25
5.	GERMANY, WEST	1.43	55.	HONDURAS	−0.26
6.	BELGIUM	1.43	56.	SRI LANKA	−0.29
7.	NORWAY	1.43	57.	MOROCCO	−0.33
8.	NETHERLANDS	1.43	58.	INDONESIA	−0.34
9.	FINLAND	1.41	59.	PAPUA NEW GUINEA	−0.34
10.	ICELAND	1.41	**60.**	**KENYA**	**−0.35**
11.	FRANCE	1.39	61.	INDIA	−0.37
12.	NEW ZEALAND	1.33	62.	SYRIA	−0.38
13.	CANADA	1.31	63.	ALGERIA	−0.39
14.	AUSTRIA	1.31	**64.**	**CAMEROON**	**−0.41**
15.	AUSTRALIA	1.29	65.	GUYANA	−0.42
16.	DENMARK	1.24	**66.**	**ZIMBABWE**	**−0.42**
17.	IRELAND	1.24	67.	NICARAGUA	−0.48
18.	UNITED STATES	1.19	**68.**	**GAMBIA**	**−0.55**
19.	SWEDEN	1.12	69.	GUATEMALA	−0.56
20.	ITALY	1.11	**70.**	**TOGO**	**−0.58**
21.	SPAIN	0.97	71.	EL SALVADOR	−0.59
22.	UNITED KINGDOM	0.94	72.	EGYPT	−0.64
23.	CYPRUS	0.83	**73.**	**MADAGASCAR**	**−0.64**
24.	TAIWAN	0.77	**74.**	**MAURITANIA**	**−0.76**
25.	GREECE	0.74	**75.**	**SENEGAL**	**−0.77**
26.	KOREA, SOUTH	0.64	**76.**	**BURKINA FASO**	**−0.77**
27.	MALAYSIA	0.60	77.	PAKISTAN	−0.78
28.	ISRAEL	0.46	**78.**	**ZAMBIA**	**−0.79**
29.	VENEZUELA	0.43	**79.**	**BURUNDI**	**−0.79**
30.	BRAZIL	0.42	**80.**	**CONGO**	**−0.85**
31.	JAMAICA	0.40	**81.**	**NIGERIA**	**−0.85**
32.	THAILAND	0.39	**82.**	**GHANA**	**−0.86**
33.	TRINIDAD and TOBAGO	0.35	**83.**	**RWANDA**	**−0.90**
34.	LESOTHO	0.35	**84.**	**NIGER**	**−0.90**
35.	COSTA RICA	0.33	**85.**	**TANZANIA**	**−1.01**
36.	CHILE	0.26	86.	HAITI	−1.02
37.	**SOUTH AFRICA**	**0.26**	**87.**	**LIBERIA**	**−1.04**
38.	MEXICO	0.24	**88.**	**BENIN**	**−1.06**
39.	TURKEY	0.21	**89.**	**SOMALIA**	**−1.11**
40.	**BOTSWANA**	**0.19**	**90.**	**GUINEA-BISSAU**	**−1.14**
41.	COLOMBIA	0.17	**91.**	**MOZAMBIQUE**	**−1.20**
42.	URUGUAY	0.17	**92.**	**ETHIOPIA**	**−1.22**
43.	ARGENTINA	0.17	**93.**	**SUDAN**	**−1.23**
44.	ECUADOR	0.15	**94.**	**MALI**	**−1.24**
45.	DOMINICAN REPUBLIC	0.11	**95.**	**UGANDA**	**−1.27**
46.	**MAURITIUS**	**0.06**	96.	MYANMAR	−1.28
47.	**SWAZILAND**	**−0.07**	**97.**	**SIERRA LEONE**	**−1.29**
48.	PANAMA	−0.16	**98.**	**ZAIRE**	**−1.37**
49.	TUNISIA	−0.18	99.	BANGLADESH	−1.40
50.	PARAGUAY	−0.19	**100.**	**ANGOLA**	**−1.60**

Notes: Bold characters denote sub-Saharan African countries.
Figures rounded to two decimal places.

**Figure 2.2   Correlation Between the Developmental Policy Index and
             Economic Growth (r=0.67)**

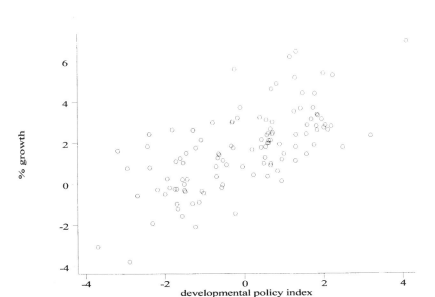

variables have a relationship that is not constant, their correlation
will be weaker than if it was linear. But the actual extent to which
they affect each other may well be stronger. Figure 2.3 clearly indicates that the relationship between the quality of governance and
economic growth is not quite linear. For countries with weak levels
of governance, improvements will be strongly associated with additional growth; but for countries that already benefit from good levels
of governance, additional improvements in the quality of their institutions may be more costly than the economic benefits they will
bring about. In a rather lapidary summary, going from the state of
nature to that of organized society has more growth benefits than
from one stage of institutional development to another. A country
with stable property rights would gain few additional investments
from further improvements in its legal system, and these very
improvements may divert resources from more productive outlets.
The optimal level of governance appears to hover around a score of 2
on the governance index. Beyond that, the marginal productivity of
governance appears negative. All the countries on the downward portion of the relationship are high-income OECD countries. For their

Figure 2.3   Correlation Between the Good Governance Index and Economic Growth (r=0.55)

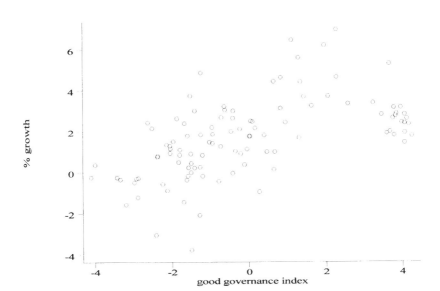

developing counterparts, however, the returns to improved governance are still overwhelmingly positive.

The relationship between overall state capacity and economic growth captures some dimensions of the growth impact of policies and of governance. As with the latter, the relationship is not quite linear. Yet the influence of policies "linearizes" the relationship and improves the overall correlation to 0.65. Figure 2.4 provides a telling summary of the findings of the last decade on the "institutional" determinants of growth and the developmental role of state capacity. In one graph, it summarizes our knowledge of the influence on growth of no less than six different policy indicators and seven different measures of governance. The strength of the association suggests that governments need not be helpless and that much of the long-run performance of their country is the result of factors within their control. It also shows how crucial it is to understand the determinants of developmental capacity.

Simple correlations provide a convenient measure and a powerful visualization of the relations between two variables. Yet several other factors are known to affect growth. First, countries at different

Figure 2.4   Correlation Between the Developmental Capacity Index and Economic Growth (r=0.65)

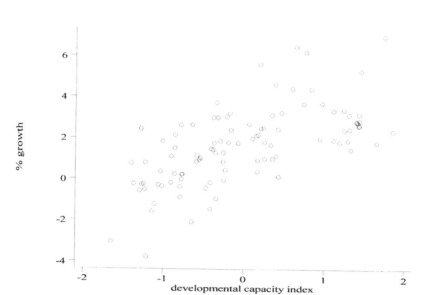

levels of income are likely to grow at different rates. Indeed, ceteris paribus, already developed countries have fewer opportunities for productive investments than those where additions to the stock of capital can still make a big difference. This is known in economics as the "convergence" hypothesis. As countries develop, the marginal productivity of capital decreases and so should their rates of growth, until such point that all countries grow at a rate equal to their population growth (since, then, only additions to the labor force provide extra contributions to output).[13]

Second, there are also structural constraints to development, such as the geographical situation of a country or its climatic conditions. David Bloom and Jeffrey Sachs (1998) have shown that the greater morbidity (malaria, infectious diseases, etc.) and weaker agricultural yields of tropical countries can be expected to reduce their growth rates. Sachs and Warner (1997a) have also found that landlocked countries grow more slowly because of their greater shipping costs and isolation from world markets.

Is the relationship between capacity and growth robust to these other factors? In other words, once we take their effects on growth into account, does capacity retain any explanatory power? The technique of regression analysis can answer this question. Regressing one dependent variable on a set of independent variables permits the identification of the latter's effects on the former, while assuming that no variation is taking place among the other independent variables. In other words, in a regression of growth on initial income level, geographic situation, and state capacity, the coefficient of state capacity will estimate its impact on growth, keeping each country's initial income level and geographical situation constant. This technique allows us to compare the explanatory robustness of each of the variables in the model and to distinguish its effects from those of the other ones.

Table 2.4 provides a set of regressions that test the robustness and distinctness of the effects of policies, governance, and capacity on growth. The first column gives a simple estimation of the effects on growth of a country's initial income level and of being an African or a high-performing East Asian country. The measure of initial income aims at capturing the "convergence hypothesis," which Barro first tested in 1991. Because convergence is likely to be nonlinear, first rising and then falling with per capita income, I added a squared measure of it to the regression (quadratic terms capture nonlinear relationships). The regression indicates that the convergence effects are not statistically significant, but the coefficients display the expected signs and suggest a weak negative effect on growth of being a richer country.[14] These variables remain statistically insignificant in each version of the model. The results of the convergence variables are not relevant to this discussion on their own, and we can therefore ignore their lack of significance. Keeping them in the estimations is important, however, as they verify that the effects of other variables are not somehow capturing income effects.

More interesting are the next two variables. These are simple regional "dummies." They tell us that, after controlling for differences in income levels, African countries grow on average 2 percent slower each year than other countries, and the East Asian dragons (which include Japan, Korea, Taiwan, Singapore, Indonesia, Malaysia, and Thailand) more than 3 percent faster. These dummies are measures of our ignorance. If their effects are significant, they are telling us that there is something negative about being an African country and something positive about being an East Asian country that our model does not capture. Observing the evolution of the coefficient of the Africa dummy will provide us, therefore, with an indication of whether the additional variables to be incorporated into the model capture the idiosyncrasies of African underdevelopment.

Table 2.4   **Estimating the Effects of Policies, Governance, and Capacity on Economic Growth (dependent variable: per capita real GDP growth, 1960–1992)**

Variable	(1)	(2)	(3)	(4)	(5)
Initial income level	-0.0322	-0.0364	-0.0391	0.0162	-0.0085
	(1.213)	(1.439)	(1.939)	(0.907)	(0.502)
Initial income level squared	0.0021	0.0021	0.0018	-0.0019	-0.0005
	(1.180)	(1.303)	(1.356)	(1.623)	(0.503)
Africa	-0.0201**	-0.0128*	-0.0059	-0.0115*	-0.0062
	(4.380)	(2.531)	(1.544)	(2.400)	(1.472)
East Asian "dragons"	0.0317**	0.0355**	0.0212**	0.0239**	0.0177**
	(6.290)	(6.861)	(5.959)	(5.475)	(5.704)
Tropical climate	—	-0.0187**	-0.0126**	-0.0105**	-0.0105**
		(5.939)	(4.765)	(3.692)	(4.081)
Landlocked country	—	-0.0027	-0.0045	-0.0002	-0.0029
		(0.838)	(1.638)	(0.097)	(1.252)
Policies	—	—	0.0092**	—	—
			(6.897)		
Governance	—	—	—	0.0058**	—
				(5.618)	
Governance squared	—	—	—	-0.0002	—
				(0.983)	
Capacity	—	—	—	—	0.0211**
					(7.866)
Capacity squared	—	—	—	—	-0.0025
					(1.620)
Adjusted R^2	0.34	0.47	0.73	0.66	0.79
N	133	126	109	105	99

Notes: OLS estimation with White (1980) heteroskedasticity-consistent t statistics in parentheses. Constant omitted.

The variables in these regressions are, respectively, RGDPCH (dependent variable), INC60, INC60SQ, AFRICA, HPAE, TROPICS, LANDLOCK, POLICY, GOVNANCE, GOVSQ, CAPACITY, and CAPSQ. See Appendix 1 for definitions, sources, and methodology.

Significance levels: * = 5%; ** = 1%.

The second column adds two additional measures to the model: an indicator of exposure to tropical climate and a dummy for landlocked countries. Both variables display negative coefficients, but tropical climate alone is statistically significant. Interestingly, however, adding the tropics variable reduces the effect of the Africa dummy from –2 percent to –1.3 percent, indicating that geographical constraints account for a substantial portion of what ails African economies, although by no means all of it.

With only five variables, this second version of the model explains 47 percent of the variation in growth across all the countries of the sample, as suggested by the adjusted R^2. The explanatory power of the model jumps to 73 percent, however, once the policy index is added in the third column. The effects of policies are large and highly significant. A one-unit increase in the index results in 0.9 percent additional annual growth. As the index ranges from about –4 to 4, a country at the top of the rankings can expect to grow by an extra 7 percent a year compared to its worst-scoring counterpart. Note, furthermore, that the Africa dummy is no longer significant. In other words, the combination of tropical climate and government policies fully accounts for what makes Africa different from other regions.[15]

The predictive powers of governance on growth, in the fourth column, are a bit weaker than the policy effects but remain highly significant.[16] Because they are not linear, it is not possible to summarize these effects with merely one figure. By means of example, however, a country scoring 2 on the governance index would grow about half a percent faster than a country scoring 1. Low levels of governance would bring about a greater effect, higher levels a weaker one.

Finally, the last column estimates the overall impact of developmental capacity on growth. Its explanatory power is strongest, accounting for 79 percent of the variation in growth across the sample. Again, the relationship is not linear, but a country scoring 1 on the capacity index would grow almost 2 percent faster, year in, year out, than a country scoring 0. Again, the Africa dummy becomes insignificant. Observe also that the East Asian dummy has fallen from 3.6 percent in the second column to 1.8 percent in the fifth one, indicating that a large part of the East Asian miracle is also a function of state capacity.

These results confirm both the importance of good policies and good governance for economic development and the view that Africa's crisis is to a large extent a crisis of capacity. In fact, capacity alone explains at least 30 percent of the variation in growth across the world. Together with a measure of the adversities of geography, it seems to fully capture the roots of Africa's predicament. Chapter 3 looks more closely at Africa's specific performance, describing both its average trend and the surprising amount of variation in state capacity from country to country.

NOTES

1. Although my definition is less encompassing than the standard concept of capacity, the pursuit of developmental goals and good governance is nevertheless so multifaceted that it ends up involving most of the

characteristics usually associated with the standard definition, including reg-
ulatory capacity, administrative capacity, technical capacity, the ability to
enforce rules, to protect property rights, to provide public order, and so forth
(see Brautigam 1996).

2. Barro (1991), Barro and Lee (1996), Sachs and Warner (1997a), to
name a few.

3. Although he is better known for his advocacy of free markets,
Smith actually stressed the need for government intervention in certain sec-
tors of the economy and in creating the context of a "well-governed society"
(Smith 1976:15) for the division of labor to take place.

4. See Amsden (1985), Wade (1990), and Haggard (1990). Note also
that these very same distortions have also been largely blamed for the East
Asian crisis of the late 1990s.

5. It should be pointed out, however, that this is probably the least
robust of the identified effects of policies on growth, as some other studies
have failed to find similar effects of trade openness.

6. This process is still largely unfinished, as witnessed by the resigna-
tion in November 1999 of the World Bank's chief economist, Joseph
Stiglitz, over his disagreement with the Bank's failure to account for the
institutional dimensions of East Asia's crisis (see *New York Times,* 25
November and 2 December 1999).

7. The United States, for example, has to a large extent equated governance with democracy and pursues it as an objective in itself, and not so
much as an instrument for economic development (see Lancaster 1993).
Under President Mitterrand, after 1990, France also made its development
aid and debt forgiveness conditional upon democratic reforms in its former
African colonies, although this policy was implemented with different
degrees of enthusiasm according to France's geostrategic interests in the
region. Gabon and Cameroon, for example, got away without true reforms,
whereas the leadership in Mali and Benin could not avoid substantial
democratization.

8. See Ndulu and van de Walle (1996).

9. With governance's impact on growth, as we saw earlier with policies, one can often argue that the direction of causality is theoretically
unclear, as it is possible that the rate of growth also affects the quality of
governance and of policy choices. Many of the authors discussed in this
chapter were aware of this potential pitfall, however, and most used statistical techniques to ascertain the direction of the causality. Even after controlling for such reciprocal influences, their results robustly indicated a causal
relationship *from* capacity *to* growth.

10. In Appendix 1, to which I relegate all technical discussions of
methodology, sources, and variable definitions, these variables are labeled,
respectively, SCHOOL, TELPW, G, OPEN, BLCK, and LLY. The index
itself is labeled POLICY. The measure of educational investment is indirect,
as it captures the mean years of educational achievement. Barro and Lee
(1996) have argued that this is a better measure of educational levels than
enrollment rates, as it also measures the quality of the educational system
and not only the number of children enrolled. It is also better than indicators
of government expenditure since a large part of the education budgets of

governments goes to teacher salaries, which in many countries are also instruments of patronage.

11. For an important discussion of these data, see Appendix 1.

12. The data sets of most of the studies mentioned as data sources for both policy and governance indicators can be downloaded from the World Bank's Economic Growth Research web page at http://www.worldbank.org/html/prdmg/grthweb/growth_t.htm. For more details on sources, variable definitions, and methodology, see Appendix 1. The variables of the governance index are labeled COMMIT, EXPROP, CORRUPT, INSTQUAL, BUROQUAL, CIVL, and HOMELANG. The index itself is labeled GOVNANCE.

13. For discussion of and evidence for the convergence hypothesis, see Solow (1956), Jones (1998), Barro (1991), and Barro and Sala-i-Martin (1995), among others.

14. The coefficient of convergence is significantly negative when the log of initial income is entered on its own. The overall goodness of fit of the regression, however, is better with a squared term. Since my purpose is to maximize the overall explanatory power of the model rather than to prove the convergence hypothesis, I use both terms in each estimation.

15. Sachs and Warner (1997a) and Barro (1997) actually reduced the Africa dummy to even greater statistical insignificance after controlling for different policies and measures of institutional quality. The reason why the Africa dummy's significance drops by less in my estimates has to do with the larger representation of African countries in my sample than in theirs. It should also be noted that some portion of the reduction in the coefficients of the African and East Asian dummies may be due to the reduction in sample size between the two specifications.

16. With governance as with capacity in column 5, I enter an additional square term to capture the nonlinearity of the relationship with growth. The square term is not by itself significant, but it improves the goodness of fit of the regression and the behavior of the residuals. In these regressions as in all subsequent ones, the residuals are well behaved, aside from problems of heteroskedasticity, which I correct with White (1980) robust standard errors.

3

The Paradox of African State Capacity

According to the September 1998 issue of *Business Traveler International*,

> Security at Lagos Airport in the Nigerian capital sunk to a new low in late June, when bandits broke into the luggage hold of an Air Afrique aircraft preparing to taxi down the runway and stole luggage as passengers watched from inside the plane.[1]

Frequent travelers to Nigeria and some other African capitals will be familiar with similar stories. They are telling examples of the failure of some African states to provide even the most basic services expected of them, the very services—the security of people and property—whose provision justifies their existence. If an African government, in peacetime, can no longer control its international airport located in its capital city,[2] can it reasonably be expected to devise and implement policies for economic development, create stable expectations for investors, guarantee property rights, and provide an efficient bureaucracy and a climate free of corruption? The answer, of course, is no. And to make matters worse, not only are many African governments unable to provide these basic levels of governance, but not a few are actively engaged in criminal activities of their own (Reno 1995; Reno 1998; Bayart et al. 1999).

Nigeria, Sierra Leone, Liberia, Somalia, the Congo Republic, former Zaire, and a handful of others are extreme cases of state failures in Africa. They represent the bottom of the range of performance of African states. Yet although the average African state is not collapsed, its capacity to provide order and security, to devise and implement policies for growth, to adopt and enforce laws, to regulate

41

markets, to control its borders and its civil servants, to credibly engage in commercial transactions, to adjudicate disputes, and to allocate resources is generally and comparatively weak. In other words, the average developmental capacity of African states is low.

Africa's weak average performance is part of our common discourse. Not only do its human tragedies receive generous media attention, but we also take for granted its enduring failure to develop when calamities are absent. On average, we are right. What is less well-known, however, is the great variance that exists across Africa in the quality of policies, governance, or more simply, in state capacity. For every failed state, there also seems to be a success story. Four African countries have grown by more than 3 percent per year in per capita terms between their independence and 1992, and seven by 2 percent or more. With population growth rates averaging 3 percent across the continent, this represents a considerable economic achievement.

The paradox of African state capacity is important if we are to make sense of Africa's development crisis. Indeed, any theoretical explanation of Africa's underdevelopment must also be able to account for developmental differences within Africa. This chapter briefly reviews Africa's average capacity failure and contrasts it with the wide range of intra-African variations in capacity, setting aside for now the disasters of collapsed states, which have been well documented elsewhere (Zartman 1995; Villalón and Huxtable 1998). Africa's success stories are identified below in order to lay the foundations toward understanding the roots of developmental capacity in Africa as elsewhere.

LAST OF THE CLASS:
CAPACITY IN AFRICA AND THE DEVELOPING WORLD

African countries generally perform worse than their counterparts elsewhere in the developed and developing world on most indicators of developmental policy and good governance. The best-performing African country on the composite policy index derived in Chapter 2 was Mauritius, which was forty-fourth worldwide. Of the twenty-five countries with the worst policies, twenty-one were African (see Table 2.1). Botswana had the best record of good governance for all of Africa, yet did no better than thirtieth among all countries of the world. Again, most of the countries with bad governance are in

Africa, sixteen out of the worst twenty-five (see Table 2.2). As for overall capacity, no African country did better than thirty-four (Lesotho) and, again, twenty-one out of the twenty-five worst performers were African (see Table 2.3). Figure 3.1 illustrates the comparative performance of African countries on the state capacity index. The vertical axis represents average rates of per capita economic growth from 1960 or independence to 1992. The horizontal axis shows countries' performance on the developmental capacity index derived in Chapter 2. As is readily visible, most African countries grow slower than other countries in the world, and most of them also display weaker levels of capacity. Africa's development crisis is indeed a crisis of state capacity.

To be sure, Africa's weak average performance was partly inherited from colonialism. Although there were variations among colonial powers, the general trend did not favor the development of African economies. As Table 3.1 makes clear, following decades of colonization, African countries were poorer than other developing countries, and their human capital foundations were weaker to begin with. (Note that OECD countries are not included in the comparison group in any of the following tables.) The undereducation of

Figure 3.1   Comparing Africa (1) to the Rest of the World (0) in Terms of Developmental Capacity and Economic Growth

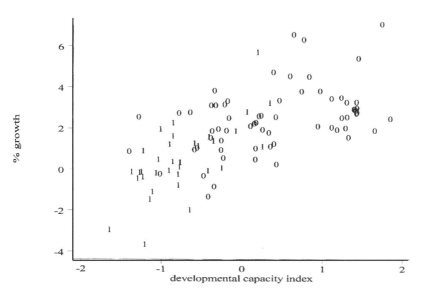

Table 3.1 How Africa Differed from Other Developing Countries at the Time of Independence

Conditions at Independence	Africa (n)		Other Developing Countries (n)		t Test P Value
Level of income in 1960 (or at time of independence) (U.S.$)**	911	(44)	2,251	(65)	0.0000
Gross primary school enrollment rates (1960) (%)**	39.47	(40)	83.59	(72)	0.0000
Gross secondary school enrollment rates (1960) (%)**	3.35	(37)	22.54	(72)	0.0000

Source: See Appendix 1, where these variables are referred to as INC60, PRIMED, and SECED.

Notes: Comparison of averages for Africa and other developing countries.

Gross enrollment rates refer to the number of children in school in percentage of the relevant age group.

P value refers to the probability that the difference between the averages is due to chance.

Significance levels: ** = 1%.

Africans at independence certainly was a liability. Their poverty, on the other hand, could have led to faster growth, as undercapitalized countries offer investments a higher rate of return than elsewhere.[3]

Africa's immediate colonial legacy is but a small part of its development failure, however. In the years following independence, African elites seem to have chosen with great consistency policies that were inimical to their development. Robert Bates (1981) has discussed the details of African agricultural policies that create rents, biases, and misallocations of resources. The famous *Berg Report* (World Bank 1981) also provided a damning indictment of African economic policies, stressing how "domestic policy inadequacies" had compounded Africa's internal and external structural problems:

> First, trade and exchange-rate policies have overprotected industry, held back agriculture, and absorbed much administrative capacity. Second, too little attention has been paid to administrative constraints in mobilizing and managing resources for development; given the widespread weakness of planning, decision making and management capacities, public sectors frequently become overextended. Third, there has been a consistent bias against agriculture in price, tax, and exchange-rate policies. (World Bank 1981:4)

A more recent assessment, by more impartial observers, confirms the diagnosis of misguided African policymaking:

Economic policy distortions in Sub-Saharan Africa have had unde-
sirable and deleterious effects on growth and efficiency in resource
use. Uncertainties arising from macroeconomic instability have
proven inimical to private investment, while distorted incentive
structures have spurred inefficient allocation of resources and hampered productivity growth. (Ndulu and van de Walle 1996:6)

The empirical evidence confirms these somber judgments. Table
3.2 shows that on most policy indicators with implications for long-
run economic growth (those that relate to the allocation of resources
between current expenditure and productive public investments and
those that introduce growth-retarding distortions), African states
have in general fared much worse than other developing countries
over the last thirty-five years or so. African governments manage to
keep their children in school only half as long as those of other
developing regions. They provide about one quarter of the infrastructure that other developing governments provide, yet they represent a
significantly higher burden on their economies in terms of their current consumption. They also introduce more distortions in their

Table 3.2   How Africa's Economic Policies Differ from Those of Other Developing Countries

	Africa (n)	Other Developing Countries (n)	t Test P Value
Average years of schooling attainment** (average 1960–1985)	2.22 (40)	4.49 (72)	0.0000
Telephones per 1,000 workers** (average 1960–1989)	10.04 (44)	40.65 (65)	0.0000
Government spending as share of GDP (average 1960 or independence–1992)**	23.86 (44)	17.67 (65)	0.0000
Ratio of liquid liabilities to GDP (average 1960–1989)**	0.19 (36)	0.34 (49)	0.0003
Exports and imports as share of GDP (average 1960 or independence–1989)	65.22 (44)	66.48 (65)	0.4406
Foreign exchange black market premium (log of 1 + premium, average 1960–1989)	0.30 (40)	0.33 (60)	0.3266
Number of instances of debt relief agreements (1980–1994)*	3.34 (38)	2.10 (74)	0.0240
Developmental policy index**	-1.37 (38)	0.23 (53)	0.0000

Source: See Appendix 1, where these variables are referred to as SCHOOL, TELPW,
G, LLY, OPEN, BLCK, DRELIEF, and POLICY.
   Notes: Comparison of averages for Africa and other developing countries.
   P value refers to the probability that the difference between the averages is due to
chance.
   Significance levels: ** = 1%; * = 5%.

financial sectors, leaving their economies with dangerously shallow financial systems. As a result, it is no wonder that they borrow from abroad with greater alacrity and end up more vulnerable to the burden of foreign debt. African countries averaged 3.3 instances of debt rescheduling from 1980 to 1994, as against 2.1 for other developing countries. Only with respect to openness to trade and distortions in foreign exchange are there no differences between African and other developing countries. Here the results are probably misleading, however. The countries from the Communauté Financière Africaine (CFA) franc zone, the monetary area of fourteen African countries linked to the French franc, have virtually no parallel exchange market because of the free convertibility of their currency. This artificially boosts the performance of Africa as a whole. As for openness to foreign trade, the fact that Africa has ratios of imports and exports to GDP similar to other regions hides differences in the content of its exports and imports. Africa exports more primary commodities than other regions and in greater concentration, and imports more consumer and manufactured goods. Hence, although Africa started worse off than other regions, its governments have done little to generate a catch-up process and have instead largely contributed to the widening of the gap between their continent and the rest of the developing world.

Over the last few years, voices have claimed improvements in African macroeconomic policies (e.g., World Bank 1995b). Recent improvements in economic performance, however, have been mostly the result of temporarily advantageous terms of trade that have boosted export revenues for many countries. Policy reform, on the other hand, has been neither as far-reaching nor as sustained as some development agencies would argue.[4] In the words of a specialist of African political economy,

> on closer inspection, it is clear that economic policy reform is not nearly as advanced as is sometimes claimed. . . . For the most part, . . . progress remains uneven and slow, with repeated setbacks. Average fiscal deficits . . . remain at an unsustainable 4.1 percent of GDP, compared to 4.7 percent in 1990. Ten countries still have deficits of at least one-tenth of GDP. Tariff structures have been simplified and average tariffs lowered, but many countries remain among the world's most protectionist, at least officially; however, the levels of custom exemptions and corruption are also among the world's highest. More complex, institutional reforms like privatization are also proceeding at a snail's pace, if at all. Moreover, it is not clear how sustainable actual reform achievements are, as struc-

tural adjustment programs remain deeply unpopular in many countries. Yet, without much deeper progress on economic reform,
growth is unlikely to persist. (van de Walle 1998:12)

African states also underprovide governance to their economies
(Table 3.3). They are more likely than other developing countries to
renounce their contractual obligations and to fail to enforce property rights. They are also more corrupt and consequently have weaker
institutions and bureaucracies in which their citizens display little
trust. They do not offer the latter many services but, on the other
hand, do not hesitate to repress them and deprive them of civil liberties. Finally, they hardly communicate with their citizens, 73 percent of whom, on average in Africa, do not speak the official language at home. Elsewhere in the developing world the figure is
about 28 percent.

Like policies, African governance has seen less substantial
progress over the last few years than is sometimes noted. If anything,
civil wars have become more widespread following the end of the
cold war and have further eroded the average quality of African governance. The politics of "warlordism" has also spread beyond the

Table 3.3   How African Governance Differs from Other Developing Countries

	Africa (n)	Other Developing Countries (n)	t Test P Value
Enforceability of contracts**	4.94 (43)	5.96 (75)	0.0004
Protection from expropriation**	5.90 (43)	6.78 (75)	0.0018
Freedom from corruption*	4.38 (43)	5.07 (75)	0.0232
Quality of (and trust in) public institutions*	4.15 (43)	5.07 (75)	0.0010
Quality of bureaucracy	4.24 (43)	4.76 (75)	0.0659
Extent of repression of civil liberties**	5.42 (39)	4.09 (55)	0.0000
Extent of linguistic alienation**	72.89 (46)	27.9 (76)	0.0000
Overall governance quality index**	-1.64 (37)	-0.46 (46)	0.0001

Source: See Appendix 1, where these variables are referred to as COMMIT, EXPROP,
CORRUPT, INSTQUAL, BUROQUAL, CIVL, HOMELANG, and GOVNANCE.

Notes: Comparison of averages for Africa and other developing countries. The first
five indicators are scaled from 0 (bad) to 10 (good) and averaged over the 1985–1995 period. Civil liberties is scaled from 1 (free) to 7 (repressive) and averaged over the
1960–1989 period. The extent of linguistic alienation is the percentage of households who
do not speak the national language at home as of mid-1990s. The governance quality index
is a summary measure of the other seven indicators with a worldwide mean of 0 and standard deviation of 1. P value refers to the probability that the difference between the averages is due to chance.

Significance levels: ** = 1%; * = 5%.

worst cases of state failure (Reno 1998). And much of the democratic progress registered in the early 1990s has stalled or been reversed.

The end result is that African states have been and remain altogether less developmentally capable than their counterparts in other areas of the third world. The average score of African countries on the index of state capacity is –0.75. For other third world countries, it is –0.06.[5] The empirical evidence therefore provides strong support for the consensual view among Africanists and development scholars that African governments bear a large responsibility in the economic predicament of their continent.

SUCCESS AMID FAILURE:
VARIATIONS IN AFRICAN STATE CAPACITY

While the story of African government failure is becoming increasingly well-known, there is an unfortunate attendant propensity among observers to subsume the entire continent under this blanket of crisis, if not chaos.[6] The news from Africa is often bad and so, progressively, has become the image of the continent as a whole. On closer inspection, however, African countries offer a wide spectrum of developmental experiences and capacity levels. For every Congo, there seems to be a Botswana, for every Somalia, a Mauritius. The best-performing African countries may not often be the fastest growing in the world or those with the absolute best institutions, but they certainly display levels of state capacity above average for the developing world.

Table 3.4 indicates that a few countries appear, over and again, as the champions of capacity in Africa. Botswana, which has the fastest rate of economic growth in all Africa, also displays the best governance across the continent. In no uncertain terms, Stephen Lewis has made clear the role of state capacity in the miracle of Botswana's growth:

> How does one explain Botswana's excellent, even extraordinary, economic performance, especially in comparison with the rest of Sub-Saharan Africa? The basic answer, I believe, is this: While good fortune plays an important role, unusually good economic policy choices were essential to achieving outstanding economic results. (1993:11)

Furthermore, state capacity in Botswana had to counteract an inaus-

Table 3.4   A Comparative Look at the Range of Developmental Performance in Africa

	All LDCs Average	Africa's Weakest	Africa's Best	Africa's Best Country
Indicators of Developmental Policies				
Average years of schooling attainment	3.49	1.26	5.37	Seychelles
Telephones per 1,000 workers	23.1	1.15	130.31	Zimbabwe
Government spending as share of GDP	20.17	44.21	11.11	Cape Verde
Financial depth (liquidity as share of GDP)	27.89	3.39	48.97	Lesotho
Exports and imports as share of GDP	65	22	140	Swaziland
Black market foreign exchange premium[a]	1.38	1.14	0.03	Gambia
Overall policy index, from −4 to 4	−0.44	−3.69	0.67	Mauritius
Indicators of Good Governance				
Enforceability of contract, from 0 to 10	5.59	1.68	8.00	Lesotho
Protection from expropriation, from 0 to 10	6.46	2.00	9.33	Swaziland
Freedom from corruption, from 0 to 10	4.82	0.00	8.33	Cape Verde
Quality of public institutions, from 0 to 10	4.74	0.83	8.33	Botswana
Quality of bureaucracy, from 0 to 10	4.57	0.67	7.33	Cape Verde
Extent of civil liberties, from 1 to 7	4.64	1.20	5.50	Mauritius
Extent of linguistic alienation[b]	44.8	95	5	Botswana, Burundi, Lesotho, Madagascar, Rwanda, Seychelles, Somalia
Overall good governance index, from −4 to 4	−0.98	−4.00	1.30	Botswana
Overall state capacity index, from −2 to 2	−0.38	−1.64	0.35	Lesotho
Annual per capita GDP growth, 1960–92 (%)	1.55	−3.79	5.59	Botswana

Source: See Appendix 1, where these variables are referred to as SCHOOL, TELPW, G, LLY, OPEN, BLCK, POLICY, COMMIT, EXPROP, CORRUPT, INSTQUAL, BUROQUAL, CIVL, HOMELANG, GOVNANCE, CAPACITY, and RGDPCH.

Notes: The first column reflects the average performance of all developing countries on each indicator. The second and third columns indicate the worst and best African performances on each indicator, whereas the fourth column names the African country with the best performance for each indicator. South Africa is excluded from the sample.

The time periods over which these variables are calculated are mentioned in Tables 3.2 and 3.3.

a. Expressed in log form. Does not include Liberia, whose dollar has been at par with the U.S. dollar since 1940, and CFA franc countries, which have fixed parity and automatic convertibility with the French franc.

b. % of population which does not speak official language at home.

picious physical setting: landlocked, vulnerable to drought, and dependent on a couple of commodities, Botswana appeared in many ways headed to the same predicament as other African countries; it literally extracted itself from its underdevelopment with good policies and sound institutions.

But it is actually Mauritius, another fast-grower, which appears to have had the most consistent set of growth-inducing policies over the last thirty years. Here again, however, independence was reached "under decidedly cloudy skies" (Brautigam 1999:141). And here again, the government extracted the country's economy from a single-commodity dependence (sugar), transforming it into a fast-growing, manufacturing-based, and export-promoting system largely patterned after the Taiwanese model and equally successful, despite a context of much higher ethnic heterogeneity (Meisenhelder 1997).

Lesotho and Swaziland are other cases in point. Lesotho has the highest overall capacity score of all African countries, the greatest financial depth, a robust system of contract laws, and linguistic closeness to its citizens. Despite a punishing dependence on the economy of South Africa (about 40 percent of its GDP is accounted for by remittances from migrants to South Africa), Lesotho has managed to provide its small economy, plagued by high population density, a poor climate, and difficult terrain, with a measure of economic diversification and a sustained rate of growth. Manufacturing, which accounted for a mere 7 percent of GDP in 1980, had risen to 18 percent of GDP by 1995, at which time industry altogether accounted for 56 percent of GDP.[7]

As for Swaziland, it is the African economy most open to international trade and most friendly toward private investments. Although it is also highly dependent on South Africa's economy, successive governments have mitigated this vulnerability by sustaining policies of industrialization that turned manufacturing into the largest segment of the economy by the 1990s (Matthews 1995). In addition, its "consistent determination to maintain an investment climate attractive to foreign business . . . has brought Swaziland a rate of post-independence capital formation not achieved in most African states" (Matthews 1995:914).

Of all the governments of Africa, that of Cape Verde has followed the greatest relative austerity since its independence in 1975, representing no more than about 11 percent of the country's GDP on average. Of course, Cape Verde benefits from remittances from its large population abroad, including in the United States (there are more Cape Verdians living abroad than at home). Nevertheless, although remittances from comparatively wealthy migrants certainly contribute to its good overall economic performance, that alone does not explain the diminutive burden that the government represents upon the economy, nor does it account for why Cape Verde is also reportedly the least corrupt of all African governments. All the other former Portuguese colonies have fared much, much worse indeed.

Despite a socialist orientation for most of the country's independent life, Cape Verde's economy remained mixed and

> there have been no attempts on the part of the government to increase its active penetration of the commercial economy. Even where enterprises are controlled by the state or where the state has a partnership interest, physical intervention is kept to a minimum and these enterprises are expected to be self-financing and, indeed, they are. . . . Even the state marketing companies . . . [are] required to turn in a profit. (Foy 1988:112)

Compare this with most of sub-Saharan Africa, where state enterprises are more often political sinecures than actual productive units.

The Seychelles also started independent life with a socialist regime and few resources on which to build a developmental strategy. Yet the government, having inherited a good educational infrastructure from the colonial era, maintained the country's superior achievements in human capital and exploited its comparative advantage in tourism. The government encouraged development of commercial links with international airlines, sponsored the creation of several hotels and other tourist attractions, expanded the port of Victoria, and financed road construction. In other words, it privileged, by and large, the development of human capital and infrastructure, providing foundations for continued growth.

But what accounts for the developmental capacity of these countries? How have they avoided the general continental tendency toward bad policies and poor governance? Where did their governments find the political capital to embark upon strategies of structural transformation and industrialization, with the destabilizing effects of the potential attendant redistribution of income and power in society? How did they resist nationalizations and their promise of easy government revenues, or expropriations and their costless acquisition of assets for government members? Where did they find the discipline to contain corruption and maintain efficient institutions? In short, what differentiates them from the rest of Africa?

African capacity success stories remind us that we cannot speak of Africa's crisis as a uniform condition of the continent. Theories that purport to explain Africa's underdevelopment with continent-wide explanations—as most do—fail to account for intra-African differences. They may discount cases of absolute failures as extremes of the continental trend, but they cannot account for success. Yet if something about Africa is inimical to development and capacity, we should find that its distribution is uneven across the continent. Africa's differential experience with capacity provides, therefore, a unique opportunity for testing theories of African underdevelopment. To be credible, a hypothesis must not only account for the difference between Africa and the rest of the world but also be able to explain the range of performance within Africa.

There should be little doubt left that Africa's development crisis is one of capacity. In Part 2, I offer a theory of what constrains the capacity of states in Africa and around the world. I hope to explain what makes Africa so much worse than other developing regions while simultaneously differentiating African capacity miracles from the continent's dismal average trend. First, it is necessary to point out how the currently prevailing theories of Africa's stagnation fail the test of accounting for both dimensions of the paradox of African capacity.

NOTES

1. *Business Traveler International,* September 1998, 10.

2. Nigeria's federal capital is now technically Abuja, but Lagos remains an important center of economic and political activity.

3. This is the convergence hypothesis briefly discussed in Chapter 2.

4. As a matter of fact, even the impression of improved economic performance in the 1990s may be somewhat overstated in the aggregate. According to the World Bank's 1999 *World Development Indicators,* nineteen African countries still experienced negative per capita GDP growth over the 1990–1997 period, while another eight of them grew by less than 1 percent per year.

5. The difference is significant at the 1 percent level. As explained in Chapter 2, the worldwide average of the state capacity index is 0, based on a sample that includes most OECD countries.

6. See, for example, Kaplan (1994) and Ayittey (1998).

7. World Bank, *World Development Indicators 1997,* 135.

PART 2

Explaining
Africa's Capacity Crisis

4

Do Social Capital and Ethnic Homogeneity Really Matter?

Joseph Schumpeter once argued that "when we succeed in finding a definite causal relation between two phenomena, our problem is solved if the one which plays the 'causal' rôle is non-economic. We have then accomplished what we, as economists, are capable of in the case in question" (Schumpeter 1983:5). To some extent, the many recent studies that have improved our understanding of the determinants of growth in Africa have followed Schumpeter's approach. They have shown that policies and governance are crucial ingredients for development and that Africa's crisis is, to a large extent, a crisis of state capacity. But rarely have they probed further and asked what in turn accounts for cross-national differences in developmental capacity. Jeffrey Sachs, for example, has argued in *The Economist* (1996) that "growth can be done" in Africa if only governments chose the right policies. But why don't they? Robert Barro (1997) has established that African governments' propensity to spend a larger proportion of their GDP than other governments contributed to their country's underdevelopment. But why do they exert such a high burden on their economies?

If we are to make sense of development, which is a multifaceted process, we need to step beyond economics and explain why some states are successful at choosing and implementing developmental policies and providing adequate governance to their markets whereas others are not.[1] We need to understand where differences in policies, governance, and capacity come from. Why do some countries systematically choose policies that are inimical to growth while others maintain the often arduous discipline of promoting it? Why do some manage to build strong institutions while others run theirs into the ground? What makes some states developmental and others not?

55

A few scholars, both in political science and in economics, have tried to answer these questions in recent years. The theory of *social capital,* which has developed since the early 1990s, has provided one answer by making the quality of institutions and policies dependent upon the prevalence of norms of trust and associative life. This effort (which is to a certain extent a revival of the civic culture argument of the 1960s)[2] has much to be commended for and has no doubt made a significant contribution to the study of development over the last few years. But the contributions of social capital theory are not without their own set of controversies, including occasional conceptual confusion, empirical ambiguities, and poor relevance to Africa.

Another recent and already quite popular theory of state capacity contends that *ethnic heterogeneity* leads to the adoption of policies that are inimical to growth and weakens the quality of institutions, as resources are diverted toward the management of polarized social relations. Unlike social capital, whose presence or absence in a given country still needs to be explained, this approach provides a more truly exogenous explanation for policy choices and governance quality. Yet the ethnic polarization hypothesis suffers from even more serious shortcomings than the social capital theory, including a simplistic view of ethnic identity and empirical fragility. Furthermore, it fails to explain variations in capacity and growth within Africa.

These two theories are certainly not exhaustive. Much has been written on the topic since some authors first suggested in the late 1970s that the so-called East Asian miracle was a function of government intervention, policy choice, and bureaucratic steering rather than of pure market mechanisms (Amsden 1979; Amsden 1985; Wade 1990). The other most common theory stresses that state capacity is a function of *governmental and bureaucratic autonomy* (Amsden 1985; Skocpol 1985; Haggard 1990; Evans 1995). Stephan Haggard (1990), for example, views the success of East Asia as the consequence of government strategies of export-led growth in conjunction with a capacity for flexible response to external shocks. The choice of these policies was in part a function of international pressures, the interplay of domestic forces, ideology, as well as the autonomy and cohesion of state actors.

What the autonomy argument lacks, however, is a plausible explanation of why autonomous agents would choose policies that enhance social welfare over policies with immediate benefits to themselves. In other words, it still needs a theory on the determinants of constraints to opportunistic behavior. Peter Evans (1995) provides an answer with the concept of *embedded autonomy.* He argues that effective state bureaucracies need not only be coherent and autonomous but also require close institutionalized links with other segments of society, specifically, in the case of Korea, which he surveyed, with the private elite and business community at the helm of the *chaebol* conglomerates. These links are shaped through a common education and a relative class identity between the state and private elites. Evans later expanded this idea and concluded that norms of trust and the "impersonal networks" on which these norms are based constitute economic assets for public institutions in societies characterized by egalitarian social structures and coherent state bureaucracies (Evans 1996a; 1996b). In other words, he related his idea of embeddedness to that of social capital. Because of this evolution of the autonomy hypothesis toward social capital theory, and because the state autonomy theory has been around longer and is better known than the ones addressed here, I do not give it further attention and turn instead to the social capital and ethnic homogeneity theories of state capacity.[3]

SOCIAL CAPITAL THEORY AND AFRICAN DEVELOPMENT

Social capital theory makes government and institutional effectiveness a function of a country's "features of social organization, such as trust, norms, and networks, that can improve the efficiency of society by facilitating coordinated actions" (Putnam 1993a:167).[4] Although social capital theory has some antecedents in French sociology in the 1970s, James Coleman (1990) articulated the first *economic* theory of social capital, which was then extended by Robert Putnam to account for the efficiency of government and democracy in northern Italy. Putnam explains north-south differences in the institutional performance of similar regional governments in Italy by contending that the "active, public spirited citizenry" of the north, marked by "egalitarian political relations" and by "a social fabric of trust and cooperation" (1993a:15) lies at the root of the north's superior institutional capacity. Generalizing the Italian case, he offers that a nation's level of "civic culture" is the main determinant of its institutional performance, a theory that also has antecedents in comparative politics (Almond and Verba 1963; 1980).

This approach (popularized by Fukuyama 1995) has contributed to the further development of the economic theory of social capital (Helliwell and Putnam 1995; Helliwell 1996; Widner and Mundt

1998; Barr 1997; Keefer and Knack 1997; La Porta et al. 1997; Collier 1998c). In this context, social capital is the resource by which civic culture contributes to political and economic development. It is a compound of trust, norms of reciprocity, participation and equality, and of associative life.[5] The idea is not too distant from what sociologist Mark Granovetter calls the "embeddedness" of economic transactions in social relations, "the role of concrete personal relations and structures (or 'networks') of such relations in generating trust and discouraging malfeasance" (1985:490), which, as mentioned earlier, also recoups Evans's (1995) idea of embeddedness.

Coleman's (1990) original work emphasized the economic mechanisms of social capital, paying less attention to institutional issues. For him, the economic resources contributed by social capital took the form of reciprocal obligations and expectations, reductions in informational asymmetries, norms of nonopportunism and effective sanctions, authority relations that overcome the free-rider problem, and "appropriable social and intentional organizations," which, set up for one purpose, actually generate social capital as a by-product (1990:306–312). Putnam's approach, on the other hand, focuses more explicitly on the effects of social capital on institutional efficiency. He sees social capital's bonds of minimal trust, norms of cooperation, stable expectations, and reciprocal obligations as inhibiting policymakers' and bureaucrats' opportunism.[6]

Current research on social capital has maintained these two approaches. The first appears to be gaining some ascendency in the contemporary literature. Francis Fukuyama (1995; 1997), John F. Helliwell (1996), John Humphrey and Hubert Schmitz (1996), Abigail Barr (1997), Ronald Inglehart (1997), and Philip Keefer and Stephen Knack (1997) all more or less bypass the institutional emphasis in their discussion of social capital's effects on growth.[7] From their perspective, social capital is credited with reducing transaction costs for private agents through trust, favoring innovation and productivity, triggering greater investment by helping people adopt longer horizons, establishing norms of cooperation, facilitating information, and resolving prisoners' dilemmas.

But the second approach, with its study of the effects of social capital on institutions, may well be more relevant to Africa's crisis, which is largely one of institutional weakness. From this perspective, in addition to the reduction in opportunism perceived by Putnam, the possible mechanisms by which social capital leads to better institutions include the greater credibility that high trust brings to the pronouncements of policymakers, thereby favoring policy design and implementation (Keefer and Knack 1997); the creation of positive expectations among citizens of each other's behavior, which "can relieve the government from the burden of enforcing compliance and free up resources"; the inducement of civic virtue and its attendant shift in individual preferences from self-interest to community-orientation; and the facilitation of coordination among elites, both within the government and with the opposition, by fostering "accommodative practices among otherwise antagonistic elites" (Boix and Posner 1998:691–692).

Both versions of social capital theory have taken the development community by storm. The World Bank and even its more conservative neighbor, the International Monetary Fund (IMF), are now commonly making references to social capital in their official discourses. The World Bank has been particularly keen to promote social capital research (see, among many, Serageldin and Taboroff 1994; Dia 1996; Serageldin and Grootaert 1997; Collier 1998c; Grootaert 1998). With assistance from the government of Denmark, it even embarked in 1996 on a Social Capital Initiative (SCI) that aimed at "defining, monitoring and measuring social capital" and at supporting "operations which promote and strengthen social capital" (World Bank 1998a). Eleven projects were selected to receive funding from the initiative:

1. Fostering social capital through federal decentralization in Mexico
2. Community action for solid waste management: Self-help in Dhaka, Bangladesh
3. Social capital development implementation study—India coal mining
4. Depletion and restoration of social capital in war-torn societies (Rwanda and Cambodia)
5. Induced social capital formation in the Andes
6. Social capital in transition (Mongolia and Russia)
7. Measuring social capital in a postcommunist society (Russia)
8. Ethnic fragmentation, political institutions, and social capital in Africa
9. Giving empirical and operational content to social capital: explaining development outcomes in Rajasthan watersheds
10. Monitoring and measuring the relative impact of social capital on decentralized water and sanitation projects (Indonesia)
11. Kenya local community action project

The papers they produced were discussed in June 1999 at a World Bank conference on Social Capital and Poverty Reduction in Washington, D.C. The Bank has also developed an extensive Web site dedicated to the dissemination of ideas and findings on social capital.[8]

Although the SCI projects are only studies at this point and do not represent actual development projects based on social capital theory, the 1999 annual report of the World Bank lists a few projects whose rationales seem at least partly to derive from the insights of social capital theory, including a $33 million loan to Guatemala to "create a more effective, accessible and credible judicial system that would foster public trust" and a $7.5 million loan to Azerbaijan to "help strengthen national identity and social cohesion" (World Bank 1999a:173, 175).

The IMF has followed suit. Concerned that the conventional approach of its structural adjustment credits has not fully succeeded in bringing back sustainable growth to recipient countries, it has recently turned its attention to "second generation reforms," that is, reforms of social, economic, and political institutions for the sustained implementation of macroeconomic policies, among which it includes building social capital (International Monetary Fund 1999).

Social capital theory has clearly become a popular and promising field of research in development studies and has entered the world of policy implementation. The World Bank and the IMF largely seem to take its developmental effects for granted. And yet upon closer look, it remains in fact a very muddled area of enquiry, fraught with conceptual problems, weak empirical support, and an apparent lack of relevance to Africa.

To begin with conceptual issues, social capital suffers from a plurality of definitions, many of which are loose and some of which are tautological. Associative life and social trust are encompassing concepts to begin with. But several authors and development agencies have gone even further, blurring concepts into one another, bringing causes and effects together, and exposing social capital theory to a significant danger of tautology. According to the World Bank's 1999 *Annual Report,* for example, social capital "refers to institutions, relationships, attitudes and values that govern interactions among people in society and contribute to economic and social development" (World Bank 1999a:122). The two main weaknesses of this definition are (1) its equation of social capital with institutions, which makes any analysis of the effects of one on the other impossible; and (2) its confinement to those institutions, relationships, attitude, and values that actually contribute to economic development, guaranteeing the effect from the alleged cause. From this perspective, if there is development, the prevailing institutions, relationships, attitudes, and values will be said to be social capital. Otherwise not. This tautological tendency is widespread in the social capital literature. It leads to confusion about whether social capital creates good institutions or whether institutions create social capital. Some authors like Fukuyama (1997) and Humphrey and Schmitz (1996) actually consider only the role of public agencies in fostering or depleting social capital and not the role of social capital in strengthening public agencies. So does the IMF when it argues that the 1994 genocide in Rwanda "caused . . . the destruction of social capital" in the country.[9] Logically, however, one would expect a nation that murders 800,000 of its own citizens to be endowed with only limited amounts of social capital to begin with. Most of the World Bank's social capital agenda also seems to be based on the assumption that it can be brought about by governments and foreign aid agencies. This is possible, but it contradicts the theory as originally exposed by Coleman (1990) or Putnam (1993a) and questions the developmental purpose of social capital.

To add one final measure of confusion, some also argue that there is "good" and "bad" social capital (Putnam 1993b; World Bank 1998a). Good social capital leads to economic growth and good institutions, whereas bad social capital does not. This appears to be an attempt of the theory to deal with mixed evidence and contradictory literature. What if the prevailing associations in a country are drinking clubs, Mafia-like organizations, or other networks of criminality?[10] Since associations such as those would presumably not serve the purposes of social capital, there is a tendency to categorize them as bad social capital and ignore them, whereas in fact they challenge the robustness of the theory. Similarly, Mancur Olson (1982) argued that associations such as unions or interest groups divert government policies toward redistribution and are thereby inimical to growth. Although this contradicts social capital theory, it is now occasionally incorporated into versions of the theory (Keefer and Knack 1997; World Bank 1998a) that contend social capital can have negative or positive effects on growth.

The empirical evidence in support of social capital theory is also problematic. Certainly, there appears to be an increasing amount of evidence in favor of the theory. Keefer and Knack (1997), for example, have offered cross-national evidence of the beneficial effects of trust in twenty-nine countries on bureaucratic efficiency, stability of property rights, and contract enforceability. These findings were based on the World Value Surveys of Inglehart (1997). In a similar vein, Raphael La Porta et al. (1997) have found trust to be inversely associated with corruption and positively associated with bureaucratic quality. Furthermore, their research also supports Putnam's (1993a) contention that hierarchical religions discourage civic participation and institutional efficiency. Finally, at the micro level Deepa Narayan and Lant Pritchett (1997) have suggested that the larger their associational activity and trust in peoples and institutions, the more income accrues to Tanzanian households.

Nevertheless, the specific evidence on the effects of social capital on economic growth is still ambiguous.[11] Neither Inglehart (1997) nor Helliwell (1996) found any positive cross-sectional relation between measures of trust and civic associations and per capita GDP growth. La Porta et al. (1997) found a weak and nonrobust relation between trust and growth. Keefer and Knack (1997) found a relationship between trust and growth (mostly mediated through investments) but not between associational life and growth. Jonathan Temple and Paul Johnson (1998) identified an effect of "previous social arrangements" on growth, but what these arrangements actually capture remains largely unanswered.

The evidence linking social capital and institutional performance is actually somewhat more compelling. Although their results may be weakened by the lack of control for other variables apart from the initial level of income, La Porta et al. (1997:336–337) nevertheless found a robust relationship between trust and a religion-based measure of social capital on the one hand, and efficiency of the judiciary, lack of corruption, and bureaucratic quality on the other. Keefer and Knack also found positive effects of trust on bureaucratic efficiency and the stability of property rights (1997:1275). Note, however, that in both these studies trust alone is found to affect institutional efficiency and economic performance. Keefer and Knack specifically found no such effect of membership in formal organizations, Putnam's (1993a) original and principal measure of social capital. The problem with trust, as opposed to associative life, however, is that it is just as likely to be the outcome of good institutions as it is to be their determinants, and consequently its exogeneity is much harder to establish. This is all the more plausible in Keefer and Knack's research since their measurements of institutional efficiency partly predate their measurement of trust. Indeed, their independent variable "trust in people" was collected by the World Values Survey (Inglehart 1997) over the 1990–1993 period, whereas their data on "efficiency of the judiciary" is an average for 1980–1983, "corruption" and "bureaucratic quality" are averages for 1982–1995, and GDP growth an average for 1970–1993. Hence, their data more likely suggest that people display trust in institutions that have demonstrably worked well and not that institutions work well when people trust them and each other. Narayan and Pritchett's (1997) findings appear more robust, although they may still be affected by one problem. In their measurements of Tanzanian villagers' associational activity, the two authors fail to take into account the possibility that social relations could be built on clientelistic patterns and that their beneficial economic outcomes could be the fruit of these patron-client networks rather than of social capital, which presupposes horizontal social relations. And although patron-client relations do tend to improve the lot of those who engage in them, they are likely to hurt the quality of the formal institutions in which they operate.

Finally, the relevance of social capital theory to Africa remains unclear. According to the theory, Africa's stagnation, poor governance, and weak state capacity derive from allegedly low levels of civic culture and social capital: vertical patron-client relations prevent effective political participation and equality; the weight of tradition stifles the emergence of modern associative life; and strong ethnic identities prevent the spread of trust in society. Blaming Africa's performance on generalized cultural features, however, fails to account for the diversity of systems, norms, and institutional traditions in Africa. Although there are cultural similarities across many parts of the continent (see Binet 1970; Alexandre 1981), even a cursory look at the classification of African political systems and cultural traits by M. Fortes and E. E. Evans-Pritchard (1941) and George Murdock (1967) reveals an impressive diversity. Hence, claims that Africans uniformly favor paternalistic rule or hierarchical social structures (Dia 1996) appear excessive and fail to account for the variance in economic performance and governance across the region. Furthermore, should Africans share any norms, these are as likely to be favorable as inimical to social capital. African systems of reciprocity are well documented (Fiske 1991; Fafchamps 1992). By way of example, *tontines,* the informal saving arrangements that Putnam (1993a) mentions as a case of associational life, are widespread in most African countries. Associative life and "networks of civic engagement" are also well developed, despite Africa's image of traditional atavism. In West Africa, for example, horizontal farmers' solidarity groups—the Groupements Naam—have existed since 1967 in about a dozen countries (Ouédraogo 1990). The prevalence of mutual aid associations across the continent (as in northern Italy) has also been well documented (Alexandre 1981:165). And recent micro evidence suggests that African producers do not lack networks of social capital (Narayan and Pritchett 1997).

In sum, there is a wide range of norms of civic and political culture across Africa, and those norms that can most be thought of as generalized would be as likely to favor as to impede the development of social capital. Bearing this in mind, the relevance of social capital theory to Africa's average stagnation could be tested by relating continental variations in social-capital-related values to variations in institutional and economic performance, instead of subsuming Africa under a blanket of low social capital. I tried such an exercise, although in the absence of appropriate data, my measurements of social capital probably stretched the concept too far for much to be read into my results. Using the finding by La Porta et al. (1997) that social capital was inversely correlated with the prevalence of Islam and Catholicism (allegedly because of their hierarchical nature) in the twenty-plus countries for which the World Values Surveys (Inglehart 1997) provide data on trust and associative life, I calculated a predicted level of social capital for African countries based on the proportion of their populations that is either Muslim or Catholic. I then used it in regressions on growth and state capacity. For what such an exercise is worth, it had no significant effect on either one.

The little empirical work that has been done so far in Africa by others using Putnam's framework also has not delivered encouraging results. Jennifer Widner and Alexander Mundt (1998) have attempted to apply a theory of social capital to analyze local government performance in Botswana and Uganda. Their first finding was that norms of social capital that were correlated in Putnam's Italian case did not cohere in their two African cases. In addition, they found no causal relationship between social capital and government effectiveness in these two countries. Finally, measures of trust turned out lower in Botswana than in Uganda, although the former's economic and democratic performance has a long track record.[12] Hence, social capital explanations of Africa's predicament appear to rely on dubious assessments of African norms and fail the test of accounting for intra-African variations in performance.

In conclusion, social capital theory does not provide a fully satisfactory answer to the puzzle of capacity and development in Africa, and possibly elsewhere. Although the theory is promising and intuitively appealing, it remains conceptually and empirically ambivalent, and its relevance to Africa is far from established.

ETHNIC HETEROGENEITY AND COLLECTIVE ACTION

The second theory of state capacity in Africa can be subsumed into the proposition that African countries adopt poor policies and have weak institutions because of their ethnic diversity.[13] Specifically, the argument holds that in ethnically fragmented societies politicians and bureaucrats tend to represent the interests of their ethnic group in the national arena. As a result, they sponsor, lobby for, and adopt policies whose benefits accrue to their constituencies but whose costs are more likely to be shared by the country as a whole. In other words, they seek to increase the share of their ethnic slice at the expense of the total national pie. To a large extent, this idea is an ethnic application of Olson's theories of collective action and of the effects of stable interest groups on policy choices (Olson 1970; Olson 1982). Donald Rothchild agrees that "ethnic groups have quite frequently mobilized behind their intermediaries to compete effectively for a proportional (even an extraproportional) share of public resources." He goes so far as to suggest that "this mobilization of group members for competition is likely to contribute substantially to the group's unity and sense of purpose over the years" and that "in this respect, ethnic groups can be likened to the interest-defined groups that they compete with for state-controlled resources" (1997:75). Along the same line, Robert Bates asserts that "ethnic groups persist largely because of their capacity to extract goods and services from the modern sector and thereby satisfy the demands of their members" (1983:161).

Another variant of the theory hypothesizes a polarization effect to ethnic pluralism. The political economy literature suggests that polarized societies are more likely to adopt distributive policies and provide weaker property rights than nonpolarized ones. Alberto Alesina and Dani Rodrik (1994), for example, argue that in democracies, income inequality favors redistributive pressures because the median voter is more likely to prefer higher levels of redistribution the greater the inequality. Keefer and Knack (1995b) take this idea a step further and investigate how income inequality creates cleavages in society that polarize social actors and policymakers, generating uncertainty about policy outcomes, the credibility of government commitment, and the security of property rights. Specifically, they hypothesize that where polarization is high, "it is more difficult for decision makers to build a consensus about policy changes that are necessary to respond to economic crises" and "property rights are less secure" (1995b:3). Income inequality is the form of polarization they emphasize, but they also consider ethnic identity and language. They find that the greater the prevalence of ethnic tension, the weaker the guarantees of property rights. They also find a U-curve relationship between ethnic fractionalization—measured by the probability that two randomly selected individuals belong to two different ethnic groups—and property rights. As ethnic fractionalization increases, property rights worsen, up to a certain level. Beyond this threshold, an increase in ethnic fragmentation improves property rights (1995b:19–20). This is consistent with the idea of social polarization, which is more likely at medium levels of ethnic fragmentation than at higher ones (Horowitz 1985).

William Easterly and Ross Levine (1997) equate ethnic polarization with ethnic diversity and suggest that both Olson's rent-seeking effect and Alesina and Rodrik's policy effects should be functions of ethnic diversity through polarization mechanisms. They contend, as a result, that "higher levels of ethnic diversity encourage poor policies, poor education, political instability, inadequate infrastructure, and other factors associated with slow growth" (1997:1205). They suggest therefore that Africa's poor record of growth and developmental policies, its "growth tragedy," is in large part the consequence of its higher levels of ethnic fragmentation.

Their empirical results appear to speak loudly. Using a measure of ethnolinguistic fragmentation similar to Keefer and Knack's (1995b),[14] they look at ethnic diversity's effects on educational policies, price distortions, fiscal policies, infrastructural investments, and violent political instability and find that it accounts for 28 percent of the growth difference between East Asia and Africa that is attributable to political or policy variables. Furthermore, when they include the direct (unspecified) effects of ethnicity on growth, the whole effect amounts to "about one percentage point of the 3.4 percentage point East Asia–Africa growth differential" (1997:1236).[15]

Most recently, Paul Collier (1998a) has also investigated the ethnic diversity hypothesis, with yet another twist. In a paper presented at the 1998 Annual World Bank Conference on Development Economics, he stresses the effects of ethnic fragmentation on political conflict and violence, which in turn relate to growth. As with Keefer and Knack (1995b), the relationship between conflict and ethnic diversity is found to be quadratic, rising at low levels of fragmentation and decreasing thereafter.

Altogether, therefore, there are three variants of the ethnic theory of bad policy and stagnation: the Olsonian rent-seeking approach, the polarization-bad policy approach, and the polarization-conflict approach. Yet their relevance to Africa's development crisis is quite problematic. First of all, they all share some historical inconsistency. Many precolonial systems in Africa, if not most "early states" around the world, were in fact multiethnic. Ethnic pluralism frequently provided the foundation of state formation, as a dominant group used other groups to break away from its own logic of lineage and into the logic of statehood by purposefully separating some public functions from the links of parenthood (see Fortes and Evans-Pritchard 1941; Claessen 1998). Ethnic heterogeneity per se is thus unlikely to be a factor of institutional weakness now when it once was the root of institutional formation.

Second, these authors tend to crystallize and simplify ethnicity, ignoring a large body of literature that stresses how ethnicity is not so much a "primordial" identity as a situational and fluid one (for Africa only, see Fortes and Evans-Pritchard 1941; Young 1976; Davidson 1992; Bayart 1993; and Gray 1995). Ethnicity is often salient in Africa, yet rarely does it relate to cases of ancestral tribal hatreds. When ethnicity is the salient component of instability, it is usually as an instrument to seize control of the state or to escape control by the state. Ethnicity provides a level of institutional identification to fall back on in times of contestation of the state. That African politics is not merely ethnic polarization can be seen in the fact that politicians usually do not simply favor their own ethnic group but build networks of support and alliances across ethnic, regional, religious, or other cleavages in order to create coalitions to support their power. Célestin Monga (1998) argues, for example, that winning elections in Africa involves support beyond one's mere ethnic constituency. Hence, ethnicity is often present in African political conflict but not so much as a factor of social fractionalization as an instrument for the contestation or the reconfiguration of power.

The equation of ethnic heterogeneity with polarization is therefore not warranted. Quite obviously, not all multiethnic societies are significantly polarized (e.g., the United States), and several ethnically heterogeneous societies are actually polarized along different lines, such as colonial languages (Cameroon), religion (Sudan), or caste (India). Most African societies are composed of several ethnic groups, sometimes dozens of them. Yet in some countries this leads to no excessive social tension (Burkina, Ghana, Tanzania), whereas in others, even the existence of only two groups has led to violent antagonisms (Rwanda, Burundi). Collier's (1998a) observation that the relationship between ethnic fractionalization and ethnic conflict and violence could actually take the shape of an inverted U-curve, rising with middle levels of heterogeneity and falling again at high levels,[16] suggests also that highly fractionalized societies such as those of Africa should be better off than those with medium fragmentation. This conforms with the situational theory of ethnicity, according to which ethnic identity is more salient when the "other" can be more easily identified in the competition for resources. A cursory look at African ethnic conflicts reveals such a pattern of high tension when there are few significant actors: Hutu and Tutsi in Rwanda and Burundi; Yoruba, Haussa, and Igbo in Nigeria; Arabs and blacks in Mauritania, Chad, and Sudan; blacks and whites in South Africa. Outside of Africa, the comparative situation of India (high diversity, low conflict) and Sri Lanka (bipolar society, high conflict) evokes a similar pattern.

Furthermore, the work of Easterly and Levine (1997) suffers from empirical shortcomings. First, their estimations fail to abolish the negative effect on growth of being an African country. In other words, even after accounting for ethnic heterogeneity and institutions, the dummy variable associated with Africa retains both its significance and its approximate magnitude, suggesting that much of Africa's stagnation mystery remains unexplained in their model. Second, the robustness of their findings is called into question when their theory is tested within Africa only. If ethnic heterogeneity is inimical to growth on a worldwide scale, it should be so among African countries as well. Indeed, although Africa is on average more ethnically diverse than the rest of the world, the index of ethnolinguistic fragmentation is nevertheless also unevenly distributed among African countries, ranging from 0.04 to 0.93. Yet the apparently strong negative relationship between ethnic fragmentation and growth that Easterly and Levine (1997) observe in worldwide, cross-sectional regressions does not survive reduction of the sample to African countries only. In other words, ethnic fragmentation is not a determinant of economic performance within Africa, and it is not therefore a robust predictor of policy choices.[17] Table 4.1 illustrates this finding.

In summary, ethnic theories of African stagnation are weak. Although collective action and polarization theories of stagnation have much intellectual appeal, ethnic heterogeneity by itself is neither a systematic criterion of social differentiation nor a necessary factor of polarization. The available evidence suggests that ethnic heterogeneity neither accounts for what distinguishes slow growth in Africa from the rest of the world, nor is able to account for differences in performance within Africa.

Table 4.1   **Growth and Ethnic Fragmentation: Worldwide and in Africa (dependent variable: per capita real GDP growth, 1960–1992)**

	Constant	Ethnic fragmentation	Adj. R^2	N
Worldwide	0.0273**	−0.0224**	0.11	120
	(9.887)	(4.252)		
Africa	0.0031	0.0006	−0.03	38
	(0.360)	(0.051)		

Notes: OLS estimation with White (1980) heteroskedasticity-consistent t statistics in parentheses. The dependent variable in these regressions is RGDPCH. The independent variable is ELF. See Appendix 1 for definitions, sources, and methodology.

Significance levels: ** = 1%.

NOTES

1. To be fair, Schumpeter's statement ended with "and we must give place to other disciplines."

2. See Almond and Verba (1963) and (1980).

3. For similar reasons, I also do not examine the work of political scientists who argued, well before economists started considering the role of policies in the process of economic development, that the structure of African polities disempowered rural masses vis-à-vis the urban elites who consequently adopted policies that favored their particular interests (Lofchie 1975; Bates 1981). In addition, although these studies did much to further our understanding of African underdevelopment, they cannot account for development success in Africa. Nevertheless, their reasoning will partly inform my argument in Chapter 5.

4. Note, however, that Coleman's (1990) definition was rather different. Social capital, according to Coleman who quoted Glenn Loury, is "the set of resources that inhere in family relations and in community social organization and that are useful for the cognitive or social development of a child" (1990:300).

5. As such, it overlaps with the idea of civil society. The more developed a civil society, the more social capital it has, since both are a function of associative life outside the state. The argument that equates strength of civil society with good governance has been made in the African context by World Bank (1992), Bratton (1994), and Harbeson, Rothchild, and Chazan (1994).

6. Putnam actually investigates the effects of social capital on democracy, but his measure of democracy is the institutional effectiveness of regional governments, as judged by local citizens. The rationale for this approach is that democratic governments provide their citizens with what they want. But in fact, what Putnam really tests for is institutional effectiveness.

7. Keefer and Knack (1997) test the effects of social capital on both institutions and growth, but their growth model is distinct from their institutional model.

8. This site, which includes an extensive bibliography, can be found at www.worldbank.org/poverty/scapital/index.htm.

9. "Rwanda. Enhanced Structural Adjustment Facility." IMF Policy Framework Paper, 1998/2000–2001/02. Available at www.imf.org/external/np/pfp/1999/rwanda/index.htm.

10. See Bayart (1999) for a similar discussion and some provocative thoughts on how social capital can be associated with criminality.

11. In fact, social capital may be thought of as more likely to affect income levels than growth. It may shift the national production function to a higher steady-state level of income without necessarily guaranteeing a faster rate of growth.

12. Not only does social capital not appear to be related to institutional performance in Africa, but in parts of the continent the growth of associative life has taken place in the shadow of state collapse, hardly the relationship predicted by social capital theory.

13. Arguably, several authors seem to consider the ethnic heterogeneity argument as a subset of social capital theory (e.g., Collier and Gunning 1997), based on the idea that ethnic fractionalization breaks down networks of social capital. The World Bank's Social Capital Initiative project number 8 also subscribes to this point of view by arguing that strong ethnic ties reduce trust between different ethnic groups at the national level (World Bank 1998a). Yet the available data does not support this hypothesis. In the 36 countries with data both on trust and on ethnic fragmentation, I found the two variables to be insignificantly correlated at -0.13. In addition, I did not find ethnolinguistic fragmentation to be a significant estimator of trust in either bivariate or multivariate regressions over the same sample. Finally, the reasonings underlying the impact of social capital and ethnic homogeneity on growth differ and, in my opinion, warrant a separate treatment. The first one stresses the reduction in transaction costs associated with trust and civic norms. It is a positive externality argument. The second, however, highlights the failure of collective action that comes from the ethnic identification of actors. It is therefore a negative externality argument.

14. Their measure of ethnic diversity is an index of ethnolinguistic fractionalization (referred to as ELF in Appendix 1) originally calculated by Taylor and Hudson (1972) and based on data from the 1963 Soviet atlas *Norodov Mirna*. The index measures, for each country, the probability that two randomly selected individuals belong to different ethnic groups. This probability increases the greater the number of ethnic groups and the more equal their size.

15. Lian and Oneal (1997), on the other hand, find no effect of ethnic diversity on growth, albeit in somewhat different specifications.

16. This idea was already discussed by Horowitz (1985).

17. The same thing happens when testing the effects of ethnic fragmentation on an aggregate measure of state capacity; it has a significant negative impact on a worldwide scale and no impact in the African subsample.

5

State Legitimacy and Developmental Capacity

> The costs of maintenance of an existing order are inversely related
> to the perceived legitimacy of the existing system.
> —Douglass North (1981:53)

Social capital theory and the ethnic homogeneity hypothesis may capture some dimensions of African underdevelopment, yet they fail to consistently explain variations in development fortunes across Africa. In this chapter I offer another theory of the determinants of state capacity and economic growth in Africa, which has relevance to other regions of the world as well. My argument highlights the peculiar genesis of the African state and the extent to which that state clashes with preexisting political institutions and political culture. It suggests that the strategies of power of domestic elites are framed by the degree of institutional congruence, or historical legitimacy, of the postcolonial state. These strategies, in turn, affect policy choices and the quality of governance. African states suffer on average from greater legitimacy deficits than other regions, and this contributes to the continent's generally weak economic performance. Within Africa, however, there is a considerable range of variation in the historical arbitrariness of the state that helps explain differences in performance among African countries.

In developing this argument, I build upon a rich body of literature on the nature of the state and political rule in Africa, especially state theories that stress the exogenous nature of the African state as well as competing ones that insist on its fusion with society. Both may be complementary, with the nature of the ongoing fusion being affected by the initial degree of exogeneity. I also use the concept of African neopatrimonial rule, the contention that African leaders tend to blur the distinction between the public and the private realm and that formal African state institutions do not accurately reflect underlying systems of power based on patronage, nepotism, regionalism, and other parallel structures. I do not impute neopatrimonialism to African cultural traits but build instead upon the work of those who present neopatrimonialism as the equilibrium outcome of the mismatch between state and society in Africa (and elsewhere). To their analysis I have added a systematic consideration of the congruence between precolonial institutions and postcolonial states across the continent (instead of a blanket statement about the imported nature of the state or the strength of societies) and a theoretical argument about how differences in state legitimacy condition strategies of power and their various effects on state capacity and economic development.

This chapter begins with an investigation of the nature of the state in Africa. How is it different from elsewhere, and how does it differ within Africa? Most African states have peculiar colonial origins, and they conflict to diverging degrees with precolonial political institutions. How does the extent of such institutional clashes affect the nature of power and, in turn, state capacity and economic growth? Linking policies, governance, and growth to levels of state legitimacy enables us to account both for Africa's weak average performance and for variations in performance within Africa.

As mentioned earlier, the definition here of state legitimacy does not involve any normative judgment on the state or the regime in power. It is, on the contrary, a structural variable determined by history: a state is deemed legitimate when it has evolved endogenously to local social relations of power and authority or when, having originally been imported, it is then absorbed by such preexisting endogenous institutions.

THE STATE IN AFRICA

Theories of development generally take the state as uniform across the world. Although variations in the performance of states are usually acknowledged, as are variations in the nature of regimes or the competitiveness of political systems, the analytical category of *state* is rarely questioned. Whether predatory or benevolent, the state is a state, and the potential relationship between predation or benevolence and the nature of the state is usually not addressed.

Yet although the international system of nations recognizes juridically sovereign states as equal entities, these states actually vary greatly in their origins, nature, and empirical effectiveness. Some evolved over centuries and were shaped by domestic relations of power and by warfare with neighboring entities, as in most of Western Europe (Tilly 1990). Others, like China, were essentially unchallenged by external factors for a very long time and developed into large-scale empires (Jones 1981). Some, such as the United States, came close to having been born of social contracts, while others were more clearly designed as instruments of domination of one group over another, like South Africa until recently. Some were once colonies, others colonizers. At any rate, there is a wide diversity of experiences of statehood across the world, and it pays to examine it more closely and think of its implications. Many sub-Saharan African states, in particular, are quite different from their counterparts elsewhere.

Before looking at the African state, however, the concept of state should be better defined. By states, I am not referring to governments, although the latter are one of the most prominent expressions and agencies of states. The terms may often be used interchangeably, but the state is actually a broader concept than government. Max Weber provides a convenient starting point with his definition of the state as a "human community that (successfully) claims the *monopoly of the legitimate use of physical force* within a given territory" (Weber 1958:78, his emphasis). The constitutive elements of this definition are a human community, a government/military, legitimacy, and a territory. Hence, the state can be thought of as a system of structures (Easton 1957), a set of institutions. It is the institutional dimension of societies, the network of apparati that make for the "public" in society. This definition, of sociological origins, has gained currency in the other social sciences. Political scientists often refer to it. Even among economists, where the confusion between states and governments perhaps remains more prevalent than elsewhere, some have nevertheless defined the state as "an organization with a comparative advantage in violence, extending over a geographic area whose boundaries are determined by its power to tax constituents" (North 1981:21), a definition that reproduces the Weberian elements of violence and territory, and in which comparative advantage in violence presumably confers legitimacy to the use of force. The World Bank now endorses an even more Weberian definition wherein the state "refers to a set of institutions that possess the means of legitimate coercion, exercised over a defined territory and its population, referred to as society" (1997b:20).

As comprehensive as these definitions appear, a complete understanding of the state's encompassing nature calls for a further element. The state is also an *idea*. Quoting Crawford Young, it is the "ensemble of affective orientations, images, and expectations imprinted in the mind of its subjects" (Young 1994:33).

> The iconography of the state is ubiquitous, visually expressed in its flag, postage stamps, coins, and currency; in textual form in its anthems, pledges of allegiance, oaths of office. In theatrical projection, the state represents itself in resplendent ceremonial: inaugurations and coronations, parades displaying its military might, rituals of national commemoration. (Young 1994:34)

The state is therefore also a conceptual category, a mental constraint. Its reach spreads from territorial and physical to ideological. Although intangible, this dimension of statehood is nevertheless crucial. It is because the state is an idea that people display feelings of patriotism and loyalty toward it. The idea of the state allows its institutions to penetrate the conscience of its citizens and to provide the frame in which they represent themselves as citizens in a political community.[1] Because of all these characteristics, the state is broader and more permanent than either governments or regimes.[2]

Most African states differ from most other states around the world along most of Weber's and Young's criteria. They are dubious communities of heterogeneous and occasionally clashing linguistic, religious, and ethnic identities; their claim to force is rarely effective and much less monopolistic; their government's frequent predatory nature fails the test of legitimate use of force; their territoriality is generally at best hesitant and contested; and their existence as an idea is usually limited to an urbanized and schooled minority. In a nutshell, most African states fall short of the requirements for statehood. They may exist as juridical entities, but they lack "empirical statehood" (Jackson and Rosberg 1982a).

In this study I argue that the empirical weakness of African states is a product of their history. The majority of contemporary African states are exogenous institutions superimposed over preexisting political structures and inherited by domestic but westernized elites at independence (Whitaker 1991; Badie 1992; Davidson 1992; Young 1994). The states that reached independence in Africa, from Ghana and Guinea in the late 1950s to Namibia in the early 1990s, were born as colonies. They did not exist before the colonial episode.

In precolonial times, the societies they now comprise were organized along different institutional lines. Some were stateless, living in small-scale institutional arrangements at the village or household level, such as the Igbo of Nigeria, the Kikuyu of Kenya, the Banda of Central African Republic, or the Lobi of Burkina Faso. Others, like the Ovimbundu of Angola, the Baoule of Côte d'Ivoire, or the Bamileke of Cameroon, were tribal. And some were organized in states but usually different ones from those that prevailed at independence: the Bakongo of Congo-Brazzaville, Congo-Kinshasa, and Angola; the Ndebele of Zimbabwe; and the Yoruba of Benin and Nigeria, to name a few. Some of these states, such as the Mossi or the Mandinka of West Africa, even developed into empires, conquering and assimilating other groups.

Colonial existence as a prelude to sovereignty is not unique to Africa, however, nor is it all that rare. Many states in Asia, the Middle East, Oceania, and the Western Hemisphere were colonies to begin with. In fact, all the states of continental North, Central, and South America were once colonies. But what is quite different is the relationship between these states and their citizenry. When the Spanish and British colonies of the Americas gained their independence, they did so as the instruments of the colonizers or their descendants. The institutions and societies pre-dating colonialism usually played no part in the new state system. They had either been assimilated, physically eliminated, or remained at the bottom of a relationship of domination with the new citizens. In other regions, such as Asia and some parts of the Middle East, the end of the colonial episode was more often (albeit certainly not always) the closing of a historical parenthesis of occupation, as preexisting states recovered their sovereignty, for example, Korea, Sri Lanka, Egypt, Cambodia, Taiwan, and Vietnam. In these cases, independence was a restoration of statehood, a "reversion" to sovereignty (Alexandrowicz 1969). As the representative of Ceylon (now Sri Lanka) argued at a committee of the General Assembly of the United Nations in 1968, his country, albeit recently independent, was to be considered an "original" state rather than a "new" one, for it had temporarily lost its sovereignty to the colonial experience rather than having gained sovereignty from it.[3]

In Africa, however, independence was hardly ever a return to history (Davidson 1992). Independence marked a change of the international status of colonies, now recognized as sovereign states, and a change in their leadership, with domestic elites replacing colonial personnel. But there was neither a return to precolonial institutional forms of sovereignty, nor an attempt by colonizers to remain at the levers of power in the new states (with the temporary exception of Rhodesia from 1966 to 1980). New domestic elites, trained in the colonizer's schools, speaking the colonizer's language, and often wearing the colonizer's clothing styles, took over the colonizer's state and made it theirs. In a word, they appropriated the imported state (Badie 1992). In doing so, they did not usually build upon their institutional past and sometimes even tried to repress it, forging ahead instead with nation-building.

The idea of the state as imported is the crucial differentiating variable of African statehood. Whereas other states were created as or were once colonies, they usually remain endogenous to their societies. Either both citizens and states were imported (as in most countries in the Americas) and the state therefore emanated from within society, or the preexisting states resurfaced after colonization (as in much of Asia, with significant exceptions such as India). The large majority of African states, in contrast, were created as instruments of military conquest, colonial domination, and economic exploitation. The colonizers went back home, but they left their states behind. New political elites who had played no role in constructing these states but had often collaborated with colonial rule took over the state.[4]

Again, this situation is not unique to Africa. A similar process took place in several states of the Middle East and South Asia, if not elsewhere. What is unique, however, is the unusual concentration of such states in Africa. Of all the regions of the world, Africa has the highest proportion of countries where the process of state creation was exogenous to their societies and where the leadership or ruling class inherited the state rather than shaping it as an instrument of its existing or developing hegemony. As a result, African states were born lacking legitimacy, meaning simply that they were not endogenous to their societies, they were not historically embedded into domestic relations of power and domination, and they therefore suffered from a dichotomization between power and statehood. Using the term coined by Kalevi Holsti, they had a deficit of vertical legitimacy, meaning that they lacked a "connection between society and political institutions" (1996:97).

These states were also usually arbitrary. As colonial creations, their boundaries were defined as the result of bargains among colonial powers, generally with little regard for either demographic, cultural, or political features. Thus they tended to lack another important dimension of statehood: the agreement as to what constitutes the community over which the state prevails. Keeping with Holsti's terminology, they had a deficit of horizontal legitimacy, meaning that they lacked "criteria for membership in the political community" beyond colonially imposed borders (1996:97).

Hence, Africa began the era of modern independence with *on average* lower levels of vertical and horizontal state legitimacy than other regions of the world. Yet although the new states had all been imported, there remained significant variations within Africa in the extent to which they conflicted with preexisting institutions and violated preexisting political communities. Indeed, African state legitimacy may have been low on average, but it was not uniformly so.

The Question of Vertical Legitimacy

The foundations of political authority in the new African states in the 1960s bore little resemblance to those in precolonial societies. Rarely, either, had the colonial state borne any relation to the economic systems, political organizations, and networks of social identification of the indigenous peoples.[5] Furthermore, preparation for independent statehood was never an original objective of the creation of colonial states; it became so as an afterthought, after World War II, under pressure from Western public opinion and the UN system. As a result of their genesis, these states lacked legitimacy vis-à-vis the societies, norms, and institutions they contained, however diminished were those that survived the colonial episode. The new states were devoid of what Stephen Cornell and Joseph Kalt (1995) call the "extra-constitutional" agreement on the structure, location, sources, and scope of their authority. To most Africans, they were but a second "public" in comparison to the institutions that had up to this time commanded their loyalties and allegiances (Ekeh 1975).

Consider the following examples to understand how independence, despite signifying the end of direct foreign domination, nevertheless turned out to be a path of political and historical alienation from the point of view of the remnants of African precolonial authority. In 1958, when it became clear that Upper Volta was moving toward increased autonomy and eventual independence from France, the Mogho Naaba, king of the Mossi (the largest ethnic group, which had developed a state formation since the sixteenth century), attempted an ill-fated coup to proclaim himself king of the new country and reassert the historical legitimacy of his rule (Bassolet 1968). He was quickly defeated by a handful of French troops, and the country's first president, Maurice Yaméogo, soon took radical measures to curb the powers of customary chieftaincies and sterilize this challenge to his rulership. In 1960, a similar will underlined the equally doomed proclamation of independence by the kingdom of Buganda in Uganda, which had been a regionally powerful state in the eighteenth and nineteenth centuries. Failure resulted this time from a lack of recognition by other states. After enjoying relative autonomy for a few years, the king had to flee in exile in 1967, and Buganda became little more than a mere geographical expression, a region of Uganda (Ofcansky 1996). In Ghana, the king of the Asante, another precolonial kingdom, refused to participate in the ceremonies of independence in 1957; he was well aware that the independence of Ghana meant the end of his hopes of regaining sovereignty, calling it "a perverse denial of the old independence" (Davidson 1992:73). David Apter quotes another Asante chief claiming "We are the rightful rulers" (1968:18). It is not my intention to take sides on the merits of these claims to legitimate rule but to show the institutional clash and incongruence brought about by colonialism in Africa and the general choice at independence to retain colonial state structures.

But is the crushing of precolonial sources of political authority any different from universal struggles for power? To be sure, modern states everywhere eradicate competing institutions as part of their own rise (Spruyt 1994). Eliminating and neutralizing rival sources of authority and territorial control may even be the essence of state making (Smith 1986:238–239). In Europe, one political institution usually asserted increased leverage and eventually imposed its domination over a territorial entity, from which emerged a hypothetical nation. Starting in the 1620s, France's Louis XIII "systematically destroyed the castles of the great rebel lords. . . . By the late 1620s, Richelieu was declaring royal monopoly of force as doctrine" (Tilly 1985:174). A similar process took place in England with the demilitarization of the great lords by the Tudors. State making unfolded later in Italy and Germany but involved a similar process of institutional monopolization. From 1859 to 1870, the state of Piedmont progressively extended its hegemony over the Bourbon kingdom of Naples and Sicily, the papal states, the grand duchy of Tuscany and duchies of Parma and Modena, and the Lombardy and Venetia segments of the Austrian empire, in order to create Italy. From 1866 to 1871, Bismarck's Prussia used commerce, treaties, and war to appropriate segments of the Austrian empire, France, and previously independent kingdoms to unify Germany.[6]

The crucial difference, however, is that the process of European state creation was endogenous, with a developing ruling class and its institutions taking over and assimilating competing social forces and swallowing neighboring territories. This was also the case in most of South and North America, where colonizers essentially eliminated preexisting peoples and their institutions to set up their own states. In precolonial Africa, state formation had often involved the subjection and assimilation of competing groups, but in postcolonial Africa, the state was first imposed from outside as an imperial extension, then was severed from its imperial core and abandoned by its creators, only to be adopted by new domestic elites who generally owed their "evolved" status to their Western education. The state was usually not the outgrowth of some domestic political institution, nor was it the political instrument of settlers (South Africa excepted). It was a colonial institution, deserted by the colonizers and inherited by a generally new African elite, against a background of preexisting institutions that, although badly battered and transformed by colonialism, had not been wiped out.[7] Hence, the problem of legitimacy.

This is not a question of states versus nations and certainly not one of modernity versus tradition. The problem is better phrased as states versus societies, but even this is still a bit off the mark. Essentially, it is a problem of clashing and mismatched institutions, contested sovereignty, and disputed allegiance. The empirical weakness of the postcolonial state in Africa is not necessarily a function of the presence of strong precolonial national allegiances, although this is occasionally the case. The empirical weakness of the African state is the consequence of its lack of institutional hegemony at the domestic level.

The discussion so far has painted an aggregate sketch of the historical conditions of African states. A more detailed picture, however, calls for recognizing a significant minority of states whose historical experiences and consequent degrees of legitimacy differ from the majority. First among these is Ethiopia, which was never colonized, although Mussolini's Italy briefly occupied it in the second half of the 1930s. The Ethiopian state must therefore be considered an endogenous institutional creation and not an import, with the caveat that it used the colonial episode to expand its territory over some former Italian possessions in today's Eritrea and Somalia, without ever succeeding in establishing effective control over these populations. As a result, the Ethiopian process of state formation took a step backward after World War II, despite the fact that the origins of the core Ethiopian state can be traced back to 4 B.C. Bearing this limitation in mind, Ethiopia is the only state in sub-Saharan Africa where state formation has truly been continuously endogenous. Liberia, the other African country usually credited with not having been colonized, does not qualify as an endogenous state since it is an imported structure (the creation of elements of the African diaspora in the United States); it has definitely clashed with indigenous institutions since its establishment in 1847. In fact, the conflict between indigenous populations and the descendants of freed slaves provided the thread of Liberia's political history until the 1990s. The 1980 coup by Samuel Doe, the first Liberian president of indigenous origin, highlighted the failure of the descendants of freed slaves to establish their hegemony after more than 130 years of independence.[8]

In addition, a few African island-states share the characteristic of having had no human settlement before the establishment of the slave trade and colonization, with the result that they cannot possibly harbor conflicts of legitimacy between precolonial and postcolonial state structures. Cape Verde was settled from 1640 onward by slaves (captured in Guinea and in transit to Brazil), Portuguese migrants, and a hodge-podge of sailors, penal exiles, and disgraced clergy, eventually leading to a population of mostly mixed origins (Bourges and Wauthier 1979:471). São Tomé and Principe followed a similar path. These two small islands were discovered by Portuguese explorers in 1478 or 1479 and then settled by Portuguese soldiers and migrants, slaves, criminals (in the 1490s each convict was provided with a slave woman for breeding purposes), and even Jewish children escaping persecution in Spain (Hodges and Newitt 1988). Portuguese explorers also discovered Mauritius in the sixteenth century. After a failed Dutch attempt at settling the island, the French established their control in 1715 and used it as a naval base throughout the eighteenth century. By the time of the French revolution, Mauritius counted 4,500 Frenchmen, 2,500 freed slaves (including workers imported from India), and 35,000 slaves from continental Africa. The British took over the island in 1810 and abolished slavery in 1834. Between 1829 and 1909, they imported some 450,000 workers from India for the sugarcane plantations, many of whom became small landowners. When the island became independent in 1968, 69 percent of its population was of Indian origins, 20 percent were of continental African descent, 7 percent were *mesticoes* (mixed racial background), 2 percent had French root, and 2 percent were Chinese traders (Bourges and Wauthier 1979:598–607). Finally, the ninety or so islets that form the Seychelles, also discovered uninhabited by the Portuguese, became a French possession in 1756 and switched to British control in 1815. The final population ended up an interracial mix of the original French colonists, their slaves from continental Africa, criminals later deported from France, and Chinese, Indians, and Malayans brought over by the British.[9] None of these four island-states can therefore be considered an exogenous institutional creation from the point of view of their population. This distinguishes them from most other African countries and provides them with a higher degree of historical legitimacy.

The two other African island states—the Comoro Islands and Madagascar—have followed a different trajectory, which more closely assimilates them into the general historical experience of continental Africa. The four Comoro Islands were settled long before colonization, but were not integrated as a unified political system by the time the Portuguese, and then the French, British, and Dutch, established contact, from the sixteenth century onward. On the contrary, they were run by conflicting Arabic sultanates (which nevertheless had a degree of kinship with each other), and some of the islands were later annexed by the Merina from neighboring Madagascar. It was not until France unified all four islands under its protectorate in 1886 that the Comoro Islands became an integrated political entity. Thus, like most African countries the islands owe their contemporary political existence to the colonial episode, although the peculiarities of their settlement and of their successive political systems make them a more ambiguous case.[10]

Madagascar is another borderline instance, although most of the evidence weighs against considering it a successor state to a precolonial political system. It comprises today several groups that had distinct political structures for most of the precolonial period. George Murdock (1967) identified eleven such groups, the largest of which is the Merina. This would suggest a presumption of illegitimacy of the contemporary state. Jean-François Bayart (1996) argues, however, that the decades preceding the arrival of the French at the end of the nineteenth century had witnessed an expansion of the Merina area of domination and their progressive incorporation of other groups into their political system. There is some debate, however, as to how far Merina hegemony had been established over the rest of the island. Unlike Bayart, Mervyn Brown (1995) argues that the forcible integration of the coastal tribes in the Merina sphere of influence in the nineteenth century never resulted in actual political unification and that the work of British missionaries, who concentrated their efforts on the Merina, actually reinforced the preexisting distinction between Merina and Côtiers (the coastal tribes).[11] The fact that Malagasy rulers have been Côtiers for the largest part of the country's independent history supports this latter point of view and justifies the narrative of contemporary Madagascar as a mostly colonial creation.

Back on the continent, there are some clear-cut cases of contemporary states that, although created by colonization, nevertheless do little institutional violence to preexisting state structures or relations of political authority. Botswana may provide the best example among them. Although Botswana was born as a British colony, more than 90 percent of its population is accounted for by the eleven preexisting Tswana kingdoms that functioned as a decentralized yet integrated political system before colonization. The British largely preserved the Tswana political structures, and upon independence in 1966, Botswana's first president, Seretse Khama, was also the son of the paramount chief of the most important of the Tswana "tribes." These circumstances led to a highly stable system that secured the replication of the preexisting Tswana hegemony within the new structures of postcolonial statehood.[12]

Similar evolutions took place in Lesotho and Swaziland. Lesotho has been a kingdom since it was integrated by King Moshoeshoe in the 1820s. South Africa failed to swallow it, and it became a British High Commission Territory (like Botswana and Swaziland) in the 1880s, under the name Basutoland. As in Botswana, the British interfered little with the traditional structure of power. One account of British rule in Lesotho describes it as a system that

> left considerable powers in the hands of the chiefs. . . . Under the paramount chiefs, authority was delegated through ranked regional chiefs drawn from the royal lineage and the most important chiefdoms. A system of customary law was adopted, with the land held in trust by the paramount chief for the people, and crucial aspects of local government were in the hands of the chiefs. The colonial government was headed by a resident commissioner and advised by the Basutoland National Council, which was led by the paramount chief and dominated by his nominated members.[13]

In 1966 Basutoland gained independence as the Kingdom of Lesotho with the paramount chief, Constantine Bereng Seeiso, becoming King Moshoeshoe II.

Similarly, the Swazi kingdom crystallized out of the fusion of several clans around the end of the eighteenth century. Its territorial integrity suffered considerably from the settlement of Boers and

British in its territory over the nineteenth century, but its political system was preserved throughout this period and the subsequent era of formal British colonization that lasted from 1906 to 1967, although the British temporarily reduced the king to the status of paramount chief. Five years after independence, King Sobhuza II scrapped the constitution inherited from the British and returned to the traditional monarchical Swazi system, a mix of royal monopoly and local government.[14]

Hence, although the contemporary states of Botswana, Lesotho, and Swaziland all are the outcome of British colonization in southern Africa, they are nevertheless embedded in precolonial relations of authority and represent the extension of precolonial states and of preexisting political hegemonies into the modern era. As such, they benefit from a degree of historical continuity and legitimacy unrivaled throughout Africa, with the exception of Ethiopia.[15]

Two additional contemporary African states had an effective precolonial existence and also represent a departure from the continental norm of postcolonial statehood: Rwanda and Burundi. Both operated as multiethnic states, with a Tutsi pastoralist aristocracy having conquered and integrated a local population of Hutu farmers (a pattern of state formation not uncommon throughout precolonial Africa). Here again, the extent to which their political systems survived colonization is ambiguous. The foundations of their political authority and the "traditional" political division of labor between the Tutsi and Hutu were considerably upset by Belgian colonialists who misperceived and reinforced the differences of status between them. This led to a challenge against Tutsi hegemony in Rwanda at the time of independence, oddly encouraged by Belgium as it departed, with the consequence that the traditional Tutsi Mwami monarchy, which had established, unified, and centralized the precolonial state, did not survive the colonial episode and was overthrown in favor of a Hutu-dominated republican system.[16] In Burundi, the Tutsi were also an aristocratic class, but both Tutsi and Hutu were under the authority of the Abaganwa dynasty, which had evolved over time into a distinct monarchical class. As independence neared, Burundi seemed set for a Botswana-like scenario.[17] The king's son, Prince Louis Rwagasore, led his party, Union et Progrès National, to a massive victory at the 1961 legislative elections and was appointed prime minister. This set the stage for a system that could have embedded Burundi back into its precolonial unified past, despite the ethnically based colonial discriminations the Belgians had implemented in Burundi at the expense of the Hutu (as in Rwanda). Two weeks later, however,

Rwagasore was assassinated and with him died Burundi's hopes for historical continuity. Instead of continuing a strategy of co-opting the structures of the postcolonial state, the king decided to challenge the rule of both the government and the parliament and further encouraged ethnic divisions in order to weaken contemporary state institutions. His strategy failed, and the monarchy was abolished in 1966, opening the door to a violent succession of Hutu- and mostly Tutsi-dominated regimes.

In both Rwanda and Burundi, the hegemony of the traditional ruling class is shattered by the process of postcolonial independence. Long-standing monarchies are abolished in both cases, and ethnic differentiation surfaces as an overriding and dividing political variable. To this extent, contemporary Rwanda and Burundi lack historical legitimacy. On the other hand, because their populations share a common multiethnic, precolonial political past and a common language, they have much deeper historical roots than the great majority of African states. As a result, they may fall short of the legitimacy standards of Botswana but nevertheless contribute to the variations in historical experiences among African states.

In the end, each of these ten countries—Ethiopia, Cape Verde, Mauritius, Seychelles, São Tomé and Principe, Botswana, Lesotho, Swaziland, and, to a lesser extent, Rwanda and Burundi—represents a certain degree of departure from the prevailing absence of state legitimacy across Africa. They benefit from a historical context in which the development of contemporary institutions of statehood has been coincidental to the historical development of relations of power. From this point of view, they are much more akin to European states than to their African counterparts.

The Question of Horizontal Legitimacy

Most African states are also territorial misfits. With borders inherited from the colonial scramble for Africa, which represent either the limits between different colonial powers' zones of influence or administrative demarcations within colonial empires, they usually lack geographical congruence with the institutions of the precolonial era. Again, their problem is not so much to be nationless states, for sociologists and political scientists agree now that the idea of a nation predating and providing the ferment to the state is often a fallacy (Tilly 1975; Breuilly 1982; Anderson 1983). In many places, "the state existed long before a sense of national community emerged," and in Western Europe itself, often credited with the birth of the nation-state, "states created nations" rather than the other way around (Holsti 1996:51–52). Hence, the question is not simply one of African states being built ahead of African nations. The problem of congruence, or horizontal legitimacy, comes from the fact that African societies were often politically defined before the creation of the colonial state and that these existing polities, vectors of political identity, did not usually provide the social foundation for modern independent African states.[18] As mentioned earlier, some of these preexisting institutions were states, others were chiefdoms, still others appeared as decentralized societies based on lineage. In many cases they were forced together under a single political structure or suffocated; in others they were split among several states or dismembered. But in either case congruence between the postcolonial state and precolonial institutions was the exception.[19]

A few country cases will help illustrate the problem of horizontal legitimacy. Somalia, for instance, is a highly homogeneous country from a cultural point of view, with its population comprising more than 90 percent of Somali. Yet it has inherited a territorial structure that fails to comprise significant segments of Somali, despite the unification at independence of British Somaliland and Italian Somalia. There are indeed substantial Somali minorities in Djibouti, Ethiopia, and Kenya (see Figure 5.1). This has made the borders between Somalia and both Ethiopia and Kenya particularly artificial, has fed wars with and within Ethiopia, and has led a Somali president to complain:

> Our misfortune is that our neighbouring countries . . . are not our neighbours. Our neighbours are our Somali kinsmen whose citizenship has been falsified by indiscriminate boundary arrangements. They have to move across artificial frontiers to their pasture lands. They occupy the same terrain and pursue the same pastoral economy as ourselves. We speak the same language. We share the same creed, the same culture and the same traditions. How can we regard our brothers as foreigners?[20]

In the Democratic Republic of Congo (formerly Zaire), not only were several precolonial kingdoms and states artificially brought together by Belgian colonialism, but many of them were also partitioned with neighboring colonies, not least the powerful precolonial kingdom of the Bakongo and the Lunda empire, both of which had existed since the sixteenth century (see Figure 5.2).[21]

These are not exceptional cases. Among the large political sys-

Figure 5.1 Partitioned Somalis

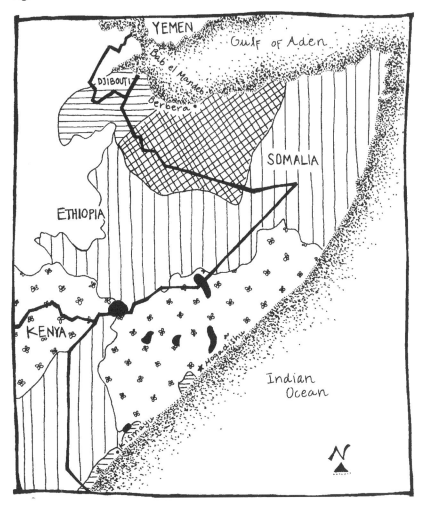

Dir

Isaq

Darod

Hawiye, Digil, Rahanwein

Non-Somali

Source: Adapted from Lyons & Samatar (1995).

Figure 5.2   The Partition of Congo's Precolonial States

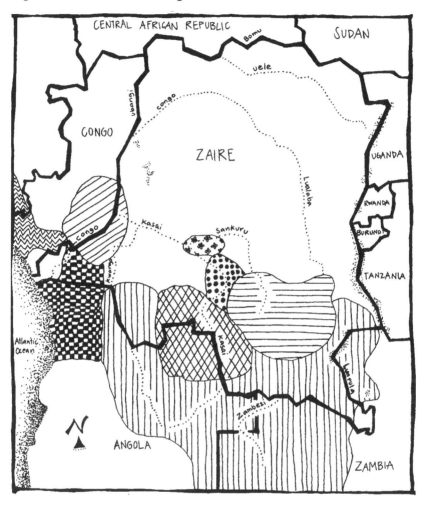

Loango	Lunda Heartland
Luba-Kasai	Kongo
Luba Kingdom	Kuba Kingdom
Lunda Empire	Tio

Source: Adapted from Library of Congress. *Zaire: A Country Study.*

tems partitioned by colonialism, one counts the Adamawa of Cameroon and Nigeria; the Borno of Cameroon, Chad, and Niger; the Malinke of Senegal, Mali, and Guinea; the Tuaregs of Mali, Niger, and Burkina; the Yoruba of Nigeria and Niger; the Ewe of Togo and Ghana; or the Chewa of Malawi and Zambia—to name but a few. In addition, colonial partition also affected a myriad of smaller groups, sometimes to a more dramatic extent. The Madara, for example, who live astride Nigeria and Cameroon, actually saw their cultural and commercial capital, Kerawa, split in two by the international border between the two countries (Barkindo 1985). Colonial partition seemed to be the norm rather than the exception. In many cases, the existence of an integrated precolonial system did not prevent partition by colonials, although the British were arguably more sensitive to ethnic and institutional identity within their colonies. With respect to their colonies' international borders, however, they generally followed the same logic of competition with other colonial powers.[22] In general, as Charles Alexandrowicz put it, "The African State entities which emerged after the Second World War . . . hardly [had] a claim to identify with the vast number of States and Chieftainships which had disappeared in the melting pot of colonial absorption" (1969:473).

Even authors who are suspicious of the exogenous view of borders in Africa concede that "there is much that is accurate about accepted wisdom on the construction of colonial boundaries," and especially their nature as the outcome of "European power-politics" (Nugent 1996:41). European colonizers typically agreed among themselves on arbitrary borders that simplified administration and enforcement. According to Sautter, "44 percent of African borders are made up of astronomical lines (meridian parallels), 30 percent of mathematical lines (arcs, curves, etc.) while only 26 percent are of geographical features" (1982:8).[23]

The greater the share of a country's population accounted for by partitioned groups, the less agreement one can expect to find as to what constitutes the community that lies at the foundation of the state, and thus the less horizontally legitimate the current state. For partitioned groups, the problem of allegiance to the new public sphere the state represents—a problem shared by all preexisting groups—is compounded by the additional alienation implied by the partition. As Robert Jackson and Carl Rosberg put it, "The social and political boundaries between these ethnic entities [divided by international boundaries, with members residing in two or more countries] may well be more significant in terms of public attitudes and behavior than are the boundaries between the countries" (1982a:5).

Once again, however, there is a fair amount of variation throughout Africa in terms of horizontal legitimacy. Some contemporary states are more congruent to their past than others. Islands usually display a high level of horizontal legitimacy with the exception of the Comoro Islands, which were divided at independence in 1975 when France retained one of its four islands (Mayotte; Mahore), and Madagascar. African islands such as Cape Verde, Mauritius, São Tomé and Principe, and the Seychelles, on the other hand, escaped the usual African deficits of horizontal legitimacy thanks to the simultaneity between their human settlement and colonial experience.[24]

On the continent, we also find a few states where the congruence between the territorial definitions of the precolonial and postcolonial systems is high. Botswana, Lesotho, and Swaziland again top the list. They were all British colonies of Southern Africa, where Britain's domination allowed some degrees of freedom to administrative units within the colonial domain. Even so, maintaining territorial integrity required considerable effort on the part of precolonial rulers. In Swaziland, for example, after a 1914 partition converted two-thirds of the Swazi kingdom into freehold concessions for settlers, the king and chiefs had to embark upon a policy of purchasing back the land from the settlers so as to restore the state closer to its precolonial territorial configuration.[25] The other vertically legitimate continental states also usually have high levels of horizontal legitimacy, with territorial boundaries that come close to precolonial arrangements. Despite the contemporary conflicts between Hutu and Tutsi, these two communities were not actually separated by colonialism but were traditionally found in both precolonial states of Ruanda and Rundi, whose boundaries are by and large reflected by today's Rwanda and Burundi (although northern Hutu populations were forcibly integrated in Rwanda under colonialism). In the case of Ethiopia, the historical continuity of the definition of the core communities that form the state suffered somewhat from the annexation of significant segments of Somali populations toward the end of the Italian colonial episode. Nevertheless, these groups, such as the Somali of Ogaden, still represent no more than a small percentage of Ethiopia's total population.

Most states that benefited from vertical legitimacy are also to be found among those with high horizontal legitimacy. This correlation between the two dimensions of legitimacy is not surprising, as one

would expect agreement about who constitutes the polity to be necessary for there to be agreement about what constitutes the state.
There are other states, however, that, although they include many
precolonial systems, split relatively few of them with their neighbors
in proportion to their overall population. Such states, among which
are Cameroon, Gambia, Mozambique, Côte d'Ivoire, and Zimbabwe,
certainly fail the test of horizontal legitimacy, as they bring together
groups that did not undergo a historical process of political assimilation; nevertheless, they avoid the extremes of horizontal illegitimacy
by not dividing more of these groups across their borders.

Although the colonial partition of Africa resulted in a low average level of horizontal legitimacy for contemporary states, a detailed
picture reveals a relatively wide variation in the experiences of specific countries, from extremes of illegitimacy such as Somalia,
Mauritania, or Guinea to states with historically well-defined polities
such as Mauritius or Swaziland.

HOW ILLEGITIMACY BREEDS INCAPACITY

"The stability of any given democracy," Seymour Martin Lipset
wrote in 1959, "depends not only on economic development but also
upon the effectiveness and the legitimacy of its political system"
(1981:64). This section demonstrates not only that the stability of
any regime depends on the legitimacy of its political system, but also
that its capacity for economic development and institutional effectiveness is constrained by its stability and, therefore, also ultimately
derives from the legitimacy of the system. In fact, the lack of state
legitimacy puts rulers in such a conundrum that they sacrifice their
regime's effectiveness and their country's development in an all-con-
suming attempt to shore up their fledgling stability and power.

As previously argued, upon independence most African rulers
inherited state structures that had little legitimacy in the minds of
their citizens, little territorial integrity, poorly defined societies, and
no sense of shared history beyond the colonial episode. These states
usually had existed for a few decades only and had often changed
shape and name in the course of this period. In Sahelian West Africa
alone, for example, France partitioned its territory into "military
regions" in the late nineteenth century, then created a governorship
for all its possessions early in the twentieth century, before setting up
the Senegambie-Niger colony, which became Haut-Senegal-Niger a

few years later. After World War I, it was split into smaller colonial units (some of which were merged again into larger units in the 1930s) before being partitioned again, along slightly different lines, after World War II (Coquery-Vidrovitch 1992). African states had been the creations of the colonizers, and their existence had been defined and backed up by the latter's power and military force. Just as the creation of domestic state institutions usually crystallizes the domination of one group over another, so too were colonial states the instrument of the domination that the colonial relationship entailed.[26] Hence, the state was an instrument of power.

The leaders of independent Africa who inherited these low-legitimacy states did not inherit the colonial power that had kept them together until then. Most of these leaders were the product of the colonial education system and usually did not benefit from precolonial power foundations. In Upper Volta, for example, the traditional Mossi leaders had deliberately kept their children out of the French schools, which they rightly perceived as challenges to their political system. This gesture of resistance turned against them, however, when independence neared, as most of the French-educated political class was by then composed of commoners with no links to the chieftaincies and no support from them either (Englebert 1996). Even when postcolonial political leaders originated from a chiefly class, as in the cases of Houphouët-Boigny in Côte d'Ivoire or Modibo Keita in Mali, that class was usually from a subnational group only by virtue of the heterogeneity of the societies comprised in the state.

Rulers of these states therefore faced a peculiar challenge, arising from the fact that the creation of their states preceded the sedimentation of relations of power in their newly and artificially aggregated societies. Their states brought together groups that until then were following different historical trajectories and building alternative political institutions. Instead of "founding fathers," they got colonial masters. Having originated outside domestic social and political relations and having failed to be assimilated within existing political and social relations, these states faced contending sources of political allegiance and did not command the loyalty of their citizens (Ekeh 1975). This is not merely a matter of weak states facing strong societies. The crux of the problem is that there were competing institutional claims to sovereignty within the state. "We have not just competing loyalties," Clifford Geertz wrote upon observing the lack of integration of the "new states" of the third world in the early 1960s, "but competing loyalties of the same general order" (1973b:261).

When leaders of independent Africa took over, mostly in the 1960s, the elation associated with the end of colonialism and the nationalist moment temporarily hid the problem of legitimacy. But soon enough, the rulers and governments of Africa discovered how little power they actually had as a consequence of the lack of legitimacy of the state they were presiding over. The impossibility of establishing even the myth of a social contract, the widespread existence of competing loyalties, and the consequent lack of hegemonic control of the state over society all conspired to undermine the power of the rulers and the effectiveness of their governments. Citizens and politicians alike conceived of the state not so much as a common instrument of collective action but, in the words of Nigerian novelist Chinua Achebe, as "they," or in other words, as having "nothing to do with you or me." It was "an alien institution and people's business was to get as much from it as they could without getting into trouble" (1960:38). The disembedded postcolonial state became either a potential resource to be appropriated or a potential instrument of domination by other groups to be resisted. Citizens and politicians feared "a loss of definition as an autonomous person, either through absorption into a culturally undifferentiated mass or, what is even worse, through a domination by some other rival ethnic, racial, or linguistic community that is able to imbue that order with the temper of its own personality" (Geertz 1973b:258–259). Jawaharlal Nehru best voiced the conundrum of the "inheritance elites" (Gellar 1973) when he noted with dismay that "face to face with centuries old India of narrow loyalties, petty jealousies, and ignorant prejudices engaged in mortal conflict . . . we were simply horrified to see how thin was the ice upon which we were skating" (Harrison 1956:3). Leaders of nonlegitimate states indeed skate on thin ice. They may themselves be bona fide and even brilliant skaters, yet their performance is inhibited by the risk that any significant move on their part will break the ice and either cause them to fall through it or further shrink the effective size of the pond they skate upon.

Policymaking almost always implies some redistributive dimension and consequent costs to specific sectors of society. Politics is usually the game of negotiating these costs and benefits, and the state is erected as both the arena and the enforcer/referee of the game. States are therefore instruments of collective action. They reduce transaction costs by preventing free riding, defining and safeguarding property rights, and controlling opportunism (North 1981; Eggertsson 1990). But as Douglass North makes clear, this last function is possible only when "ideological convictions . . . constrain individual maximizing" (1981:44). In other words, enforcement of the game will be possible only when the contractual relations are perceived as legitimate. In states mired with competing loyalties, however, not only are rules of the game not agreed upon, but there is not even a consensus about playing the game at all because the players never come together willingly. Opposition to government policies by groups that perceive themselves as losers tends to translate into opposition to the state itself, or at least to its executive branch as a whole, leading more often than not to government overthrows, communal violence, or even attempts at secession. The disaffection of citizens for the arena of national politics reduces the power and the capacity for political action of the "inheritance elites." The lack of legitimacy of the political system as a whole reduces the loyalty of citizens vis-à-vis state institutions perceived as alien and makes them more likely to choose "exit" rather than "voice" options when faced with policies or leadership they disapprove of.[27] This situation represents much more than a mere challenge of integration for the rulers of these states. It is often argued that keeping together centrifugal societies is the core problem of African leaders (Hyden 1983a; Sandbrook 1986), but their problem is in fact much simpler and more overwhelming. Leaders of nonlegitimate states simply face a crisis of power. Ruling over a nonlegitimate system undermines the very essence of their own power—even if they were themselves legitimately elected—and dramatically reduces their freedom of political action and the range of feasible policies.

Hence, the president and his men are quickly faced with resistance to policies and reform, political deadlocks, coups, and even secession attempts or civil wars, reminding them that the inheritance of the colonial state in no way implied the inheritance of power. Examples from the first decade of African independence unfortunately abound and usually paint a tragic picture of the power gap of inheritance elites.[28] Africa experienced its worst period of instability in the 1960s, when it was also the most unstable of all developing regions (Campos and Nugent 1997). The preponderance of coups d'état over apparently benign matters of domestic politics was but one of the mildest manifestations of the politics of low-legitimacy states. In Benin, discontent in unions and political deadlock among the main parties resulted in military coups in 1963 and 1965. Unrest over austerity programs and rumors of an impending military reshuffle also led to a government overthrow in the Central African Republic in 1966. Complaints by unions about unemployment and government incompetence were also responsible for the Congolese

(Brazzaville) coup of 1963. In Gabon, army discontent with low pay and slow promotions resulted in a coup in 1964, although it was promptly overturned by French military intervention. Asante disgruntled at Kwame Nkrumah's cocoa policies were in part responsible for his overthrow in 1966. In Togo, President Olympio was assassinated in 1963 in a coup launched by Togolese veterans of the French army upset at their lack of reintegration in the national military. In 1966, the army also took over in Upper Volta, after unions demonstrated against government austerity.

In each case, either the opposition forces called for military intervention instead of working within the formal political system, or the armed forces alone took advantage of their control over the instruments of force to rearrange the outcome of the political process in their favor. Either way, and without passing judgment on their policies, the governments realized how little room they had to maneuver because of the absence of a social contract empowering the state to coordinate problems of collective action.

In other instances, violent overthrows resulted not so much from disputes over government policies but from competing attempts by subnational groups to control the state. Northern Chadian Muslim groups attempted to overthrow the southern-based government of Tombalbaye in 1963, 1965, and 1967. Rivalries between President Massemba-Débat, a southerner, and Captain Ngouabi, a northerner, were also partly responsible for the latter's 1968 coup in Congo. Equatorial Guinea, which had become independent barely a year earlier, had its first coup in 1969, partly as a consequence of the president's attempt to promote his Fang ethnic group's control over the civil service. In Côte d'Ivoire, there was a major plot against the government in 1963 because of fears of domination by president Houphouët-Boigny's Baoule group. Kenya had enduring conflict between Kikuyu and non-Kikuyu elites throughout the 1960s. In 1961, officers of northern Somalia staged a coup attempt because of their dissatisfaction at being commanded by officers of the south. In 1969, the Somali army took over to prevent the fractionalization of the country among competing clans. In 1966, Ewé dissatisfied with the government attempted a coup in Togo and were also instrumental in the overthrow of Nkrumah in Ghana. In Uganda, an uneasy arrangement in which the traditional king of Buganda, the Kabaka, was also president of Uganda came to an end when Prime Minister Milton Obote overthrew the president in 1966 and established a unitary state, hampered as he was by the enduring power of Buganda.

Things get more serious when conflict over the state takes on a more sustainably violent overtone. By 1968, large-scale fighting had erupted between the government of Chad and the northern National Liberation Front (FROLINAT) following perceptions of neglect and excessive taxation by the north. In Cameroon, the Duala- and Bamiléké-based Union des Populations du Cameroun (UPC) launched occasional guerrilla attacks against the government throughout the 1960s, in part for fear of the domination of the north-ern-based Ahidjo administration. In Nigeria, the Tiv launched an armed rebellion from 1961 to 1965, and in Sierra Leone, violence erupted in 1968 by Mendé elements dissatisfied with the non-Mendé nature of the Siaka Stevens government. In Sudan, Morrison et al. confirm that "communal instability is partly the result of the colonial legacy in which many small-scale societies of Nilotic peoples in the south (who have resisted arabization by the northern Sudanese) were attached to the predominantly Arab north" (1989:635).

Finally, although these attempts were thwarted by the rigidities imposed by the Cold War and neocolonial interventions, many groups simply tried to break away from the arbitrary postcolonial African state. The best-known examples are Katanga and Biafra, but they are not alone. In the former Belgian Congo, the failure of the central administration to Africanize the national police force led to an attempt at secession by Katanga within a week of Congolese inde-pendence (though not without Belgian encouragement). Virtually no effort was made by Katanga politicians to solve the problem in Kinshasa (Young 1983). Later, as the Congolese crisis further unfolded, supporters of Lumumba engaged in armed rebellion against the Kasavubu government, whose legitimacy did not extend beyond the Bakongo regions (Verhaegen 1966). In Nigeria, the attempt at secession by the Igbo of Biafra from 1966 to 1970 was but the most visible mark of contestation of the state and of the Haussa domination in the 1960s. Other cases of secession attempts include the Ewé of Ghana, partitioned with Togo, who were responsible for recurring irredentist violence throughout the 1960s. Earlier, when Nkrumah had lowered the price of cocoa in order to extract a surplus from agriculture to be reinvested in industrial development, the Asante already had openly called for secession (Apter 1968). Attempts to secede were also made by the Agni of Côte d'Ivoire in 1959 and again in 1969. Somali irredentism affected Kenya and Ethiopia. In Zambia, the Barotze clamored for secession while the state violently clashed in the 1960s with church groups that refused to recognize its political supremacy. In Angola, the baKongo exerted substantial irredentist pressure. In fact the Uniao des Populacoes de Norte Angola (UPNA), founded in 1954 by Holden Roberto (which would later become the FNLA—Frente Nacional de Libertacao de Angola), had reunification of the baKongo people as its first objective.

The pattern that emerged in the 1960s was therefore one in which the state failed to be perceived as a neutral arena or a third-party enforcer but rather as an instrument and resource for promoting subnational interests. There was no agreement as to the mechanisms of the political system because the latter was perceived as an alien colonial creation. Consequently, the state failed to become a leviathan endowed with powers of conflict resolution, and policies that hurt the interests of some groups resulted in attempts by these same groups either to overthrow the government or secede away from the state. This dramatically reduced the power and capacity of the rulers in their policymaking activities.

Note, however, that although many of the above examples have an ethnic content, they were not about alleged ancestral tribal hatreds or so-called primordial sentiments. The problem of the ruling elites was not to pacify feuding societies. On the contrary, the ethnic violence or ethnic origins of coups relate directly to issues of control of the state. The alien nature of the state leads each group to attempt to appropriate it or to fear appropriation by others and break away from it. This is the direct consequence of the state's lack of historical legitimacy in the eyes of its citizens, of the absence of a social contract among constitutive groups of society.

Hence, the power of the leaders of low-legitimacy states is fragile, their capacity for policymaking limited. More than other rulers, leaders of nonlegitimate states have to strive to establish control over their state and to impart it with the power to act over their societies. This is their challenge and the prime motive of their actions.[29] Faced with such a power gap and widespread instability, these leaders eventually adjusted their strategies. They learned. They sought ways to shore up the foundations of their regimes. As Bayart (1993) puts it, they engaged upon a "hegemonic quest."[30] Their objective became to stabilize their grip on the state and the state's grip on society by creating a social basis for their rule. Obviously, they could not and would not restructure the states they had inherited, so they either tried to restructure their alleged nations, to reshape them in the mold of imported states, or resign to themselves to accommodate their diverse components.

The Politics of Illegitimacy

Faced with the dilemma of having inherited states without power, modern African leaders typically embarked on one of two alternative paths. They either tried to legitimate the state by forcing a new national identity upon their societies, or used its resources to create and sustain networks of support for their regime.

In the first instance, which James Coleman and Carl Rosberg (1964) referred to as the "revolutionary-centralizing trend," the modern elites, dissociated from the customary sources of power, attempted to launch revolutionary processes of national integration by imposing the new state on the lives and minds of their citizens. This was the era of "nation building" that led to a climate of confrontation between state and society, in which precolonial systems were most strongly battered. Revolutionary movements often accompanied this approach, but under the communist or socialist veneer, the true ideology was one of national integration. Examples of this approach included the Sékou Touré regime in Guinea, Modibo Keita in Mali, Maurice Yaméogo in Upper Volta, Julius Nyerere in Tanzania (especially with his policy of *ujamaa,* which brought farmers together in new villages away from their usual social structures and which refused to recognize traditional political structures), and Kwame Nkrumah in Ghana, among others. Even Mobutu of Zaire tried this approach for a while when he changed his country's name, forced his citizens to change their name, set up a *parti unique,* and made membership in it automatic for all ("The MPR presents itself as a large family to which all Zaireans without exception belong. All Zaireans are born equal members of the MPR").[31] All these regimes had in common their desire to quash competing centers of institutional allegiance (ethnic identification and ethnic-based political parties were often banned, as were customary chieftaincies), to force their societies into a new mold, to impose a symbiosis between state and society in which the burden of the adjustment was placed upon the society.[32] What these leaders were doing, in the words of Nkrumah, was to "seek ye first the political kingdom" and hope that all else would be granted to them thereupon. Often they sought to clothe themselves in the legitimacy of the past. They renamed their countries after ancient kingdoms, although these had little or nothing in common with their contemporary states; this is how Ghana, Mali, and Benin came to be. Or they renamed themselves after unifying political figures of precolonial times, as when Ahmed Sékou Touré borrowed his last name from

Almany Samory Touré, the great West African Muslim leader and resistance fighter to colonialism.

This approach to political power more often than not implied a charismatic component as leaders sought additional avenues for the creation of allegiance. The bond between the leadership and citizens involved by the charismatic relation to some extent reduced the power gap of leaders like Nkrumah, Azikiwe, Kenyatta, Nyerere, or Sékou Touré. The limits of charismatic leadership are narrower, however, than the enthusiasm they generate may suggest. In most of these cases, the charisma acquired through the nationalist phase of the decolonization process did not endure through the realities of power and rule. The charismatic relation momentarily hid the problem of state illegitimacy but did not do away with it. To some extent, the failures of Nkrumah, Nyerere, and Sékou Touré were by and large the result of their own incompetence as economic policymakers, but they also illustrate how state illegitimacy caught up with charismatic as well as other leaders of independent Africa, weakening their true power and constraining the policy options available to them.

The nation-building approach to state power was rarely successful, and many of the instances of instability related earlier had nationalist leaders as their victim. Yet these policies were an attempt at overcoming the incongruence of state and society, at legitimating the state by changing the society and shaping it in its image. When they failed it was because the resilience of alternative loyalties remained too high.[33] While many observers expressed an initial faith in the process of integration of new states (Emerson 1960; Zolberg 1966), it did not take long for the most perceptive ones to notice the progressive abortion of the process. As early as the late 1960s, Geertz (1973a:236), for one, acknowledged the stalling of the "forward motion of the nation as a whole" in new states. Failure was either the overthrow of the political elite or a progressive abandonment of the integrative purpose and a parallel deliquescence toward mere authoritarianism, where political survival took precedence over political construction (e.g., Sékou Touré in the last half of his rule). In other cases, societies disengaged from the state's grip and escaped back into preexisting patterns of social interactions, as with the resurgence of Tanzania's "economy of affection" in the wake of the failure of *ujamaa* (Hyden 1980).

Failures of nation building led these African elites to the conclusion that somehow they must accommodate or domesticate the competing foci of domestic power and allegiance. This strategic reversal brought them closer to their counterparts who had from the beginning followed the approach that Coleman and Rosberg (1964) labeled the "pragmatic-pluralistic pattern" of rule. These leaders attempted to substitute the instrumental legitimacy of neopatrimonial policies for their lack of moral claim to rule, and they resorted to clientelistic networks to prevent state fragmentation. This soon became the most frequent type of rule in Africa and has been recognized by Africanists as the "fusion" (Lonsdale 1981; Boone 1994) or the "reciprocal assimilation" of elites (Bayart 1993). The point is for the contemporary leadership to establish alliances with other elites, be they regional, ethnic, customary, or otherwise, who control the loyalty of some segments of society. In doing so, these loyalties are co-opted for the national regime, which thereby stabilizes its rule and reaches some level of social foundations. These competing elites are enticed into the national system with political sinecures, financial largesse, pork, and other forms of patronage. What is actually being established here is a multilevel network of patron-client relations starting between the national politicians (patrons) and competing elites (clients), and building upon regional networks where the latter elites have traditionally played the role of patrons.[34] The formation of the ruling class is therefore predicated upon a system of nonformal political and economic relations that take true precedence over the formal political system. These networks take place in the margins of the formal institutions of statehood and provide foundations to the power of elites but not to the postcolonial state itself. This is the true root of African neopatrimonialism (Médard 1982; Hyden 1983a; Sandbrook 1985; Sandbrook 1986; Lewis 1996; Bratton and van de Walle 1997).

Such neopatrimonial strategies can take place irrespective of the formal political system, be it electoral, as in Senegal, where Léopold Senghor gathered the support of the Muslim Brotherhoods by guaranteeing their monopoly of the peanut trade; authoritarian, as in Zaire, where Mobutu Sese Seko repeatedly "purchased" the collaboration of the opposition from different regions; or a mix of both, as in Nigeria, where either "democratic" or military regimes have attempted to establish the shared hegemony of central political elites and their northern Haussa counterparts. Truly, appearances are deceptive with African regimes, and their formal characterization along the democracy-dictatorship or the conservative-progressive scales does not fully reveal the essence of their power.

The fusion of elites provides elements of stability to the rulers. Goran Hyden (1983a:73), for example, uses a similar concept to explain why ethnic conflicts are not more prevalent in Africa. To the competing elites it gives a measure of participation and of government accountability and reduces their alienation from the imported state. This is how one is to make sense of the frequent participation of opposition figures in African governments: Abdoulaye Wade in Senegal before he became president, Etienne Tshisekedi and Nguz Karl I Bond in Zaire, Joshua Nkomo in Zimbabwe, Herman Yaméogo in Burkina, Laurent Gbagbo in Côte d'Ivoire, and so forth.

But why would African leaders not attempt to boost their power and build acquiescence to their rule with developmental policies instead of neopatrimonial ones? Why not generate loyalty out of development, legitimacy out of efficiency? After all, it is often argued that the performance and efficiency of some East Asian regimes provided them with legitimacy, despite their lack of democratic credentials. The truth is that quite a few African policymakers tried, especially those who chose the "revolutionary" nation-building approach to their conundrum. But creating legitimacy out of efficiency is a catch-22 in the context of low-legitimacy states. Indeed, legitimacy results in time $t+1$ from the efficiency displayed in time t. But successful implementation of developmental policies in time t requires a certain preexisting level of state legitimacy and of societal loyalty, which these states did not benefit from to begin with. Under conditions of weak initial legitimacy, bureaucrats are insufficiently loyal to the state and private agents too distrustful of its institutions. This makes it difficult for state elites to implement developmental policies and provides an incentive for them to pursue instead nation-building or elite-fusing strategies of power consolidation. Hence, the potential returns of building legitimacy out of development are low, which raises the relative returns of either the nondevelopmental version of nation building or the neopatrimonial option. Altogether, the "reciprocal assimilation of elites" (Bayart 1993) turns out to be the most widespread strategy because it is the least costly and the most likely to succeed. Most social revolutions fiddled away into fusion of elites, as attested to by claims of widespread corruption in model social revolution states such as Sékou Touré's Guinea or Julius Nyerere's Tanzania.

In contrast, the leaders of more legitimate states did not usually confront a hegemonic crisis. Although their states had also been colonized, they were either composed of new populations without previous allegiances (e.g., most of the islands off the coast of Africa) or had been reappropriated by preexisting political systems (Botswana, Lesotho, Swaziland).[35] In place of the colonial domination, these leaders were generally able to substitute the historical legitimacy of their right to rule, and within the relative lack of arbitrariness of their colonial boundaries they found preexisting polities over which to rule. Consequently, they felt no need to build nations out of artificial states, nor did they have to resort to distributing the resources of the state to competing groups in order to maintain tolerance of their rule. On the contrary, they were able to adopt, and derived more benefits from adopting, developmental policies and from reinforcing their formal institutions.

Both the nation-building and neopatrimonial responses to the illegitimacy of political structures inherited from colonial domination dictated to African elites a specific set of policies. These policies had, in turn, damning implications for the capacity of their states and their economic prospects. As demonstrated next, in nonlegitimate states development was sacrificed on the altar of power.

The Policies of Illegitimacy

Although the hegemonic strategies of the rulers of nonlegitimate states may have helped provide their regime with some level of stability and control over society, they have tended to ruin the capacity of their formal state institutions to design and implement sound economic policies and to provide good governance to markets. The need for a hegemonic "quick fix," brought about by the inheritance of artificial colonial states, bears a large responsibility for the choice of policies inimical to development (Sandbrook 1986). African rulers of nonlegitimate states have truly lacked the leverage to choose policies for growth, so weak have been the foundations of their power. They have chosen policies to foster a sense of nationhood or to elicit the support of a selected few crucial constituencies. But as power became the purpose of public policy, development became its victim.

Those who chose the nation-building approach typically followed an increasingly interventionist course under the guise of numerous ideologies from "African socialism" to "state capitalism."[36] State-society relations were structured from the top down, and the imposition of the state onto society required an expansion of the realm of the former. Single parties were one of the crucial instruments of this process (Zolberg 1966), and the distinction between the party, the nation, and the state was usually blurred.

The expansion of the public sphere tilted economic systems away from private enterprise and market mechanisms, which had rarely been predominant to begin with during the colonial period. The few existing foreign investments ran a high risk of expropriation, both on ideological grounds and for the revenue they could contribute to the public sector (e.g., Congo-Kinshasa in 1971). Waves of nationalization swept many countries (Ghana from 1957 to 1966, Congo-Brazzaville in 1970, Benin in 1975, Guinea-Bissau, Angola, and Mozambique from 1975 to the early 1990s). In rural areas, there were cases of forced villagization and resettlements, as in Tanzania in 1967 and Zimbabwe from 1980 onward, and agricultural extension services everywhere imposed state control over "free" farmers. Land too was occasionally nationalized (Congo in 1966, Burkina Faso in 1984).

Although some of these interventionist policies did respond to an ideological rationale (initially largely shared by foreign donors) and to the idea that modernization was to be brought about by the state in the absence of a sufficiently developed indigenous entrepreneurial class, they also went hand-in-hand with the political imperative of nation building and state control of society. The usually poor record of both agricultural production and industrialization in Africa actually derives from this mixed motive. The nation-building imperative substituted political criteria for economic considerations in the type of interventionist policies that were followed. Public investments, for example, favored projects that fostered a sense of statehood or that furthered the controlling capacity of the state, over those with better economic returns. The African state, deprived of a "cultural frame in which to define itself" (Geertz 1983:1443) or a "master fiction" to "operate as the unchallenged first [principle] of a political order, making any given hierarchy appear natural and just to rulers and ruled" (Wilentz 1985:4), developed a tendency to multiply theatrical displays of statehood and sovereignty such as white-elephant development projects, imperial coronations, unnecessarily large armed forces, national airlines, glamorous presidential palaces, and maisons du peuple. Similarly, in its permanent quest "to control the social system by means of a strong bureaucracy" (Badie and Birnbaum 1979), the nation-building state also overdeveloped its bureaucracy and turned the state into a burden for the economy (Barro 1990; Findlay and Wilson 1984), although ideology also played a role in this expansion of the public sphere. This evolution went together with an increase in the personal nature of presidential rule, as the person of the president became the rallying point of the new national identity, the smallest common denominator of the alleged nation (see Jackson and Rosberg 1982b). As a corollary to national integration defined as allegiance to one man, political repression also became more pervasive and civil liberties declined. Control turned to predation.

But people everywhere escape oppression if they can. In Africa too, the nation-building oppression of its citizens by the state resulted in attempts by the former to escape. Robert Bates reminds us that farmers "dodge and maneuver to avoid the deprivations inflicted upon them by public policy" and "use the market against the state, thereby evading some of the adverse consequences of government policies" (1981:87, 82). They do so in part by reducing output, migrating out of the countryside, returning to subsistence lifestyles, or joining the informal sector. Consequently, policy aberrations on the part of governments are more likely to result in exit patterns than in attempts at reform. There is some evidence that the informal sector is particularly large in Africa. J. J. Thomas (1992:67) has shown that the percentage of working population in the informal sector in a sample of eleven (nonlegitimate) African countries averaged 49.1 percent, as against 37.4 percent in a sample of seven Asian countries. In Zaire, the central bank reported in 1992 that as much as 72 percent of GDP was accounted for by informal activity and subsistence agriculture (Economist Intelligence Unit 1994). This may be evidence of the massive evasion of Africans from economic domination by the state. Yet this is not a zero-sum game. The African citizens who try to improve their lot by escaping the state-sponsored formal economy live in a second-best economic world. In transferring away from some activities and into others, they both generate and encounter substantial efficiency losses, transaction costs, and innovative failures. The main costs are associated with the absence of a legal system able to guarantee contracts, the lack of well-defined property rights, and the difficulties in enforcing agreements. This prevents effective specialization and division of labor and leads to economies performing well below their possibilities.[37]

In the end, the African "integrative revolution" (Geertz 1973b) turned into the disintegration of the state. Seeking control of the political kingdom exacted an unbearable price on the kingdom itself. The means destroyed the end. In the process of building up their power, the leaders of illegitimate African polities who chose the nationalist route actually tore down their states.

For the regimes that have followed the fusion of elites approach, the use of state resources to finance the co-optation of competing centers of legitimacy became the instrument of choice.[38] Neopatrimonial policies involving corruption, nepotism, ethnicity, factionalism, and patronage have provided substance to networks with competing elites. Yet as widespread as "corrupt" practices are in these states, it may not be their regimes' defining characteristic; such policy opportunism exists elsewhere and also answers to different logics (Sindzingre 1997; Wedeman 1997). What is most crucial about African neopatrimonialism, however, is that it does not operate in the margins of state institutions, as an illegal and repressed vice, but actually attaches itself to formal political structures, parties, and bureaucracies in order to link the centrifugal components of the state with its new core. In essence, it transforms the nature of these institutions, turning them from their original purposes of representation, management, enforcement, or conflict resolution, into instruments of distribution, co-optation, or reward. The formal state becomes the tool of informal strategies of power. African politics deserts the state and erects a "shadow" counterpart to it (Reno 1995) by using its very resources.

Here too the means of modernization—accommodation—threaten its very end. The ultimate consequence of neopatrimonial rule, which has occurred with increased frequency over the last decade, is the collapse of the formal state.[39] Before that occurs, however, there is a slow but steady deterioration of the quality of governance. The efficiency of the bureaucracy as measured by its capacity to design and implement policies vacillates. The law turns irrelevant. Trust in institutions, weak to begin with, further evaporates and leads to additional corrupt practices by citizens who perceive that the "laws of the village" have become powerless "in the affairs of the nation" (Achebe 1966:167). Governments become unable to take sustained action, to make credible commitments, and to enforce the rules of the game. Meanwhile, their spending rises in proportion to the size of the economy. Long-term investments such as education and infrastructure are neglected to the benefit of current expenditure on wages, consumption, and for the creation of ever more agencies to provide prebends (see Joseph 1987). As Geertz put it with respect to Indonesia, also an artificial creation of colonialism, "Governmental structures—national councils, state planning commissions, constitutional conventions, and so on—have multiplied like weeds in a neglected garden" (1973b:282). And Sheldon Gellar noted in the 1970s that "in all but one or two West African states, there was a rapid expansion of the state bureaucracy . . . after independence" (1973:399).

As the foundations for growth weaken, resources dry up and governments turn to foreign financing. They commit to reforms imposed with aid, but often backtrack when these reforms threaten their system. Out of twenty-six countries that had entered adjustment programs with the World Bank by the early 1990s, for example, eleven had actually recorded a macroeconomic policy deterioration, and nine had implemented less than a third of the required macroeconomic reforms (World Bank 1994a:261).[40]

In a nutshell, the instrumental legitimacy of systemic patronage, while substituting for the lack of political legitimacy of the state, introduces a systematic bias in policy choice away from long-term-growth enhancing policies and leads to a decrepitude of the national institutions. Hence, the attempts by elites to remedy their power deficit leads to the ruin of the state itself. It is not so much that Africans have a natural propensity to understand power and politics as acquisition instead of as instruments for social transformation, as Bayart (1993) may argue, but rather that the inheritance of illegitimate political structures constrains African political elites to use their institutions as resources to shore up their power.

Understanding institutional illegitimacy as the root of political behavior in these African states sheds a new light on the variance in policy choice and institutional quality across Africa. Not all African states suffer from the same level of incongruence with their precolonial institutions, nor do they all have equally arbitrary polities and similar vacuums of social contracting. And we can at least partly explain their differences in state capacity in terms of their differences in state legitimacy. Leadership quality may well have some relevance too (Sandbrook 1986), but without a social agreement on the rules of the game or the shape and size of the field, players and referees are equally helpless, however good they may be. Hence, the nature of the state is the ultimate constraint and determinant of the political behavior of elites, other things being equal. Before turning to aggregate evidence in support of this proposition, I compare the experience of the Democratic Republic of Congo (formerly Zaire) and Botswana, to convey a more intuitive understanding of the relationship between legitimacy and capacity in Africa.

WHY CONGO IS POOR AND BOTSWANA IS RICH

Botswana and the Democratic Republic of Congo (henceforth, Congo) have had drastically divergent development paths since their independence in the 1960s. Botswana has grown by an average of

5.6 percent per year (in real per capita terms), while Congo has made
no significant developmental progress and has actually registered a
decline by many measures. At independence in 1966, Botswana's per
capita income level was equivalent to the purchasing power of $577
in 1995 U.S. dollars. Six years earlier, Congo's per capita income
had been grossly similar at $489. By 1995, however, Botswana's
GNP per capita had risen to $5,580, whereas Congo's was rather gen-
erously estimated by the World Bank to still stand at no more than
$490.[41]

Why such divergent paths? Both countries are rich in natural
resources. Botswana produces more diamonds than any other country
in the world and is a major cattle exporter. Congo is also a major
player in world diamond markets and produces numerous additional
minerals such as copper, cobalt, gold, and zinc. In addition, it has
timber and coffee resources as well as a vast hydroelectrical potential
that could supply electricity to all of southern Africa. If Botswana's
miracle is one of natural resources endowment, then it should have
been dwarfed by development in Congo. And if Congo's predicament
is the result of commodity dependency or of deteriorating terms of
trade, then it should have been accompanied in its fall by Botswana.
Other differences in natural or social conditions shed no further light
on their divergent development fortunes. Botswana is actually more
vulnerable to weather patterns, having suffered from several
droughts since independence and having a large portion of its territory covered by desert. It also is landlocked, while Congo has access to
the ocean at Matadi. It is unclear whether Botswana benefits from
higher levels of social capital than Congo. As mentioned earlier,
Jennifer Widner and Alexander Mundt (1998) have found social capital to be relatively low in Botswana, whereas there is ample evidence that associative life is vibrant in Congo, especially in the wake
of the collapse of the formal state. Botswana is more ethnically
homogeneous than Congo, but not so much as one would expect.
Using the index of ethno-linguistic fragmentation, which measures
the probability that two randomly selected individuals would belong
to different ethnic groups (see Chapter 4), Botswana scores 0.51 and
Congo 0.90. Even this difference may be an overstatement, capturing
linguistic variations that do not truly reflect cultural differences. Jan
Vansina has argued indeed that "the cultures of the Congo resemble
each other strongly" (1966:10). There is no straightforward answer
from conventional theories as to why Congo should be so much
poorer than Botswana.

Differences in leadership styles have also been pointed to on occasion. Botswana's Seretse Khama and Ketumile Masire are well-known to have been leaders of great personal integrity, whereas Mobutu was largely a bandit who not only stole from his country but even encouraged his people to steal ("just steal a little at a time," he warned them). But was Mobutu an evil man from the beginning? Why would Lumumba, another character of integrity, have appointed him as his military chief of staff in 1960 if there were suspicions about his morality? In fact, there was little to suggest when Mobutu took over in 1965 that he was a crook. To the contrary, he appeared to many as a stalwart of uprightness amid the political immaturity of the Congolese political class. Instead, he grew into the role of crook over time, a trap that Botswana's leaders mostly avoided. I argue below that the degeneration of Congo's leadership, policies, and, eventually, institutions was the consequence of the nation-building and neopatrimonial logic of power brought about by the lack of historical legitimacy of the postcolonial state. In contrast, the quality of leadership and the construction of state capacity in Botswana are directly related to the embeddedness of its postcolonial state into pre-colonial patterns of political authority.

Congo was created by Leopold II, king of the Belgians, as a private commercial venture. Henry Stanley had been commissioned to explore the basin of the Congo River, and the resulting Congo Free State was created in 1885 as the personal property of the king. According to Winsome Leslie, "The focus was on extraction of resources, the unification of the territory through military conquest, and the economic destruction of pre-existing kingdoms" (1993:8). Leopold divided the country into districts headed by commissioners, ignoring preexisting ethnic boundaries and crushing the authority of local chiefs. "The aim," Leslie writes, "was the creation of a unified territory, even at the cost of the destruction of existing polities" (1993:9). The Belgian government acquired Congo as a colony in 1908, after the repressive excesses of Leopold's private state brought about widespread condemnation of his administration of the country. Colonial rule continued the institutional destruction of local societies, however, forcing local systems into submission and substituting a new political hierarchy for the existing political orders. Traditional chiefly authority was undermined: "Custom was recognized and respected only at the level of the *chefferie*, even though tribal chiefs had been entrusted with the welfare of entire tribes in precolonial times" (Leslie 1993:12). Leaving so much destruction in its path, it comes as no wonder that the Belgian colonial state became known to the Congolese as Bula Matari, the crusher of rocks (Young 1994).

The formation of a modern Congolese elite involved a certain level of dissociation with customary authority. The very few Congolese who had access to education became *évolués*—evolved individuals—a term that emphasized their dissociation from traditional structures and socialized them in looking down on their previous identity and that of their compatriots. As Mahmood Mamdani (1996) has brilliantly argued, the *évolués,* by their very dissociation, became the future citizens of a state defined by colonialism, whereas the rest of the indigenous population remained mere subjects, deprived of historical agency. The naming of their capital as Léopoldville gives a taste for the alienation the Congolese must have felt for the system in which they now lived.

Until the very last minute, the Belgians had no intention—and no plan—to surrender control over Congo and to grant independence to its citizens. Ruling with an iron fist in a paternalistic glove, they provided the Congolese with little education and did not allow local elections until 1957. It was riots in 1959 that shocked them into a rapid and confused process of decolonization. A roundtable was convened in early 1960 with a handful of political leaders and independence was granted a mere six months thereafter. The songs of Joseph Kabasellé, "Table Ronde" and "Indépendance Cha-Cha," convey the bittersweet taste of independence for the Congolese.

Colonization had destroyed the preexisting systems of power but provided no alternative path to political socialization at a hypothetical Congolese level, since Africans had been kept in an artificial state of political childhood until the end of the 1950s. Searching for solidarities in their uprooted urban environment, *évolués* began to organize politically on a mostly regional or ethnic basis.[42] Joseph Kasavubu's *Alliance des Bakongo* (ABAKO) represented the Bakongo population. Moïse Tshombé's *Confédération des Associations Katangaises* (CONAKAT) drew its support from the southern Katanga province. Antoine Gizenga's Parti de la Solidarité Africaine relied on Kwilu. Even Patrice Lumumba, usually considered the most "national" of Congolese independence leaders, drew a disproportionate amount of support from his Equatoriale province. Most of these parties only reluctantly played the game of Congolese politics, and mostly to avoid seeing the control of the state wrested away by other groups. Otherwise, there were few deep or preexisting conflicts between these regions and ethnic groupings, but it was the superimposition of Congo as the political arena that created antagonisms of self-determination. ABAKO had a strong preference for regional autonomy and tolerated national integration only if there was to be a confederation. CONAKAT supported the independence of Katanga. What the Congolese wanted was to return to the mastery of their own destinies, and the most obvious path for most of them was to do so at the level of their specific culture area, even though their new elites had been largely dissociated from traditional structures of political authority.[43] As René Lemarchand wrote in the early 1960s, "Behind the fragmented pattern of modern associational development in the Congo lies the precolonial past. It has shaped and continues to influence the group loyalties and the political perspectives and behavior of most Congolese" (1964b:560). Despite similarities among Congolese, there was little redeeming value in the eyes of most to keep Congo as a unified political system. It had been the creation of King Leopold and represented little more than a product of the colonial scramble for Africa. Moreover, to the Africans it had mostly brought about domination, exploitation, violence, and suffering. Although the logic of decolonization pushed Congo toward becoming a successor to the colonial state, its lack of historical legitimacy shattered the transition.

Within a week of independence in June 1960, the army mutinied, in a typical example of how political demands turn into challenges of the entire system in nonlegitimate states. A few days later, this mutiny had become a secession attempt by Katanga as a whole under the leadership of Moïse Tshombé. Meanwhile, President Kasavubu and Prime Minister Lumumba were at each other's throat, alternately dismissing one another in September. The stalemate led supporters of Lumumba to declare Stanleyville, in his province, the legitimate capital and to launch de facto another secession movement. By January 1961, the province of Kasai had begun a secession of its own. The following four years saw widespread chaos compounded by numerous foreign interventions and resulted in Mobutu's takeover in 1965.[44]

Although justly reviled across the board, Mobutu is also widely credited with having pacified Congo and maintained its territorial integrity. He did so with a mix of authoritarianism and co-option, of nation-building politics and accommodation of competing elites (see Callaghy 1984). History will judge whether the preservation of the postcolonial state justified the developmental costs it has exacted upon the Congolese. My purpose here is only to show the connection between the preservation of power in an illegitimate state and its economic decline. Mobutu's approach truly mixed the two dimensions of the politics of illegitimacy discussed earlier. He began with a pseudonationalistic strategy embodied in the 1967 *Manifeste de la N'sélé,* which soon turned into a personality cult that even Mao would have envied. He attempted to forge a Zairean nationality by increasingly resorting to the fiction of a national family, with him as father and his own mother, Mama Yemo, as a founding national figure, and by forcing new "African" identities and party membership upon Congo's *citoyens* (Schatzberg 1989). In addition, he literally purchased the support of regionally based elites by building networks of patronage and clientelism that allowed them to systematically plunder the state to the benefit of their region, their people, and themselves.

Both dimensions of Mobutu's strategy of power irresistibly led to economic decline, as Janet McGaffey (1987 and 1994) has well documented. The nationalist/Mobutist phase, which culminated in the 1970s, implied a destruction of the existing structure of property rights and a host of economically unsound public investments. Land was nationalized in July 1966, and all unexploited concessions reverted to the state within a month. In 1967, the giant mining company Union Minière du Haut-Katanga (UMHK) became a nationalized Gécamines. There was no socialist ideological underpinning to the nationalization. As Kamitatu Massamba (1976) has argued,

> The decision to nationalize UMHK was a political act, deliberately and carefully prepared. Its objective was less for the decider [Mobutu], the recovery of the economic independence of the Nation, than the consolidation of presidential power, the budgetary underpinning of which was basically constituted by fiscal levies on UMHK. . . . The second political aspect of nationalization was the presidential determination to remove from UMHK the capacity to offer financial backing to potential political opponents of the regime.[45]

Following this wave of nationalizations, which established state control of economic resources without either a well-conceived plan for what to do with them or even the bureaucratic capacity to do much, the Mobutu regime embarked upon a series of white-elephant projects that had more to do with an affirmation of sovereignty and power than with sound economic rationales. These included the Maluku steel mill, which was bankrupt within a few years (Young writes that it produced "low-grade steel at eight times the cost of better quality imported steel"[46]); the giant Inga dam, which has since functioned at a minimal fraction of its capacity; the Inga-Shaba power line, which was more an instrument for control of Shaba (former Katanga)—to which power delivery could be suspended by Mobutu if need be—than a needed infrastructural development; and numerous stadiums and monuments to the "Guide."

The neopatrimonial phase of Mobutu's power, which peaked in the 1980s, involved a further deterioration of property rights, increased recurrent government spending and employment, and (progressively) truly generalized corruption. "Zaireanization," in 1974, marked the beginning of this phase of the regime and involved the confiscation of assets of foreigners and their redistribution to regional elites and clients of the Mobutu regime. V. S. Naipaul (1979) has described the absurdity of the process in his novel *A Bend in the River:*

> I suppose you know why you come back, *patron.* . . . Because you have nothing to come back to. You don't know? Nobody told you in London . . . ? You don't have anything. They take away your shop. They give it to citizen Theotime.

Meanwhile, the size of the government sector in proportion to the rest of the economy kept on growing. Government consumption, which had represented 9 percent of GDP in 1965, had reached 24 percent by 1988 (World Bank 1990b). Most of this financed the creation of prebends and networks of nepotism and regional favors. In March 1995, during a desperate attempt by the Kengo government to shore up public finances, an internal audit found that half the 600,000 civil servants employed throughout Zaire's eleven provinces were fictitious, a finding that even union leaders did not contest (Economist Intelligence Unit 1995:29).

The perpetuation of Mobutu's power not only shattered conventional notions of property rights but also created absolute precariousness of life for individuals, leading to widespread economic insecurity and compensating acts of corruption. Mobutu's brand of reciprocal assimilation involved an intense rotation of associated elites in order to avoid the development of competing foci of power. Aware of the fragility of their position, political appointees maximized their pursuit of material resources while in office. At the lower levels of the state apparatus, the rank and file of civil servants, rarely paid and equally vulnerable, also used their limited access to instruments of power in order to appropriate resources from private citizens. Simple citizens, in turn, coped with the endless arbitrariness of government by resorting to "Article 15" or "Système D" (local expressions that refer to fending for oneself), by "beating" the system irrespective of the formal body of laws, rules, and regulations.

Mobutu's own acquisition of wealth only partly followed a logic of personal enrichment. Although he owned prime real estate in Belgium, France, Florida, and elsewhere, the U.S.$14 billion he was believed to have diverted from Zaire's public coffers could not be found after his death, despite inquiries in Switzerland, Belgium, and the United States. Bank secrecy regulations probably contributed to hiding some of it, but it is also possible that not much was left of Mobutu's embezzlements. Their purpose was political; their aim was to finance allegiance, buy compliance, and silence opposition. Mobutu redistributed his wealth. He was the center and the engine of a power mechanism that consisted of extracting resources from the state and redistributing them to segments of society whose support was needed or whose opposition had to be tamed. The system worked wonders for Mobutu, who stayed in power more than thirty years, and for the idea of Zaire, which survived repeated challenges. The Zairean state was not so lucky. In the process of subduing dissent against himself and Zaire, Mobutu exhausted the state, all but surrendered its capacity for public policy and governance, and killed the goose that laid the Zairean egg. In the end, Congo never recovered from its original deficit of legitimacy.

Politics and policies in Botswana provide a stark contrast to those in Congo. On the continuum of historical legitimacy of states, Botswana lies at the opposite end too. The Tswana kingdoms predated colonization by the British. In comparison to Belgium's rule in Congo, British colonialism in Bechuanaland was mild and almost welcomed by the Tswana, who actually requested the establishment of a British protectorate as a defense against encroachments by Boer settlers from the Transvaal. Once the protectorate was established, the Tswana successfully resisted occasional attempts by the British to absorb them into South Africa. Instead, the traditional political system endured throughout the colonial episode and resumed its sovereignty upon independence. The economic exploitation of the colony also was milder, with a more limited transfer of wealth from colonized to colonizer than elsewhere. For example, African ranchers still owned 90 percent of the cattle at the end of colonization (Stedman 1993).

Upon independence in 1966, the continuity of politics was epitomized by the election as president of Seretse Khama, formerly the heir to the Ngwato kingship, whom the British had forced to renounce chieftainship in 1956 after he married a white woman. Khama's marriage in the end was symbolic of his joint appeal to traditional rural populations and urbanized classes, and it further contributed to linking Botswana's past to its present. In addition, the Botswana Democratic Party of Seretse Khama was headed by large cattle owners like Khama himself (the largest in the country), reproducing into the modern era the underlying structure of Tswana hegemonic class domination (see Samatar 1999). Continuity took place not only among the leadership but also within local political institutions. At the village level, the traditional *kgotla* (village council) system of direct democracy was maintained. John Holm (1993) has shown that participation in *kgotla* politics correlates, not surprisingly, with participation in the democratic institutions of the postcolonial system. In addition, traditional institutions, including the chieftaincy, have also been used to administer justice, leading to greater trust in the judicial system and better enforcement of laws, including property rights, which are crucial for economic activity (Dia 1996).

As in Congo, the governments of Botswana have not hesitated to intervene in the economy over time (Picard 1987; Harvey 1992; Lewis 1993). Unlike Congo, they have done so in ways that have fostered development, diversification, and, eventually, a measure of industrialization. Economic policy has been proactive, exploiting Botswana's initial comparative advantage in meat production, generating a surplus from it, and using it to finance a break from commodity dependence. The Botswana leadership's control of the cattle industry, initially the main resource, favored the adoption of policies based on the country's economic strength. Developing the meat processing and exporting capacity did not threaten the dominant position of the Tswana and actually reinforced the foundations of their power.

In the 1960s, the government invested in slaughterhouses to attain international standards of meat quality and to develop meat exports (Morrison 1993). Developing the meat industry not only favored the dominant class but also reproduced the traditional pattern of economic relations in Tswana society by preserving the interests of small producers too. The government set up and used the Botswana Meat Commission (BMC) "to deliver the services necessary to maintain patterns of accumulation in the livestock industry, as well as the position of large traditional and commercial producers, without wrecking the public purse and alienating the majority of small producers," certainly an uncommon feat among African marketing boards (Samatar and Oldfield 1995:653). These authors also note that the political climate in Botswana, including the status the chiefs derived from their successful resistance to British attempts at incorporating Bechuanaland into South Africa, "facilitated the development of such an effective and legitimate national institution." To this day, the BMC "has remained sensitive to the needs of producers" (Samatar and Oldfield 1995:662) and has consistently followed world prices. In addition, it has returned all surplus to farmers. The authors conclude in a manner supportive of the legitimacy hypothesis: "The BMC has been able to strike a fine balance between reproducing current socio-economic inequalities without unduly alienating and forcibly dispossessing the poor. Although these structural conditions severely curtail significant improvements in the economic well-being of small producers, most seem to feel that they have a stake in the system" (Samatar and Oldfield 1995:666).

But although meat is the backbone of the Botswana economy, its relative importance soon decreased to the benefit of diamond mining. The stability of the leadership, brought about by the hegemony of political institutions, allowed successive governments to look beyond the short term and devise policies that encouraged accumulation of resources and structural transformation of the economy. Diamond mining and exports provided the second stage of this economic strategy. Botswana started diamond mining in 1971, and within a few years it became the greatest contributor to GDP and exports. Unlike Congo, which expropriated foreign mining investors in 1966 and then "Zaireanized" the businesses that remained in the hands of foreigners in 1974, the Botswana government established joint ventures with South Africa's De Beers, the world's primary distributor of diamonds.

Most interesting, however, is the set of macroeconomic policies that accompanied the development of mining. Revenues from diamond exports were managed with great conservatism and used by the government to accumulate foreign exchange reserves. This was made possible by the fact that, unlike in Congo, the government did not face demands for redistribution by competing elites whose loyalty it had to buy.[47] The elite in power was, by and large, the only game in town. The reserves helped weather subsequent recessions brought about by droughts or by downturns in world diamond prices. Furthermore, when recessions did hit, as happened with the drought of the mid-1980s or the slowdown in diamond demand a few years earlier, the adoption of austerity measures by the government did not result in widespread contestation and challenges to either the regime or the state. After revenues from diamonds fell by 40 percent in

1981, for example, the government adopted a drastic series of austerity measures in 1982, including credit ceilings, interest rate hikes, frozen wages, reduced spending, and a devaluation. No serious political upheaval ensued. It is doubtful many other African governments could have gotten away with these kinds of policies.

Having first used the mining industry and its capacity to respond to economic shocks to favor accumulation, the Batswana leadership eventually embarked upon further diversification by breaking free from the constraints of natural resource economies and sponsoring the development of manufacturing. Since the 1990s, Botswana hosts vehicle assembly plants for Hyundae and Volvo and several light manufacturing plants in its Selebi-Phikwe regional development project, and it announced plans for a textile factory for Gabarone in 1997.

The path from the traditional cattle industry to manufacturing motor vehicles suggests a capacity to diversify and to invest the surplus of existing economic activities into new ones—a capacity that other African countries cannot politically afford. Implied by such development choices is the relative level of autonomy of the leadership and bureaucracy from competing interests and loyalties, which the legitimacy of political institutions brings about (see Isaksen 1981). State legitimacy lifted the policy constraints on elites that most other African states face. Because the leadership did not need to establish its own hegemony over society and competing loyalties, it faced fewer incentives to introduce growth-inimical distortions and to divert state resources. This is not to say that there has been no corruption in Botswana. But there appears to be less of it than elsewhere in Africa (Botswana averages 6.59 on the ICRG freedom-from-corruption index as against 4.38 for all of sub-Saharan Africa and 0.1 for Zaire), and it is also less systematic than elsewhere. When there is corruption, it is more likely to represent abuses of power by some politicians or civil servants than to be the manifestation of a system of political survival based on redistribution of state resources.

*   *   *

How do differences in state legitimacy account for some of the differences in state capacity and growth between Africa and the rest of the world, and within Africa? The answer lies in the manner in which deficits of state legitimacy condition the economic policies that rulers choose and the quality of the governance they provide. The more likely a state is to have evolved endogenously to local relations of power, and to represent therefore either the instrument of an established hegemonic group or the joint solution to a collective action problem among competing groups, the freer its rulers are from the imperative to consolidate their power, and thus the more likely they are to adopt policies with a longer time horizon.

States lacking this initial allegiance find it difficult to implement developmental policies and to foster their power by "delivering the goods" of growth and welfare. They derive more benefits, in terms of their power, from taking the opposite route and using state resources to pursue their quest for hegemony, either by attempting to reshape their societies into a new state-defined mold or by establishing new networks of support based on patronage, nepotism, regional preferences, and other forms of neopatrimonial policies. Because these strategies of power imply a biased set of policies and a "highjacking" of state institutions, the capacity of the state, weak to begin with, is further eroded, sometimes until its actual collapse. Economic performance is first affected by the poor policy choices leaders make and by the deteriorating quality of governance they provide, and second, by the mechanisms of escape that societies use to respond to the state's failure to govern, such as an increase in informal economic activity, a return to subsistence farming, or the substitution of smuggling for trade.

The initial degree of state legitimacy at independence is therefore a determinant of the pressing nature of leaders' quest for increased power and of the relative returns, in terms of power, of developmental versus neopatrimonial policies. In countries where no hegemony is yet established, leaders will be more likely to adopt neopatrimonial policies because the latter will provide them with the instrumental loyalty of some groups in society. In countries where the state developed over time as the instrument of the ruling class, there is greater social allegiance to the state, and the power of rulers can be further enhanced by developmental policies.

The crucial point here is that the payoffs of different policies depend on state legitimacy. In the low-legitimacy setting of most postcolonial African states, neopatrimonial policies yielded the greatest relative short-term payoffs to elites in terms of consolidating their power. They bolstered domestic support by directing public resources to private actors through unofficial channels and networks, allowing official development policies to languish. As time passed, these neopatrimonial strategies increased existing levels of corruption, contributed to the erosion of quality in the bureaucracy, and diminished public trust in the rule of law, leading to a vicious cycle of diminishing state capacity. In the worst cases, state collapse became the ultimate consequence of low state legitimacy.

Using Michael Mann's distinction between "despotic power," or the power of elites to do things without "routine, institutionalized negotiation with civil society groups," and "infrastructural power," which is "the capacity of the state actually to penetrate civil society and to implement logistically political decisions throughout the realm" (1986:113), my argument is that in nonlegitimate states, the construction of despotic power takes place at the expense of the infrastructural power of the state. In cases of endogenous state development, the two will probably develop together. But in imported states, leaders inherit an institutional infrastructure without historically developed despotic power. By using nonproductive interventionist and neopatrimonial policies to establish their own power, they run their state's infrastructural power to the ground.

Catherine Boone (1994) makes a similar point but focuses on agricultural policies rather than on state capacity. She sees the crux of the power struggle of African elites as surplus extraction from agriculture in order to create the financial means of their fusion. This prevents accumulation, investments in technology, and increases in agricultural productivity, eventually ruining the chances to develop an endogenous capitalist class that could be the engine of capitalism. Boone rightly insists—in contrast to theories that make the African state an institution "suspended, as it were, in mid-air above society" (Hyden 1983a:69)—that the African state is rooted in society, grounded in rural institutions. The state penetrates society to extract financial resources.[48] The representatives of rural institutions penetrate the state as one end of patronage relations. What Boone and Bayart before her do not establish, however, is how the nature of this reciprocal penetration is a function of the imported nature of the state.[49] Hence, the state may no longer be suspended in midair above society, but the nondevelopmental nature of its endogeneization derives from its lack of original congruence with society. There is therefore no necessary contradiction between a view of the African state as imported and as grounded. But a distinction between state and power offers a clearer picture: the graft[50] of the imported state never truly "takes" because the successful power strategies of its elites kill it. The state remains exogenous as the power of its elites gets grounded in domestic institutions. Hence, the appropriation of the state is contradictory to its developmental capacity.[51] To borrow a conceptual distinction from Berman and Lonsdale (1992), in the context of imported institutions the process of state "formation," which gives "to a minority of autochthons the historical opportunity to use to their advantage the new institutions" (Bayart 1996:7), results in the weakening of state "construction" and therefore of the state itself and its capacity to design and implement policies for development.

What distinguishes this theory from the usual neopatrimonial argument is its more general character and its flexibility to variations in the African historical setting. It brings in an explicit consideration of the match between precolonial and postcolonial institutions as the determinant of the power conundrum of elites, thereby going beyond the uniform "transplanted institutions" hypothesis (Sandbrook 1986; Dia 1996). It thus reconciles two strands of literature in African studies: the one that stresses the hegemonic quests of elites as determinant of their political behavior (Lonsdale 1981; Bayart 1993; Boone 1994) and the one that insists on the imported nature of the African state as the root of policy deviances (Hyden 1983a; Whitaker 1991; Davidson 1992). Furthermore, this model operates within the rational-choice assumption that leaders care about their power and want to maximize their time in office. In other words, it links the likelihood of developmental policies to the elites' self-interested considerations of power rather than to considerations of national integration or conflict resolution. As a consequence of these features, it can account for both Africa's specificity in the world and the diversity of developmental records within Africa.

NOTES

1. Sindzingre (1998) provides a thoughtful discussion of the links between the idea that citizens develop of the state in Africa and the credibility of economic reforms.

2. By logical extension, state legitimacy is also different from and broader than government or regime legitimacy.

3. See A/C 6/SR 1036 (discussion of the Report on Succession of States and Governments in respect of Treaties by Sir Humphrey Waldock, Special Rapporteur, cited in Alexandrowicz 1969:465).

4. Even when the new elites had fought the colonial state, as in Guinea-Bissau, Mozambique, or Angola, or had failed to collaborate until the end with the colonial enterprise, as in Guinea, they nevertheless fought to appropriate these very states that had oppressed them, captured, as was African liberation, by the parameters of colonial domination (see Mamdani 1996 for a similar point about ethnicity).

5. Although colonialism used local systems to extend its rule (Boone 1994; Reno 1995; Mamdani 1996), it did not base its rule upon them or their legitimacy.

6. For summaries of the Italian and German unifications, see Craig (1972).

7. In many cases, these elites were literally new, creations of the colonial education systems, with no previous claim to rule. In some cases, the emerging leaders actually enjoyed some traditional sources of authority, as Félix Houphouët-Boigny in Côte d'Ivoire, for example, who had the status of tribal chief in his Baoule group. Yet neither the Baoule nor the planters he is often said to have represented had developed any historical hegemony over other Ivorian groups by the time of independence.

8. For a comprehensive history of Liberia, see Liebenow (1987).

9. "Seychelles." *Britannica Online* www.eb.com:180/cgi-bin/g?DocF=micro/539/70.html [accessed 04 June 1998].

10. For more details on the history of the Comoro Islands, see Newitt (1984).

11. More of relevance to this question is in Allen (1995).

12. On the traditional Tswana system and its implications for today's statehood, see Samatar (1997). Sillery (1952) describes the collaborative brand of British colonialism in Botswana, whereas Morrison (1987) shows the relative lack of intrusiveness of the colonial state in Botswana.

13. "Lesotho. History: Basutoland (1871–1966)." *Britannica Online* www.eb.com:180/cgi-bin/g?DocF=macro/5005/94/140.html> [accessed 05 June 1998].

14. For more on Swaziland, see Booth (1983).

15. I do not discuss South Africa because it was a clearly illegitimate state in the eyes of the majority of its population until the early 1990s. It has now become a more ambiguous case. The longer duration of its existence than other African states and the process of reconciliation between descendants of settlers and indigenous populations undertaken by the African National Congress government militate in favor of greater legitimacy. The continued tension between the state and certain groups with strong preexisting identity, such as the Zulu, calls for caution, however. Because of its peculiar historical trajectory and because the empirical chapters of this book cover the 1960–1992 period, at which time South Africa could not be considered a legitimate state structure, I exclude it from much of this discussion.

16. See Lemarchand (1970), Bourges and Wauthier (1979), and Pabanel (1991).

17. Of course, this comment benefits from hindsight. Botswana would not become independent until 1966.

18. They may no longer have been able to provide that foundation, because the colonial episode and the frequent collaboration of traditional elites with the colonial enterprise had challenged their own foundations (Mamdani 1996). Yet bypassing them altogether in favor of the colonial legacy furthered the alienating effects of independence.

19. "Political suffocation" and "political dismemberment" are expressions from Geertz (1973b:264).

20. Late Somali president Abdirashiid Ali Shermaarke, quoted in Said S. Samatar (1985:155).

21. Admittedly, Bakongo had lost most of its luster by the nineteenth century and had become little more than a culture area.

22. See Brownlie for a list of the minority of African boundary cases where "substantial (though not necessarily exclusive) reference was made to tribal distribution in delimitation of borders" (1979:6).

23. For country-by-country descriptions of the colonial treaty origins of contemporary African boundaries, see Brownlie (1979).

24. See previous section for details.

25. See Booth (1983) for a more detailed account of Swaziland's history.

26. This was despite the official colonial discourse that they were instruments for the development of the local populations.

27. The expressions "exit" and "voice" are from Hirschman (1970) and refer to the two possible attitudes he identifies in response to organizational decline. In the first case, one goes shopping elsewhere, abandoning the ship. In the second, there is an attempt to remedy problems by participation.

28. Unless otherwise indicated, the details of the following examples were drawn from Morrison et al. (1989).

29. This is true whether politicians care about power for its own sake or for the accomplishment of broader goals. Should they be altruistic and in politics only to further the common good, they still need to shore up their power if they are to accomplish these goals. Hence, the assumption that their prime motive is to maximize power is robust to different ideologies and personal characteristics of rulers. It can safely be assumed to be universal and does not necessarily involve the pursuit of self-interest.

30. Although the expression "hegemonic quest" was coined by Bayart (1993), with apparent inspiration from Gramsci, he does not make this quest a function of the power vacuum of the postcolonial state. He sees it instead as an ongoing historical process begun before colonization, between competing elites and in which the new state is but an additional element, a reframed arena. Bayart minimizes the contemporary relevance of the colonial experience, a position he further amplifies in a later book on the *Graft of the State* (1996). He also rejects the idea of a particularism of African politics. I borrow my conceptual framework from Bayart's hegemonic quest and from those who earlier voiced the same idea in different words, such as Lonsdale (1981), but unlike Bayart, I make it a function of the power-statehood dichotomy brought about by the colonial moment. I disagree with his dismissal of the analytical relevance of imported statehood for Africa. Although hegemonic quests are universal, only in nonlegitimate imported states do they take place after the creation of the state, within an already crystallized institutional framework and in the context of alternative "publics" (Ekeh 1975). The next section will show that the consequences of this African reversal of the usual historical sequence are far-reaching in terms of state capacity and economic development.

31. A party official, quoted in Schatzberg (1989:71).

32. In a world where the ideology of the nation-state is paramount, these leaders found much understanding within and outside of Africa for their efforts to integrate disparate societies (see Emerson 1963; Zolberg 1966; Geertz 1973b, to name a few).

33. There have been, however, occasional resurgences of such approaches to power throughout the postcolonial era, including Ratsiraka in Madagascar and Sassou-Nguesso in Congo in the 1970s, and Sankara in Burkina Faso in the 1980s.

34. For the traditional preponderance of patron-client relations in rural Africa, see Fafchamps (1992).

35. Bayart (1993) labels this strategy "conservative modernization," or the assimilation of the imported state structure by traditional elites. As mentioned earlier, this is a rare outcome in Africa, for it depends on the historical legitimacy of the inherited state structure, which is the exception rather than the norm. Furthermore, conservative modernization solves the legitimacy problem of the imported state only when a *national* customary aristocracy inherits the state and fully endogenizes it into the preexisting institutional structure. Should conservative modernization take place on a more limited scale (i.e., one traditional aristocracy among several takes over), then the postcolonial state would remain illegitimate. This can be argued to have been the case in the first phase of Cameroon's independence, where Ahidjo represented the traditional power aristocracy of the north but failed to bring the anglophone west, the Bamiléké mountain region, or the south and coastal areas into his project of statehood. This led to a rise of regional, linguistic, and ethnic fragmentation. A similar process may have taken place in Senegal, where the *marabouts* may have co-opted the modern state (see Boone 1992; 1996) but failed to integrate Casamance into their hegemonic project, leading to fledgling legitimacy and enduring secessionist tendencies.

36. I do not question the ideological good faith of the leaders who chose these sets of policies. I contend that they were compelled to take either a nation-building or a fusion of elites approach. Choosing one did not prevent them from voicing ideological preferences. In fact, the class identification of Marxist ideology provided the potential ferment for the creation of a new identity. "African socialism" was the official ideology of Nyerere's Tanzania. "State capitalism" was the official label of the economic system of Sankara's Burkina.

37. See De Soto (1989).

38. The categorization of leaderships as nation building or elite fusing is ideal-typical. In practice, they all contained some elements of each.

39. Seventeenth- and eighteenth-century France suggest, however, that neopatrimonialism can coexist with some very real state building. But neopatrimonialism built the power of the French kings, upon which they built the state. In contemporary Africa, where the state precedes the formation of power, the neopatrimonial achievement of the latter threatens the effective existence of the former.

40. See Whitaker (1991) on the relationship between the nature of the African state and the implementation of structural adjustment policies, and Sindzingre (1996) on the effects of these policies on the perceptions ("representations") African bureaucrats and society develop of the state and their relationship with it.

41. All these figures are in Purchasing Power Party (PPP) dollars. The estimates for 1966 and 1960 are from the Penn World Table (NBER 1994). The 1995 estimates are from the World Bank's *World Development Indicators 1998*.

42. See Young (1976) for the role of urbanization in the salience of ethnicity.

43. Tshombé, however, was united by marriage with the traditional Balubakat political hierarchy.

44. See Young (1965), Young and Turner (1985), and Schatzberg (1991).

45. Kamitatu Massamba (1976), "Problématique et rationalité dans le processus de nationalisation du cuivre en Afrique Centrale" (Ph.D. diss., Institut d'Etudes Politiques de Paris), quoted and translated by Crawford Young (1996:24).

46. Young (1996:31).

47. The same freedom from the demands of reciprocal assimilation or nation building, which allowed the government to use diamond revenue for the future, also contributed to an allocation of aid flows toward education, health care, and roads to rural areas, or in other words, the formation of human and physical capital.

48. The fact that the state, weak or strong, legitimate or not, has the capability to penetrate society to extract a surplus, weakens, in my opinion, the traditional approach of "state capabilities" (Migdal 1988), which considers extractive power one such capability. A governance-centered concept of state capacity, as I use here, considers instead the developmental capacity of states.

49. This is the reason why they cannot account for variations in patterns of elite fusion and in institutional performance across Africa. "The general argument comes at the expense of systematic attention to variation of setting, circumstance, and manner *within* the African context, and at the cost of analyzing the infinite variety of ways in which these social and political realities were actually constructed and contested on the ground" (Boone 1994:110–111).

50. As in skin graft, not yet as corruption.

51. This may already have been true in colonial times. Although colonial force was the ultimate instrument of domination, local administrators nevertheless also relied on strategies of mutual accommodation with local elites, mostly to reduce the fiscal demands of their domains upon the metropolitan budget. These arrangements belied colonial developmental claims and set the pattern for future leaders. For the example of Sierra Leone, see Reno (1995). For a more theoretical statement, with a Marxist bent, see Berman (1992).

PART 3

Confronting the Evidence

6

Accounting for Africa's Development Crisis

To test the theory of developmental legitimacy by using empirical analysis requires two steps: First, creating a quantitative measure of state legitimacy based on a historical review of the origins of states, country by country (along criteria derived from the argument in Chapter 5), then comparing the performance of legitimate and non-legitimate developing countries on the main indicators of policies and good governance. Having established that states behave in significantly different ways according to their level of historical legitimacy, it is possible to estimate the actual impact of legitimacy on economic growth, partly as mediated through its effects on state capacity—in other words, to assess how much faster legitimate states grow, keeping other relevant factors constant. Once legitimacy is accounted for, being an African country demonstrably has no particular negative effect on growth. Hence, if something truly makes African economies different from the rest of the world, this model seems to capture it.

MEASURING STATE LEGITIMACY

How to capture in a measurable way the idea of the social endogeneity of state structures, of the historical continuity of institutions, which characterizes the concept of state legitimacy and from which point of view Africa so much differs from the rest of the world? How to differentiate countries of the world according to the origins and embeddedness of their state? To answer this empirical puzzle, I created a simple dichotomous variable (a dummy variable that takes either the value 0 or 1), bestowing upon each state of the world a stamp of "legitimacy" or "illegitimacy," according to five criteria that address the historical continuity of state institutions (for noncolonized areas) or the level of embeddedness of postcolonial states into precolonial relations of authority. When these criteria together suggest a discontinuity in the evolution of state institutions, a "clash" between precolonial and postcolonial political institutions, then a country scores 0 on the legitimacy variable. When there is no conflict between imported and domestic institutions, then a country scores 1.[1] Tables 6.1 and 6.2 summarize the methodology and the specific country scores, while Figure 6.1 illustrates the logic of the variable. Ideally, a continuous variable would have been preferable in order to capture the different nuances in legitimacy among states. But difficulties in measurement and the increased danger of subjective biases prevented adopting this form of operationalization. In Chapter 7, however, I use a nonsubjective continuous measure of horizontal legitimacy in Africa, which reinforces the findings of the legitimacy dummy.

The first criterion differentiates countries that were colonized in modern times from those that were not. In this context, the term *colonized* should be interpreted loosely to cover also other forms of substantive foreign occupation and domination in which a foreign power determines the nature of the state (e.g., East Germany). If a country was not colonized in modern times, there is a presumption of endogeneity of the state, of continuity or endogenous change of political institutions, of state legitimacy. Many European countries are considered legitimate on this account, together with places like China, Ethiopia, Iran, Japan, Nepal, Saudi Arabia, Thailand, Turkey, and Yemen, all of which were never colonized. Some of these places certainly fell at times under the influence of foreign powers, but this did not involve effective colonization in the sense of reshaping political domestic institutions.

The second stage considers the case of countries that, having been colonized in modern times, recovered their previous sovereignty upon independence. In other words, they were returned to their preexisting institutional existence. In these restored states, the colonial episode is but an institutional parenthesis. These are not new states, although their formal independence may have been only recently recognized by the international system of nations. Indeed, some of them saw juridical acknowledgment of their existence postponed by foreign colonization, but all had established an empirical presence before the colonial episode and recovered it when it ended.

Table 6.1   State Legitimacy Decision Tree

Question	Answer	Next step	Countries scoring 1
1. Was the country colonized in modern times?	N = 1 Y = 0	If yes, go to question 2.	*Afghanistan,* Austria, Belgium, China, Denmark, Ethiopia, France, Germany (West), Hungary, Iceland, Iran, Italy, Japan, Nepal, Netherlands, Norway, Poland, Portugal, Russia, Saudi Arabia, Spain, Sweden, Switzerland, Thailand, Turkey, United Kingdom, Yemen, Yugoslavia
2. When reaching independence, did the country recover its previous sovereignty, identity, or effective existence?	Y = 1 N = 0	If no, go to question 3.	*Albania,* Bahrain, *Bhutan, Brunei,* Bulgaria, *Cambodia,* Egypt, *Estonia,* Fiji, Finland, Greece, Korea, *Kuwait, Latvia, Lithuania, Mongolia,* Morocco, Myanmar, Oman, *Qatar,* Romania, Taiwan, *Tonga,* Tunisia, *United Arab Emirates, Vietnam, Yemen (South)*
3. If the country was created by colonialism, was there a human settlement predating colonization?	N = 1 Y = 0	If yes, go to question 4.	*Antigua and Barbuda,* Cape Verde, Mauritius, *São Tomé and Principe,* Seychelles
4. Did the colonizers (and/or their imported slaves) reduce the preexisting societies to numerical insignificance (or assimilate them) and become the citizens of the new country?	Y = 1 N = 0	If no, go to question 5.	Argentina, Australia, Barbados, Belize, Brazil, Canada, Chile, Colombia, Costa Rica, *Cuba, Dominica,* Dominican Republic, El Salvador, *Grenada,* Guyana, Haiti, Honduras, Israel, Jamaica, Mexico, New Zealand, Nicaragua, Panama, Paraguay, *St. Kitts–Nevis, St. Lucia, St. Vincent and the Grenadines,* Suriname, Trinidad and Tobago, United States, Uruguay, Venezuela
5. Does the postcolonial state do severe violence to preexisting political institutions?	N = 1 Y = 0	End.	Bangladesh, Botswana, Burundi, Czechoslovakia, Ireland, *Kiribati,* Laos, Lesotho, *Maldives,* Malta, Pakistan, Rwanda, Singapore, Sri Lanka, Swaziland

Note: Countries without data on either one of the policy index, the governance index, or growth are listed in italics. They are not included in the sample on which the empirical results of this book are based.

Many Asian countries fall into this category, including Bhutan, Brunei, Cambodia, Fiji, Korea, Mongolia, Myanmar, Taiwan, and Vietnam. Quite a few Eastern European, Central Asian, and Middle Eastern countries can also be found here. Oman, for example, is a traditional imam-chief system with centuries of history (Holsti 1996:102).

Figure 6.1   State Legitimacy Decision Tree

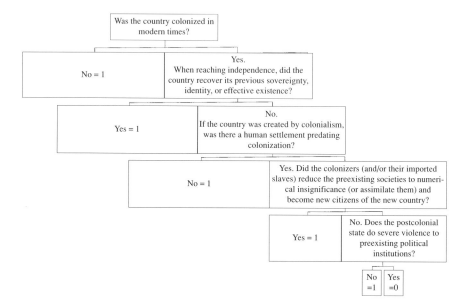

Countries deemed legitimate according to these first two criteria approximate the idea of nation-state suggested by Rupert Emerson:

> Where the state has survived for many generations reasonably intact within an approximation of the same frontiers, as is the case with France, England . . . , Ireland, Spain, Portugal, Egypt, China, Japan, and certain others, the argument is so obvious as to need no elaboration. In such cases the territory claimed as the national homeland is substantially identical with that enclosed within the boundaries of the state. Poland, Hungary . . . , and Bulgaria may serve as good examples of states which vanished from the historical scene for longer or shorter periods of time but left behind them firmly established national precipitates. (1960:115)

The third stage asks whether, if a country was created by colonialism, its territory comprised any human settlement beforehand. This step addresses the case of desert islands that were first populated through colonialism and the slave trade. The underlying assumption is that there can be no conflict with preexisting institutions in countries that were not settled by human civilizations before colonialism. The four African island-states discussed in Chapter 5—Cape Verde, Mauritius, São Tomé and Principe, and the Seychelles—fall here, together with Antigua and Barbuda.

More often, however, a country that was created by colonialism will have had preexisting human societies on its territory. In stage four, I ask whether, in the establishment of the modern state, these societies were marginalized either through a policy of extermination or through diseases or other source of demographic change and, upon this marginalization, the postcolonial state was then engendered by the former colonizers or the slaves brought there by colonialism. In such cases, which include most of Latin America, Israel, the United States, Canada, Australia, and New Zealand, the current country is deemed historically legitimate because it is endogenous to its current population. The fact that it was superimposed over preexisting systems is attenuated by the destruction or neutralization of these systems. Both the state and the society are new, and the former derives from the latter.

Finally, if a country was created by colonialism but its preexisting political institutions have endured, it is deemed legitimate only if it does not do severe violence to these previous institutions, that is, if it embeds its own authority into their historical legitimacy. African colonies that closely matched preexisting kingdoms or states, such as Botswana, Lesotho, and Swaziland, fall into this category. I have also included Burundi and Rwanda, although they are less clear-cut cases. Although Rwanda and Burundi were preexisting states, Belgian colonialism so thoroughly manipulated their political mechanisms that the foundations of political authority no longer were the object of a consensus by the time independence came in 1962 (see Pabanel 1991; Lemarchand 1970). I included them, however, first because Crawford Young (1988) and Jean-François Bayart (1996), two of the most prominent Africanists in the world, assess them as legitimate along these lines. Second, when in doubt and as the last resort, I make a reverse selection on the dependent variable, looking at the record of capacity and growth and giving the country the score that will least support the hypothesis. Such an approach may decrease the magnitude and significance of my empirical results but it improves their robustness. Altogether then, the total of legitimate states in Africa amounts to ten:

1. Botswana
2. Burundi
3. Cape Verde
4. Ethiopia
5. Lesotho
6. Mauritius

7. Rwanda
8. *São Tomé and Principe*
9. Seychelles
10. Swaziland

Table 6.2 shows the regional breakdown of countries scoring 0. Although Africa has the largest concentration of such countries, all regions of the world include some of them. Most OECD countries scored 1, however. (In order to make sure that my empirical results did not capture a rich country–poor country dichotomy, I have either withdrawn the OECD countries from the sample or added a variable controlling for each country's income level in all the following estimations.) In Latin America, countries with more than one third of "Indian" indigenous population scored 0 (according to the fourth criterion). These were Bolivia (70 percent Indian), Guatemala (47 percent), Peru (40 percent), and Ecuador (38 percent) (Kurian 1997:46).[2] Asia also has a rather large proportion of illegitimate states, among which are some of its most important countries: India, Indonesia, Malaysia, and the Philippines. India may well have had a certain cultural homogeneity pre-dating colonization, but

> this amorphous spiritual identity had found virtually no expression in political unity. The characteristic political condition was a shifting array of states and principalities, of conquests and alliances, which enabled the British to utilize Indians in the conquest of the country and lent color to the trite comment that India was only a geographical expression. (Emerson 1960:122-123)

Indonesia and the Philippines are more akin to African states, and Malaysia is a collection of Malays, Chinese, and Indians brought together by the idiosyncrasies of colonialism but each having a deep communal attachment that preceded it.

One can probably quibble over whether a country should score a 1 at one stage or another of the five-step decision process, which is necessarily sensitive to judgment calls, but I hope the overall idea of state endogeneity or exogeneity will have been captured at one of the five stages. There were certainly some difficult cases to decide. Pakistan and Bangladesh, for example, did not lend themselves to straightforward decisions. Pakistan was created in 1948 to allow Muslims to have self-government away from the Hindus of India. Its territory is based on the regions where Muslims predominated. On the one hand, as Emerson argued almost forty years ago, "There is no good reason to assume any traditional identification of a Pakistani

Table 6.2   "Nonlegitimate" States, by Region

Africa	Angola, Benin, Burkina, Cameroon, Central African Republic, Chad, Comoro Islands, Congo, Côte d'Ivoire, Djibouti, *Equatorial Guinea,* Gabon, Gambia, Ghana, Guinea, Guinea-Bissau, Kenya, Liberia, Madagascar, Malawi, Mali, Mauritania, Mozambique, *Namibia,* Niger, Nigeria, Senegal, Sierra Leone, Somalia, South Africa, Sudan, Tanzania, Togo, Uganda, Zaire, Zambia, Zimbabwe
Asia	India, Indonesia, Malaysia, Papua New Guinea, Philippines, *Solomon Islands, Vanuatu*
Europe	Cyprus, East Germany
Latin America and the Caribbean	Bolivia, Ecuador, Guatemala, Peru
Middle East and North Africa	Algeria, Iraq, Jordan, *Lebanon,* Libya, Syria

Note: Countries without data on either one of the policy index, the governance index, or growth are listed in italics. They are not included in the sample on which the empirical results of this book are based.

nation still in the making with even an approximation of the divided lands which came to it" (Emerson 1960:107). On the other hand, the fact that Pakistan willfully extracted itself from a British-created colonial structure suggests a certain level of endogeneity of the state, even if religious differentiation was the only principle underlying it. At any rate, Pakistani Islam had strong nationalist undertones.[3] In addition, although the Pakistani did not have a separate political identity before British colonization, Muslim rulers had controlled the area for centuries, despite majority Hindu populations. Fearful of seeing independence bring about Hindu rule, the Muslim nationalist movement opted for partition from India. In the end, the origins of Pakistan suggested a relatively endogenous process of state formation and the creation of a structure that does not do violence to preexisting forms of political authority.

Yet this leaves open the question of Bangladesh. Because of similar religious feelings, Bangladesh at first joined Pakistan in partitioning from India and became Eastern Pakistan. In 1971, however, it broke away from Pakistan because their religious similarities were insufficient to compensate for stronger cultural differences. Because Bangladesh's "national character dates to the ancient past" and "consists in three distinctive attributes—a land, a language, and a religion,"[4] I opted to consider it a historically legitimate state. I was reinforced in this decision by my principle of adverse selection on the dependent variable (see above), since Bangladesh has a relatively poor record of state capacity and economic development.

I relied on the same logic used for Pakistan and Bangladesh to give Singapore the stamp of legitimacy. Singapore was not an integrated political system before settlement by the British in 1819. Sultans from Malaya exerted limited leadership over it, but it was only weakly institutionalized. During British colonization, the demographic picture was radically altered by heavy Chinese immigration. Singapore first joined the Federation of Malaya upon independence but then seceded from it in 1965 with the agreement of the Malaysian government, as both sides acknowledged the artificiality of the union.

In Africa, some would argue that Somalia, which is rather culturally homogeneous, had a unified precolonial existence. Abdi Ismail Samatar makes a strong argument, however, that

> Somali chieftainship was not an indigenous institution. . . . Chiefs truly acted as creatures of the colonial state. . . . The constellation of the colonial state, colonial chiefs and the tribalization of the moral and political order, and the slow but steady commoditisation of the pastoral and peasant economy transformed the nature of Somali social order. (1997:694)

In addition, these chiefs presided over competing subpolities rather than being effectively integrated into a larger national system. Indeed, the impending disintegration of the country along warring clan lines precipitated the 1969 military takeover. Hence, Somalia's relative cultural homogeneity has historically carried less weight than its political and institutional diversity.

Do missing countries constitute a bias in the sample? In other words, do the countries for which data are missing have something in common that could alter my findings? Missing data certainly deprive us of useful information, but in this case there does not appear to be a systematic bias associated with this problem. First of all, few important countries are missing in any given region, with the exception of Central Asia, where there was no data for any country, simply because none of them was independent during most of the period reviewed here.[5] Once these new states have accumulated long enough time series to rule out the economic variations due to the business cycle, it will be interesting to see whether differences in their performance also relate to their historical status before Russian and Soviet imperialism.

Second, a closer look at the countries for which data are missing does not reveal any systematic trend. Using alternative estimates of growth that were available for some of these other countries resulted in all cases in "better" statistical results, in the sense that the effects of legitimacy on development were even more pronounced and the residual effect of being an African country less so.[6] Filling the missing data with these alternative estimates of growth, I also compared the performance of legitimate and nonlegitimate states by region and found results largely similar to those I present in this chapter.[7]

Finally, I divided the countries with missing data into a legitimate and a nonlegitimate subgroup and, using miscellaneous alternative measures of growth, tested whether these two groups performed differently. Of the twenty-nine legitimate states, I found data for twenty. Of these, twelve had positive growth and eight negative growth, with the average performance at 1 percent average annual GDP growth. Among the twelve nonlegitimate countries, eight had no data from any source; of the remaining four, three had negative growth, and the four of them averaged –1 percent annual growth. As shown below, these results are consistent overall with my findings that, other things being equal, legitimate states grow faster than their nonlegitimate counterparts.

Note again that the state legitimacy variable as I derived it ignores the nature of the political regime. It does not measure regime legitimacy but the legitimacy of the structures of statehood, for which it substitutes with the idea of historical endogeneity of the state, or historical continuity of its institutions. Where do state structures come from? Did the state historically arise parallel to relations of power, to the construction of political hegemony in society? If there was colonialism, was it but a parenthesis in the long-term history of the country, or does it define its current existence and status? These are the questions the legitimacy variable tries to address and measure. The evolution of illegitimate states ex post facto independence is not considered here. What the variable captures instead is the static condition of the state at independence, the institutional premise of politics, and the nature of statehood as colonial domination ends or in 1960, whichever comes later.

DEFICITS OF LEGITIMACY, FAILURES OF CAPACITY

How does the performance of legitimate states differ from that of nonlegitimate ones on matters of policy choice and governance quality? Are there significant differences in their levels of developmental capacity? Table 6.3 suggests answers to these questions. The first two columns compare the average performance on indicators of policies and good governance, of countries scoring 0 and countries scoring 1 on the legitimacy variable. The third column shows the probability that this difference is not statistically meaningful and that it is only the result of sampling error, a term that refers to the fact that even two samples randomly selected from a single population will be slightly different from one another. A value of 0.0100, for example, would indicate that there is only a 1 percent chance that the two groups come from the same population. Table 6.3 includes only developing countries in order to preclude the possibility that these

Table 6.3   Comparing Policies, Governance, and Growth Among Legitimate and Nonlegitimate States in the Developing World

Variable	Nonlegitimate States (n)	Legitimate States (n)	P Value
Policies			
Average years of schooling **	2.99 (37)	4.61 (46)	0.0001
Telephones per thousand workers (infrastructure)**	16.96 (45)	54.50 (40)	0.0001
Current government spending (% GDP)**	22.66 (50)	18.06 (59)	0.0012
Foreign exchange distortions† (log scale)	0.31 (46)	0.34 (53)	0.2854
Openness to international trade (% GDP)*	59.04 (50)	71.86 (59)	0.0500
Depth of financial sector (log scale)*	1.28 (42)	1.43 (43)	0.0354
Foreign indebtedness (rescheduling instances)**	3.64 (45)	1.86 (64)	0.0016
Policy index**	−1.09 (43)	0.14 (48)	0.0000
Governance			
Enforceability of contracts (1-10)**	4.84 (51)	6.15 (64)	0.0000
Risk of expropriation (1-10)**	5.73 (51)	7.02 (64)	0.0000
Extent of corruption (1-10)	4.51 (51)	5.01 (64)	0.0689
Quality of institutions (1-10)**	4.01 (51)	5.22 (64)	0.0002
Quality of bureaucracy (1-10)*	4.15 (51)	4.81 (64)	0.0256
Civil liberties (1-7, smaller = freer)**	5.20 (46)	4.15 (47)	0.0001
Linguistic alienation (% pop.)**	71.14 (55)	22.38 (65)	0.0000
Governance index**	−1.55 (43)	−0.44 (39)	0.0001
Developmental capacity index**	−0.64 (40)	−0.09 (37)	0.0001
Years of civil wars*	8.25 (64)	4.58 (92)	0.0187
Per capita GDP growth**	0.49% (50)	2.44% (59)	0.0000

Notes: The first two columns compare the average performance of countries in both samples on each indicator. In the third column, P values refer to the probability that the observed difference is due to chance, based on one-tailed t tests with equal or unequal variances according to F tests performed on the sample variances. Numbers in parentheses are the number of observations in the sample.

The variables in this table are respectively SCHOOL, TELPW, G, BLCK, OPEN, LLY, DRELIEF, POLICY, COMMIT, EXPROP, CORRUPT, INSTQUAL, BUROQUAL, CIVL, HOMELANG, GOVNANCE, CAPACITY, WARCIV, and RGDPCH. See Appendix 1 for data source, definition, and methodology.

Significance levels: ** = 1%; * = 5%.
† Difference not in the hypothesized direction.

findings would simply reflect a difference between rich and poor countries.[8]

In all but one instance, legitimate states perform better than their nonlegitimate counterparts, and for all but one case this difference is statistically significant. Among the policy indicators, the evidence in favor of the hypotheses in Chapter 5 is robust. Nonlegitimate states tend to invest less in education because it has few direct returns to their weak leadership. If they invest in education, it is more likely to be on salaries of teachers (who may form a constituency of the modern state) than on educational quality, and this translates in low achievement figures. This bias, together with the requirements for pork and large bureaucracies that neopatrimonialism implies, leads to a greater government propensity for current spending at the expense of long-term investments such as infrastructure development. Infrastructure has no immediate return to the rulers and may actually hurt them in the long run. One is reminded of Zaire's late President Mobutu's quip to his Rwandan counterpart, embattled with a civil war: "I told you not to build any road. . . . Building roads never did any good. I've been in power in Zaire for thirty years and I never built one road. Now they are driving down them to get you."[9] Governments of low-legitimacy states are also more likely to set up barriers to trade, as these provide the rents governments need to finance their networks of patron-client relationships and to introduce distortions into their financial sectors, directing credit along criteria that are more likely to favor political motives than considerations of present value. Finally and not surprisingly, these governments tend to get more deeply indebted, partly as a financing mechanism for their consumption, partly as a compensation for the shortages of foreign exchange that may accompany their trade policies. Furthermore, their indebtedness is less bearable to their economies because they tend to use their available credit to finance nonproductive projects whose purpose is more likely to be an assertion of their sovereignty (e.g., the relocation of a capital away from the colonial site, as in Côte d'Ivoire's Yamoussoukro or Nigeria's Abuja, or the construction of multiple presidential palaces, as in Saddam Hussein's Iraq) or a means to extend their hegemony (Mobutu's Inga dam aimed at controlling the supply of power to secessionist Shaba), than improvements in their country's productive capacity.

As a result of their leaders' instability and their use of the state for building social foundations to their power, nonlegitimate states also score consistently and significantly lower than their legitimate counterparts on all indicators of good governance. Their capacity to enter contractual arrangements is thwarted by their leaders' needs to accommodate the fluctuating demands of their unstable constituencies. They have little respect for private property as it represents untapped resources for their networks. Rotation in the lower levels of power is also rapid because leaders fear the rise of alternative power. Thus, lower-level politicians maximize their economic accumulation during their short time in office, further weakening whatever limited sense of private property may have prevailed.[10] Corruption, patronage, nepotism, and other forms of neopatrimonial behavior become endemic as they provide the very mechanism by which power survives in nonlegitimate states. As time passes, these neopatrimonial strategies contribute to the erosion of the quality of the bureaucracy and diminish the quality of public institutions and public trust in the rule of law.

Citizens of legitimate states also enjoy greater civil liberties. In addition to neopatrimonial strategies of power, leaders of nonlegitimate states are also more likely to resort to repression in the process of nation building or as part of the personalization of their rule. In fact, corruption and repression are the manifestations of the two distinct options of leaders of nonlegitimate states: the fusion of elites (Lonsdale 1981; Boone 1994)[11] or the nation-building approach. In the first case, the resources of the state are used to placate alternative sources of legitimacy and power (for example, Ahidjo's Cameroon). In the second, leaders attempt to impose national unity by force (Sekou Touré's Guinea). States that choose nation-building strategies find that repression is crucial to mask their lack of national cohesion, or at least to control their centrifugal tendencies. Hence, the lower the legitimacy, the greater the propensity to repress. Should a low-legitimacy state choose the neopatrimonial route, however, as in more democratic countries, corruption will then be more likely to occur (e.g., India or Senegal). As a result, an illegitimate state environment may lead to either repressive systems or corrupt systems. Indeed, whereas corruption is strongly correlated with repression ($r=0.74$) among legitimate countries worldwide, there is no significant correlation ($r=0.10$) between the two variables among nonlegitimate ones. Although this does not necessarily support the above hypothesis, it suggests at least that the logic of corruption and repression is different in nonlegitimate countries, where both phenomena are less likely to go hand in hand and more likely to represent alternative strategies of power.

Finally, nonlegitimate states owe their existence to the colonial episode, and their elites are usually the fruit of colonial education policies. As a result, they are more likely to adopt the language of the colonizer as their official tongue than that of their own people. The proportion of people who do not speak the official language of the state at home is more than three times greater in nonlegitimate countries than in legitimate ones, leading to greater citizen alienation and lesser government accountability.

Table 6.3 also offers striking evidence that nonlegitimate states suffer from civil wars at about twice the rate of their legitimate counterparts. This supports Kalevi Holsti's (1996) contention that post–World War II wars have been struggles over the state rather than traditional struggles among states over power or resources, as realist theory would have it. It also reinforces the argument of Chapter 5 that the lack of agreement about the rules of the political game in nonlegitimate states results in a greater likelihood for challenges to policies to metamorphose into challenges to governments and states themselves.

In view of the differences between legitimate and nonlegitimate states on all these indicators of state capacity and political stability, it comes as no surprise in the end that the former grow more than four times faster than the latter (2.44 percent v. 0.49 percent average annual growth).

LEGITIMACY AND GROWTH

A deficit of state legitimacy reduces a country's potential for economic growth because it distorts its government's choice of policies and harms the quality of its governance. Leaders of states with low legitimacy resort to neopatrimonial policies to substitute instrumental legitimacy for the lack of moral foundations of their power. They need the resources of rents, taxation, and other forms of legal and illegal extraction to finance their networks of patron-client relations. These resources are diverted from more productive outlets. As a result, as shown in the previous section, they are more likely to distort markets, engage in excessive public spending in proportion to the size of their economy, neglect infrastructural and human capital expenditure that have longer-run payoffs, and raise tariffs or otherwise discourage the openness of their economy. In addition, they are likely to use the institutions of the state for their private power-building motives, having inherited the state without its usual historical power foundations. The quality of public institutions deteriorates accordingly, while the expectations of public behavior and the performance of the bureaucracy suffer. Corruption, nepotism, and sinecures become widespread, and the overall quality of governance goes down.

When policies are predatory and governance is weak, citizens and economic agents shy away from investing, stay clear of government-sponsored markets and economic institutions such as the banking system, and tend to withdraw into the informal economy. This too affects a country's economic performance. Shrinking private investments reduce the stock of capital available for future growth. Escape into the informal sector increases the transaction costs faced by economic operators, magnifies the uncertainty of economic activity, and compounds the vulnerability of citizens to the arbitrariness of state agents.

It is via its impact on state capacity (both policies and governance) and its consequent propensity to favor the disengagement of citizens from the realm of the "public" that state illegitimacy breeds economic stagnation. Investigation of this combined influence on growth will follow a simple and logical approach. First, I estimate the actual effects of state legitimacy on state capacity and its components. How much of the cross-country variations in the policy, governance, and capacity indices is accounted for by state legitimacy, and what is the actual contribution of legitimacy to capacity? Answers to these questions are revealed by modeling the relationship between capacity and legitimacy. Using regression analysis, I predict the actual effects of legitimacy on capacity. Because there are many other factors that probably also contribute to a country's level of state capacity, my predictions capture only part of the variance in state capacity across countries of the world. In fact, the difference between a country's predicted and actual levels of state capacity can be conceived of as the dimension of its capacity that is not a function of state legitimacy. This is called the residual of the regression. Later, I jointly model the effects of state legitimacy and of the residual of state capacity on growth (together with several other variables that are also known to influence growth). In this manner, the total impact of legitimacy on growth can be isolated, both as it operates through capacity and outside of it.[12]

Table 6.4 shows the results of the regressions of state legitimacy on policy choices, the quality of governance, and overall state capacity. The predictive powers of legitimacy are considerable. In each case, state legitimacy explains 30 percent or more of the variance of the respective indices (as measured by the "adjusted R^2"). For a

Table 6.4   The Effects of State Legitimacy on Policies, Governance, and Capacity

Dependent variable	Legitimacy effect	t statistic	Adjusted R^2	N
Policy index	1.7512**	(7.479)	0.30	114
Governance index	2.5754**	(7.614)	0.30	106
Developmental capacity index	1.0656**	(7.042)	0.33	100

Notes: Intercepts not reported. OLS estimations with White (1980) heteroskedasticity-consistent t statistics in parentheses. The policy and governance indices range from about –4 to 4. The state capacity index ranges from about –2 to 2.

Significance levels: ** = 1%.

The three dependent variables are respectively POLICY, GOVNANCE, and CAPACITY. The explanatory variable is LEGIT. See Appendix 1 for data definitions, sources, and methodology.

single explanatory variable in a cross-sectional setting, this is rather good. Legitimate states score 1.75 points higher than nonlegitimate ones on the policy index, which represents 22 percent of the range of the index; 2.58 points higher on the governance index, a 32 percent advantage; and 1.07 points on the overall capacity index (27 percent).

Specific regressions on the indicators that comprise these different indices suggest that the strongest policy effects are mediated through education and infrastructure, the two measures of investment in capital (human and physical), and through current government spending. The legitimacy effects on trade and price distortions were weaker. One possible explanation is that trade and foreign exchange policies require an active management capacity that, as the findings on governance suggest, nonlegitimate states are short of. In contrast, neglecting education and infrastructure and letting government consumption run amok require only abstaining from active management, which is consistent with the use of states for neopatrimonial purposes and their consequent "collapsed" nature (Zartman 1995). Among the components of the governance index, legitimacy has its strongest impact on governments' capacity to enforce and commit to contractual arrangements, the risk of expropriation, and the overall quality of institutions and level of citizens' trust in them.

Chapter 2 discussed the importance of developmental capacity for economic growth; the above section demonstrated the effects of state legitimacy on developmental capacity. Bringing these together now allows assessment of the actual impact of state legitimacy on

economic growth. Like Table 2.4, Table 6.5 presents a basic model of
economic growth to which I progressively add variables measuring
policies, governance, and state capacity. The difference is that I now
do so first without, then with state legitimacy in the estimations. The
purpose of this approach is to identify the additional explanatory
power of the model that results from including state legitimacy
among the explanatory variables.

The first column in Table 6.5 reproduces the basic model of
Table 2.4. The first two variables tell us that a country's long-run rate
of growth (measured here over the 1960–1992 period) is inversely
related to its initial level of income (rich countries grow more slowly
than poor ones, if other things are equal, because they have fewer
opportunities for additional productive investments). The third and
fourth variables stand in for the growth effects of simply being an
African or a "high-performing" East Asian country (World Bank
1993). Again, these regional dummies essentially are a measure of
our ignorance. They do not specify what it is about being an African
country or an East Asian dragon that is inimical or favorable to
growth. They just identify such effects, indicating thereby that
important variables remain that our model has not yet captured,
which contribute to differentiating the growth performance of these
two regions. Setting aside differences in the other variables included
in this model, we can expect an African country to trail other countries' rate of growth (not including the historically fast-growing East
Asian economies) by about 1.3 percent each year. The implication is
that even though African economies have grown somewhat on average over the last thirty years, the gap between them and the
economies of the rest of the world has nevertheless increased as they
have lagged behind the growth performance of other regions.

The fifth variable indicates that a country with its territory
entirely exposed to a tropical climate will grow much slower, year in,
year out, than a nontropical country, partly because of reduced agricultural productivity and increased morbidity (Bloom and Sachs
1998). The sixth variable suggests that landlocked countries also
grow more slowly than those with access to the seas, but this relationship is statistically weak and does not permit strong inference.[13]
Together, these six variables explain a little less than half the variation in long-run growth among the 126 countries of the sample.

In the second column, I observe the same model with the addition of the policy index, modified to take into account only the portion of the index not affected by state legitimacy. Despite this reduction in scope, it remains a strong determinant of growth, with a

Table 6.5 Measuring the Overall Impact of State Legitimacy on Economic Growth

Dependent Variable: Average Annual Per Capita GDP Growth, 1960–1992

Variable	(1)	(2)	(3)	(4)	(5)	(6)	(7)
Initial income level	-0.0364	-0.0485*	-0.0366	-0.0150	0.0174	-0.0212	0.0051
	(1.439)	(2.238)	(1.576)	(0.686)	(0.850)	(0.943)	(0.281)
Initial income level squared	0.0021	0.0027	0.0014	0.0005	-0.0020	0.0008	-0.0015
	(1.303)	(1.914)	(1.010)	(0.374)	(1.510)	(0.601)	(1.333)
Africa	-0.0128*	-0.0143**	-0.0032	-0.0160**	-0.0099	-0.0154**	-0.0057
	(2.531)	(3.294)	(0.815)	(2.956)	(1.973)	(2.856)	(1.273)
East Asian "dragons"	0.0355**	0.0286**	0.0217**	0.0316**	0.0236**	0.0296**	0.0166**
	(6.861)	(6.080)	(6.587)	(5.566)	(5.586)	(5.772)	(4.826)
Tropical climate	-0.0187**	-0.0177**	-0.0119**	-0.0175**	-0.0100**	-0.0175**	-0.0099**
	(5.939)	(5.912)	(4.301)	(5.889)	(3.283)	(6.094)	(3.679)
Landlocked country	-0.0027	-0.0016	-0.0054*	0.0015	-0.0010	0.0022	-0.0037
	(0.838)	(0.459)	(2.175)	(0.481)	(0.432)	(0.596)	(1.667)
Policies[a]	—	0.0048**	0.0088**	—	—	—	—
		(4.089)	(6.971)				
Governance[a]	—	—	—	0.0018	0.0053**	—	—
				(1.599)	(5.056)		
Governance squared[a]	—	—	—	-0.0004	-0.0005	—	—
				(1.215)	(1.853)		
Developmental capacity[a]	—	—	—	—	—	0.0079**	0.0205**
						(3.257)	(7.860)
Developmental capacity squared[a]	—	—	—	—	—	-0.0006	-0.0013
						(0.381)	(0.850)
State legitimacy	—	—	0.0207**	—	0.0202**	—	0.0263**
			(5.583)		(5.074)		(6.110)
Adjusted R²	0.47	0.63	0.74	0.57	0.67	0.63	0.78
N	126	109	109	105	105	99	99

Notes: Intercepts not reported. OLS estimation. Figures in parentheses are White (1980) heteroskedasticity-consistent *t* statistics.
Independent variables are respectively INC60 INC60SQ, AFRICA, HPAE, TROPICS, LANDLOCK, POLICY, GOVNANCE, GOVSQ, CAPACITY, CAPSQ, and LEGIT. See Appendix 1 for data definitions, sources and methodology. Significance levels: ** = 1%; * = 5%.
a. Orthogonal to state legitimacy, meaning the portion of policies, governance, and capacity that is *not* a function of state legitimacy.

one-point increase in the index leading to almost a half percent growth rate. Adding this measure of the quality of government policies considerably improves the "goodness of fit" of the model, raising the adjusted R^2 to 0.63. Note, however, that controlling in this manner for the residual policy index does not reduce the negative effect on growth of being an African country. This contrasts with the findings of Chapter 2, where adding the full policy index to the same model resulted in the statistical vanishing of the negative Africa impact. The resilience of the "African effect" in this case indicates that the remaining variations in policies across countries, after accounting for differences due to state legitimacy, are no longer associated with any particular African characteristic. In other words, the portion of the worldwide variance in policy choices that was specific to African countries was mostly the same portion that is also specific to the absence of state legitimacy. Note also that the adjusted R^2 rose to 0.73 after the introduction of the policy index in Table 2.4, whereas its increase is limited to 0.63 in this case.

Column 3 confirms these important findings. Adding the state legitimacy variable to the previous model obliterates the statistical impact of the Africa dummy and raises the model's overall explanatory power to 74 percent of the worldwide variation in growth. Furthermore, the results show that legitimate states grow more than 2 percent faster than nonlegitimate ones each year, which is a very substantial effect, bearing in mind that the average rate of growth of all countries of the world during the 1960–1992 period was about 1.8 percent and that the average African rate of growth was barely better than 0.5 percent.

The fourth and fifth columns follow the same methodology, substituting the quality of governance for policy choice. The results are essentially the same. Again, state legitimacy contributes more than 2 percent to annual growth and the African impact is no longer statistically significant.[14] The last two columns provide the most parsimonious model, capturing both residual policies and governance with the index of developmental capacity. In this model, the one with the best explanatory power (albeit a smaller sample size), the growth impact of state legitimacy rises to about 2.6 percent per capita GDP growth per year, and the magnitude and significance of the Africa dummy once again become inconsequential.

The results of Table 6.5 provide, therefore, consistent evidence in support of the state legitimacy hypothesis. The overall impact of state legitimacy on growth, some of which is indirectly mediated through state capacity, amounts to at least 2 percent per year, even after controlling for convergence, climate, landlocked status, regional location, and dimensions of state capacity.[15] This is equal to about 40 percent of the difference between the average rate of growth of African countries and the average rate of growth of the high-performing East Asian economies. Equally important, factoring in state legitimacy eliminates the negative impact on growth of being an African country. Until now, many empirical studies of growth had identified such an African effect (Barro 1991; Mauro 1995; Easterly and Levine 1997; Temple and Johnson 1998). A few studies (including Sachs and Warner 1997b) had managed to eliminate its statistical significance by adding measures of policy choices, institutional quality, and climate to their model. Yet, because they did not explain why policies and institutions were worse in Africa than elsewhere, they had in fact failed to truly elucidate the mystery of the Africa dummy. Instead, showing how state capacity depends in large part on state legitimacy contributes, I hope, to an understanding of where the true root of African underdevelopment lies.[16] The World Bank (1989:60) may have been right when it stated that "underlying the litany of Africa's development problems," there is a crisis of governance. But going a step further, it seems that underlying this crisis of governance (and more broadly, of developmental capacity), there is a crisis of legitimacy.

REVISITING THE SOCIAL CAPITAL AND ETHNIC THEORIES OF AFRICAN STAGNATION

How do these findings compare with empirical evidence in favor of the competing theories of social capital and ethnic heterogeneity? Is the legitimacy hypothesis robust to controls for these other variables? Or could the effects of the legitimacy dummy substitute for possibly greater levels of social capital among legitimate states? And is it not also possible that legitimate states are more ethnically homogeneous, reinforcing rather than challenging the ethnic heterogeneity hypothesis? The best way to answer these questions is to perform some joint statistical tests on these variables and to compare their effects. For example, if the effects of legitimacy on capacity disappear upon introducing a measure of social capital in the estimations, then we can infer that state legitimacy has no individual explanatory power aside from capturing social capital effects. If the impact of social capital vanishes, on the other hand, we conclude that legitimacy is a more robust predictor of developmental capacity. The same reasoning can be applied to comparisons with ethnic heterogeneity.

Unfortunately, very limited cross-sectional data on social capital are available. The World Values Survey (Inglehart 1997) measures trust and organizational membership in up to forty-three countries, most of which are developed ones. Only five of these score 0 on the state legitimacy variable, however, making it hard to provide a meaningful statistical contrast between the two theories within the context of the World Values Survey data. Nevertheless, making the best use of what is available, Table 6.6 compares the effects of social capital and state legitimacy on capacity for the limited number of countries for which data exist.

The results are quite interesting. By itself, trust is a systematic determinant of policy choices, good governance, and state capacity (left-hand side of Table 6.6). This apparently solid relationship tends to support Robert Putnam's theory. It suffers, however, from the caveat that the measurement of social capital (1990–1993) is not clearly exogenous to that of governance (1984–1995).[17] The fact that Philip Keefer and Stephen Knack (1997) found no capacity effect of associative life (a more clearly exogenous component of social capital) reinforces this misgiving. In addition, the effects of social capital on capacity do not translate into a relationship between social capital and growth. Some other unspecified effect apparently cancels out the beneficial impact of social capital on governance, resulting in an unclear effect on growth altogether (not shown).[18] Furthermore,

Table 6.6   Comparing the Effects of Social Capital and State Legitimacy

Dependent variable	Single-variable regressions			Multivariate regressions			
	Trust	Adj. R^2	N	Trust	Legitimacy	Adj. R^2	N
Policy index	0.0194* (2.436)	0.08	31	0.0115 (1.723)	2.0264** (3.744)	0.51	31
Governance index	0.0803** (6.082)	0.46	28	0.0689** (6.290)	2.5874** (4.335)	0.65	28
Developmental capacity index	0.0247** (4.562)	0.33	27	0.0190** (4.469)	1.1610** (4.131)	0.64	27

Notes: OLS estimations. Numbers in parentheses are White (1980) heteroskedasticity-consistent *t* statistics. Constants omitted. The dependent variables in these regressions are, respectively, POLICY, GOVNANCE, and CAPACITY. The independent variables are TRUST and LEGIT. See Appendix 1 for definitions, sources, and methodology.

Significance levels: * = 5%; ** = 1%.

when one looks at the simultaneous effects of both trust and state legitimacy (right-hand side of Table 6.6), the impact of trust is significantly reduced. In the case of policies, it no longer has a statistically significant effect. With respect to governance and capacity, it loses some of its impact but remains significant. In contrast, state legitimacy has a significantly positive impact in addition to the trust effect in each case. Bearing in mind that legitimacy is unambiguously exogenous to policies and governance, these results suggest it is a more robust explanation of state capacity than trust (given the limitations of the available data).

In addition, trust itself could be partly determined by state legitimacy.[19] To the extent that legitimacy measures the lack of arbitrariness of states vis-à-vis societies, it is likely to be associated with a greater trust of institutions and of the different components of society for each other. This association may explain why the effects of trust shrink upon controlling for legitimacy.

In fact, the evidence provided by Putnam himself can be read in a manner that does not necessarily support the civic culture hypothesis. Throughout his book are remarks that in fact advocate a legitimacy-like argument more than a cultural one. For example, a statement such as "the role of collective solidarity in maintaining the civic order marked the northern cities as *sui generis*" (1993a:130), would better serve an argument of institutional embeddedness than of cultural orientation. It could well be that the greatest difference between the Italian north and south is the fact that the city-states, guilds, and communes of the north were endogenous political institutions, whereas the south was under the tutelage of a Norman emperor, an exogenous ruler, and his imported state structure. As Putnam writes later: "In the Mezzogiorno . . . virtually all the successive dynasties that controlled the South were alien" (1993a:136). And projecting the argument to the contemporary period, it can be argued that the unification of Italy in the 1860s was also to a large extent alien to the south. After all, Cavour was from Piedmont and Garibaldi from Nice. The oft-quoted saying that "Italy was made before the Italians" takes on a new resonance in this light. It is still unclear whether the southerners were ever truly made Italian or whether they continue to face state institutions they perceive as somewhat illegitimate to their society. The southern origins of the Mafia—a proto-state organization—do not conflict with such a claim.

Yet social capital cannot altogether be dismissed by these results, as it retains a significant impact of its own on governance and developmental capacity. The results of Table 6.6, however, support the contention that state legitimacy is a more robust predictor of state capacity than is social capital. Social capital theory suffers from some conceptual problems, and the quantitative evidence for it is based on few countries and subject to weaknesses with respect to the direction of causation. Nevertheless, giving social capital the benefit of the doubt, there appears to be room for both theories as determinants of state capacity.

It is worth stressing that the essential difference between the social capital and the state legitimacy theories is that the latter makes no claim about the necessary cultural contents of institutions or cultural outlook of societies. All that is believed to matter is the match, the congruence, the endogeneity, the institutional "ownership," irrespective of the number of civic associations, the level of trust in society, and other dimensions of civic culture and social capital. Yet the legitimacy argument remains a cultural theory in the sense that it posits the necessity of cultural embeddedness of institutions, but it does not rank cultural features in terms of their alleged developmental qualities.

How does the ethnic heterogeneity theory fare under a similar comparison? And if ethnic heterogeneity does not matter to the extent hypothesized by William Easterly and Ross Levine (1997), as suggested in Chapter 4, then how do we explain their rather robust empirical findings? It is actually possible that Easterly and Levine (1997) partly captured legitimacy effects through their ethnolinguistic fractionalization variable. African states do tend to have greater ethnic diversity than other countries of the world, and the fractionalization variable thus captures some African effect. But this effect could in fact be the preponderance of low-legitimacy states in Africa. The ethnolinguistic fractionalization (ELF) index and the state legitimacy dummy actually correlate at -0.57. Arbitrary states created by colonialism are more likely to incorporate a wide array of different ethnic groups than their endogenous counterparts. This is why ELF could be a proxy for state legitimacy. But rather than ethnic polarization, what is captured is the neopatrimonial dimension of policies and governance in nonlegitimate states.

The empirical results of Table 6.7 lend support to this hypothesis. As with social capital, the left-hand side of Table 6.7 shows the predictive power of ethnic fractionalization on policies, governance, capacity, and growth for a worldwide sample of countries. In each case, it is a highly significant negative predictor. Yet on the right-hand side, I ran exactly the same regressions but added state legitimacy as an explanatory variable. The striking result is that ethnic

Table 6.7   Comparing the Effects of Ethnic Heterogeneity and State Legitimacy

Dependent variable	Single-variable regressions			Multivariate regressions			
	Ethnic	Adj. R^2	N	Ethnic	Legitimacy	Adj. R^2	N
Policy index	−2.6118** (6.411)	0.25	108	−1.1612 (1.943)	1.3114** (3.660)	0.35	108
Governance index	−3.5068** (5.380)	0.20	103	−0.9477 (1.062)	2.2758** (4.575)	0.33	102
Developmental capacity index	−1.4756** (5.703)	0.23	97	−0.4905 (1.413)	0.9000** (4.464)	0.36	97
GDP growth	−0.0224** (4.252)	0.11	120	−0.0056 (0.743)	0.0165** (3.522)	0.22	120

Notes: OLS estimations. Numbers in parentheses are White (1980) heteroskedasticity-consistent *t* statistics. Constants omitted. The dependent variables in these regressions are, respectively, POLICY, GOVNANCE, CAPACITY, and RGDPCH. The independent variables are ELF and LEGIT. See Appendix 1 for definitions, sources, and methodology.
  Significance levels: ** = 1%.

heterogeneity no longer is a significant predictor in any of the regressions. State legitimacy, on the other hand, is robust in the presence of the ethnic fractionalization variable and retains a significantly positive influence in each of the regressions. In other words, when comparing the explanatory power for development of ethnic fragmentation and state legitimacy, legitimacy is the horse that wins the race.[20]

   Together these results cast doubt upon the validity of the ethnic theory of African stagnation. They compound misgivings about conceptions of ethnicity in Africa as a primordial determinant of interethnic competition and conflict. There is no question that Easterly and Levine (1997) captured an empirical relationship in their study, but all indications converge to suggest that this was the state legitimacy effect, which they did not theorize. The polarization theory of ethnic fractionalization, on the other hand, is not borne out. As will be shown in Chapter 7, measures of institutional diversity and of simple linguistic diversity are better predictors of poor governance.

NOTES

   1. The main sources I used in deriving this variable were the *Encyclopedia Britannica*, Emerson (1960), Young (1988), Morrison et al.

(1989), Holsti (1996), Bayart (1993), Bayart (1996), Kurian (1997), and miscellaneous Library of Congress *Country Studies.*

2. See also De Soto (1989) for a discussion of the lack of legitimacy of the state in Peru.

3. "Pakistan" Britannica Online. <http://www.eb.com:180/cgi-bin/g?DocF=macro/5004/ 83.html> [accessed 25 August 1998].

4. "Bangladesh: History," *Britannica Online* <http://www.eb. com:180/cgi-bin/g?DocF=macro/5000/58/21.html> [accessed 25 August 1998].

5. This is why no Central Asian states are included in Tables 6.1 or 6.2.

6. These other estimates were those used by Bruno and Easterly (1996) and Easterly and Levine (1997), both of which are derived from World Bank National Accounts data. I chose growth data from the Penn World Table (NBER 1994) in my estimations throughout this book because they provided the greatest sample size and the weakest estimates of the legitimacy effect, hoping thereby to reinforce the robustness and replicability of my results. See Appendix 1 for further discussion of the data.

7. In one case only, using Bruno and Easterly (1996) to compare the growth of legitimate and nonlegitimate states in the Middle East and North Africa, did the latter perform better than the former. This was due to the inclusion of Kuwait, whose growth was estimated to have averaged –6 percent per year over a period that covers the Gulf War and its aftermath.

8. Including OECD countries produces equal or better results.

9. Quoted in Robinson (1997a).

10. See Schatzberg (1989) on this mechanism in Zaire.

11. Bayart (1993) calls this the "reciprocal assimilation of elites."

12. Econometricians say that capacity and legitimacy are now "orthogonal" to each other, which means that they are no longer correlated. From a technical point of view, this solves the problem of multicollinearity that arises when two explanatory variables are related to each other. Multicollinearity does not affect the overall predictive capacity of the model, but it deflates the magnitude and the significance of the coefficient of each of the related variables, preventing an accurate assessment of their respective effects. Making them orthogonal to each other by previously regressing one on the other solves this problem, provided the direction of causality between the two variables can be clearly established, as in the present case.

13. Sachs and Warner (1997b), however, find this variable to have a significantly negative effect on growth. The difference in significance may be due to the larger sample size of my estimations.

14. The reduction of the African impact is less in this case, however, falling from –1.6 percent to about –1 percent and keeping a marginal level of significance (10 percent).

15. Several additional variables were also controlled for but are not reported here because of their statistical insignificance, including the rate of population growth, ethnic fragmentation, the prevalence of civil wars, the size of the country, and political assassinations. In addition, similar regressions were run with data from the World Bank's *World Development Indicators 1999* CD Rom covering the period 1961–1997. These generated

consistent results with actually larger and more significant legitimacy effects. Note also that although these estimations may not appear to be conventional growth models, the policy and capacity indices nevertheless capture the determinants of physical and human capital usually included in growth regressions.

16. Note that state legitimacy also systematically reduces the positive impact of the East Asian dragons dummy, although it certainly does not affect the strength of its statistical significance. Nevertheless, state legitimacy appears to explain some, if by no means all, of the East Asian miracle.

17. This problem is most particularly associated with the paper by La Porta et al. (1997). Keefer and Knack (1997) partly correct for it by including an earlier set of World Values Survey from 1981. Nevertheless, there were only twenty-one countries in the 1981 World Values Survey, and their regressions are based on a sample size of twenty-nine, suggesting that for at least eight countries TRUST was measured ex post to growth (which they average over the 1980–1992 period). Given the relatively small size of the sample, this can turn out to be a problem. In my estimations, trust is mostly measured ex post facto.

18. I failed, therefore, to confirm the results of La Porta et al. (1997:336) and of Keefer and Knack (1997:1261) on growth. The latter, however, restricted their sample to twenty-nine (out of forty-three countries in the World Values Survey), looked at growth over the 1980–1992 period only, and used a somewhat different specification, controlling for primary and secondary school enrollment and for the price of investment goods relative to the United States.

19. In a simple bivariate regression on trust, state legitimacy increased the proportion of "trusting" people by 9 percent, a statistically significant result.

20. In addition, in all the multivariate regressions on growth or capacity previously discussed here, not once did adding ethnic fractionalization (ELF) either significantly alter the coefficient of legitimacy or result in a significant effect of its own. Also, ELF had no significant effect on good governance in Africa when added to the explanatory variables in Table 7.4 in Chapter 7. Only when it was substituted for the other measures of social heterogeneity did it become statistically significant, but this resulted in a large decrease of the adjusted R^2.

7

Success and Failure
Among African States

Chapter 6 demonstrated how Africa's relative lack of state legitimacy contributes to its weak economic performance compared to other developing regions. Here I attempt to show how variations in levels of state legitimacy among African countries also account in large part for differences in state capacity and economic performance across the continent. This is a usually overlooked aspect of both theoretical and empirical studies that aim to explain Africa's overall stagnation. And yet because there is such a substantial variance in development across Africa, any hypothesis that purports to differentiate the continent from the rest of the world must also be able to account for differences in performance within Africa.

First, I compare policies and governance between legitimate and nonlegitimate African countries. But the variable used in Chapter 6 really captures only what Kalevi Holsti (1996) called the vertical dimension of state legitimacy, the agreement on the right to rule, the continuity of political cultures and institutions, and the contents of the social contract. As argued in Chapter 5, however, there is also a crisis of horizontal legitimacy in Africa or, in other words, a crisis as to what constitutes the polity, the community that comes together to negotiate the social contract. The arbitrariness of Africa's colonial borders has brought together peoples that belonged to separate political institutions and partitioned some that belonged together. I add therefore a measure of the horizontal legitimacy of African states and estimate its effects on state capacity. As the data will show, there is no stronger determinant of good governance in Africa. Finally, I assess the total effects of vertical and horizontal legitimacy on growth in Africa.

VERTICAL LEGITIMACY AND
DEVELOPMENTAL CAPACITY IN AFRICA

As established earlier, the tendency of African states to lack historical legitimacy is one crucial reason why Africa's economic development is lagging behind that of other regions of the world. Here I
investigate the robustness of the legitimacy-capacity relationship by
assessing its ability to differentiate developmental performance
among African states. To recap our findings thus far: The range of
Africa's economic performance is surprisingly broad, varying from
–3.7 percent to 5.6 percent average annual per capita GDP growth
from independence to 1992; African state capacity is not a uniform
failure, and policy choices and the quality of governance also are
subject to large variations across the continent; and, finally, social
capital theory and the ethnic heterogeneity hypothesis are unable to
account for these differences. Now I test the proposition that these
variations in African state capacity are related to different levels of
state legitimacy among African states.

The measure of vertical state legitimacy used in Chapter 6
remains at the core of the empirical analysis in this section. As a
reminder, ten African countries score 1 on this variable: Botswana,
Burundi, Cape Verde, Ethiopia, Lesotho, Mauritius, Rwanda, São
Tomé and Principe, Seychelles, and Swaziland. These include the
countries listed by Jean-François Bayart (1996:14) as being "political
formations" that "pre-existed the forcing [of Africa] into dependence,"[1] those listed by Crawford Young (1988:33) as having had
"pre-colonial existence," and islands that were not settled before
colonialism or slavery and where there can be no conflict of authority between precolonial and postcolonial systems.

Table 7.1. compares seven of these ten countries (the only ones
for which data was available) with about thirty of their nonlegitimate
counterparts. It provides a first level of confirmation that African
legitimate states systematically and significantly outperform nonlegitimate ones in terms of policy choices, governance, and state
capacity. The difference in terms of the policy index represents 28
percent of the variation in the index across Africa. Table 7.1 does not
show the details of policy performance, but a closer look at the component variables of the index would indicate that, within Africa too,
legitimate states invest more in education, make public investment
decisions based on more productive than political criteria, and are
better able to forgo current consumption. Nonlegitimate African

Table 7.1   Comparing Policies, Governance, and Capacity Among Legitimate and Nonlegitimate African States

Variable	Nonlegitimate states (n)	Legitimate states (n)	P Value
Developmental policy index	−1.53 (31)	−0.69 (7)	0.0570
Good governance index*	−1.88 (30)	−0.61 (7)	0.0269
Developmental capacity index*	−0.86 (28)	−0.34 (7)	0.0347

Notes: The first two columns compare the average scores of nonlegitimate and legitimate African states on the three indices. In the third column, *P* value (one-tailed) refers to the probability that the difference between legitimate and nonlegitimate states is due to chance. The variables are, respectively, POLICY, GOVNANCE, and CAPACITY. See Appendix 1 for definitions, sources, and methodology.
Significance levels: * = 5%.

states are more likely to adopt distortionary policies such as overvaluing their exchange rate in order to protect the purchasing power of narrow urban constituencies born of clientelism and prebendalism. They instruct their banks to lend to political clients and fail to enforce repayment terms, leading to distorted and ailing financial sectors. Supporting the existence of inefficient industries whose origins were at least partly motivated by patronage and regional distribution of state resources, their economies are also less likely to be open to international competition. When they borrow abroad, it is for projects whose economic rationales are weak and actual implementation dubious, leaving their governments with a debt service they cannot afford and leading to substantially more frequent episodes of debt crisis than their legitimate neighbors.

The fact that policymaking in Africa can be partly differentiated along the lines of state legitimacy is a potentially important theoretical insight. State legitimacy apparently provides the missing element in theories of urban bias (Lipton 1977), agricultural pricing distortions (Lofchie 1975; Bates 1981), or other generally predatory behavior in Africa. The fact that the absence of state legitimacy is a good predictor of these policy distortions sheds light on why they are so prevalent in Africa. Why is it, otherwise, that African states are more likely to tax their farmers and protect their urban minorities than most other countries in the world, if not because they need these resources to build up a ruling class to fill in the hegemonic vacancy of their illegitimate states? Note that the cases Robert Bates (1981) studied were all nonlegitimate states: Ghana, Nigeria, Kenya, Zambia, and Tanzania. To show how legitimate and nonlegitimate

African states differ on these characteristics brings home the point that the imported nature of the state drives these policies, and not some intrinsic African quality.

With respect to the quality of their governance, the difference between the average performance of legitimate and nonlegitimate African states amounts to 24 percent of the total range across the continent. Again, digging deeper than the aggregate comparison provided by Table 7.1 offers useful insights. A look at the component variables of the governance index reveals that legitimate African states are better leviathans, enforcing property rights more consistently. Their institutions, including their court systems, are better and their citizens have more trust in them. They also tend to be less repressive of their citizens' civil liberties. In contrast, lack of a stable hegemonic class in nonlegitimate states leads to arbitrary personal rule, random policy turnabouts, and weak property rights, all of which make the state an unreliable partner and a weak provider of public goods. Furthermore, and most fundamentally, citizens (or subjects?) in nonlegitimate states hardly understand their governments to begin with. Indeed, about 84 percent of the population of nonlegitimate states speak a different language at home than the country's official language. For legitimate ones, the number is 25 percent only. In other words, the citizens of states whose continuity has survived the colonial ordeal are significantly less alienated from their public authority than those of states created by colonialism, which typically embraced the language of the colonizer.

There is, however, virtually no difference in the extent of corruption among both groups of countries within Africa. This is a bit surprising in view of the neopatrimonial hypothesis that makes corruption a central element of the mechanism by which low legitimacy leads to economic stagnation. One possible reason for this may be that perceptions of corruption among legitimate African states are affected by the reputation of the "rotten" ones. In other words, less corrupt legitimate states possibly find it hard to escape from a presumption of corruption in Africa.[2] Another possibility is that corruption levels are overall similar across subsamples but that their nature is more systemic in nonlegitimate states, leading to negative effects on the government's capacity to enforce contractual obligations and to provide stable property rights, two variables that are most strongly affected by legitimacy differences within Africa. This in turn more seriously affects prospects for growth than the nonsystemic corruption of legitimate states, which is but an opportunistic deviance of policymakers and bureaucrats.[3]

Table 7.1 makes a clear statement about the explanatory power of state legitimacy in African state capacity. Yet it also reminds us to keep the legitimacy argument within its own limits. State legitimacy is a crucial determinant of state capacity in Africa but not the only one. Legitimate African states still score, as a group, below the worldwide average score, as indicated by the negative values. This remaining shortfall is partly due, however, to the poor policy and governance performances of Burundi, Ethiopia, and Rwanda, each of which has been the theater of civil violence and repressive policies, and whose governments have consequently been distracted from economic policymaking. Nevertheless, it also reminds us that other variables are at play in determining the level of state capacity in Africa. I suggest below some alternative determinants of African governance and compare their explanatory power to that of state legitimacy.

HORIZONTAL LEGITIMACY AND DEVELOPMENTAL CAPACITY IN AFRICA

Moving away from the study of state legitimacy on a worldwide scale and focusing on Africa alone allows for the introduction of a measure of horizontal legitimacy, or the extent to which there is agreement on what constitutes the political community underlying the state (Holsti 1996). As a proxy for this concept, I created a continuous variable that measures the percentage of a country's population belonging to an ethnic group that was *not* partitioned by colonial borders.[4] Hence, the greater the variable, the less arbitrary the state's territory and the greater the fit between the postcolonial state and precolonial political communities. Practically, I calculate the value of this variable, which is between 0 and 1, as 1 minus the percentage of a country's population that belongs to an ethnic group split by colonially imposed borders. It operationalizes horizontal legitimacy by measuring the degree of congruence between precolonial and postcolonial polities.

Concepts of societies, institutions, political identity, and the like are fluid and subject to competing definitions. The argument that Africans identify politically with their ethnic group is subject to much debate, especially with respect to the origins, meaning, and very existence of ethnic identity. Several scholars have convincingly argued that ethnic groups and identities were to a large extent creations of the colonial period (Davidson 1992; Bayart 1993; Gray

1995), and political anthropologists have long claimed that ethnic identity has situational dimensions, varying with the circumstances individuals face (Fortes and Evans-Pritchard 1941). This point is illustrated by Crawford Young's (1976) mention of an instance, while on fieldwork in Congo, when he was asked by a soldier which one of two local conflicting ethnic groups he belonged to, despite being quite obviously white and a foreigner. The salience of ethnic identity is indeed variable and often depends on exogenous factors.[5] In addition, in institutional terms ethnic identity is no guarantee of political identity. Many precolonial African societies were lineage-based and did not have organized political structures outside the family.

Yet ethnicity displays some stability and permanence over time and, in a flexible interpretation, most probably provides a good proxy for the sense of precolonial political identification of the citizens of contemporary African countries, although it will be more artificial at times than at others. A considerable amount of overlapping exists between so-called ethnic groups and precolonial political groupings, which justifies using ethnicity as a proxy for the latter. Furthermore, when several groups coexisted in a system, their partition by colonial borders implies necessarily that their political system too was partitioned, and hence the ethnic proxy adequately captures the political divisiveness of colonial borders.

I used data on the ethnic distribution of contemporary African countries (Morrison et al. 1989) to compute the percentage of their population that belongs to an ethnic group split between at least two countries, and then subtracted this percentage from 1 in order to get a positive measure of horizontal legitimacy. The identification of split groups was mostly obtained from A. I. Asiwaju's *Partitioned Africans* (1985),[6] but when information about preexisting political institutions was straightforward, it was simply substituted for the ethnic data. For example, there are Hutus and Tutsis in both Rwanda and Burundi, but they were not partitioned by colonialism. On the contrary, both Rwanda and Burundi pre-dated colonialism as multiethnic political formations. In such cases, I give precedence to political institutions rather than ethnic identities. The resulting variable is therefore a proxy for the congruence of modern African states vis-à-vis precolonial institutions. A country's score on the horizontal legitimacy variable is independent of its level of ethnic heterogeneity. Somalia, for example, where more than 90 percent of the population is Somali, nevertheless scores very low on the horizontal legitimacy index because there also are Somali in Djibouti, Ethiopia, and Kenya, suggesting that, although very homogeneous ethnically,

Somalia remains highly arbitrary as a state from a territorial point of view. This is also true for another of its ethnic groups, the Affar, who are present in neighboring countries. As a result, almost 98 percent of Somalia's population was split by colonially imposed borders, leading to a score of only 2.5 percent on the horizontal legitimacy variable, which stresses the near-total incongruence to precolonial institutions.[7]

Another case in point is the Comoro Islands. In this case, an ethnically heterogenous group of four islands, settled since the sixth century by successive currents of migration from the Arab, Asian, and African worlds, proclaimed independence from France in 1975, but one of its islands, Mayotte (Mahoré), was retained by the French after a referendum denounced by the United Nations. Although the islands' ethnic heterogeneity would make it impossible to identify what groups are split by the French retention of Mayotte, the existence of a political split as a result of the colonial episode militates for a low score on the horizontal legitimacy scale.

Note, finally, that this variable does not take into account groups that are divided by contemporary borders because of precolonial events or postcolonial migration. For there to be a deficit of state legitimacy, the split must have intervened as a consequence of the colonial moment. Lesotho and Swaziland, for example, are peopled almost exclusively by Sotho and Swazi, groups also found in South Africa. Yet the presence of Sotho in South Africa is mostly accounted for by the progressive contraction of Basutoland between 1836 and 1868 because of continuous encroachments by Boers and the Orange Free State. Colonization by England, however, implied the annexation of the kingdom as it was then and no further partition of the Sotho. Thus the presence of Sotho populations in South Africa is more a function of relations between two independent states (and of postcolonial migration patterns) than a matter of colonial partition.[8] The same is true of the Swazi. The frontiers of Swaziland were actually defined by the British in 1881 and 1884, that is, before they colonized it in 1890. The purpose of establishing these frontiers on behalf of Swaziland was to counter the encroachments and territorial ambitions of Transvaal (Brownlie 1979:1313).

Country scores on the horizontal legitimacy variable are presented in Table 7.2. They are rather uniformly distributed with a bit of leftward skewness: fifteen countries score above 0.75; twelve between 0.5 and 0.75; nine between 0.25 and 0.5; and ten below 0.25. Many of the high-scoring countries are also those that benefit

Table 7.2   Horizontal State Legitimacy in Sub-Saharan Africa

Cape Verde	1.0000	Burkina Faso	0.5735
Madagascar	1.0000	Liberia	0.5635
Mauritius	1.0000	Guinea-Bissau	0.5575
São Tomé & Principe	1.0000	Angola	0.5250
Seychelles	1.0000	Nigeria	0.4888
Swaziland	1.0000	Chad	0.4793
Lesotho	0.9900	Zambia	0.4428
Rwanda	0.9900	Sudan	0.4159
Burundi	0.9800	Namibia	0.3810
Ethiopia	0.9493	Zaire	0.3734
Botswana	0.9035	Malawi	0.3400
Cameroon	0.8565	Gabon	0.3262
Gambia	0.8290	Niger	0.2906
Mozambique	0.8048	Congo	0.2474
Côte d'Ivoire	0.7616	Senegal	0.2022
Zimbabwe	0.7500	Central African Republic	0.1865
Tanzania	0.7406	Equatorial Guinea	0.1500
Benin	0.6746	Mali	0.1346
Ghana	0.6609	Djibouti	0.1137
Kenya	0.6428	Guinea	0.0867
Sierra Leone	0.6363	Mauritania	0.0352
Uganda	0.6341	Somalia	0.0250
Togo	0.5912	Comoro Islands	0.0000

Sources: Created and calculated by the author from data in Asiwaju (1985), Morrison et al. (1989), Grimes (1996), CIA (1997), Reddy (1994), Murdock (1967), *Africa South of the Sahara* (1997), and miscellaneous Library of Congress *Country Studies* (various years).

Note: This variable, labeled HLEGIT in Appendix 1, is defined as 1–the percentage of a country's population whose ethnic group is split across colonially imposed borders.

from vertical legitimacy. Vertical and horizontal legitimacy are to some extent two sides of the same coin, as argued by Holsti (1996:97), since the lack of agreement on what constitutes the polity is unlikely to lead to any agreement on the foundations of authority and political institutions. It comes as no surprise that both variables are relatively highly correlated ($r=0.68$). States that score 1 on vertical legitimacy average 0.98 on horizontal legitimacy, whereas those that score 0 on the former average 0.46 on the latter. Yet they capture close but distinct realities, and as we will see, their effects also differ.

Table 7.3 compares the average performance of countries with high levels of horizontal legitimacy to those with low levels. I chose 0.75 as a cutoff point between low and high legitimacy because a visual inspection of the data suggested it is the threshold at which legitimacy begins to make a difference (see Figure 7.1). Once again, the results provide rather broad support for the legitimacy theory of

Table 7.3   Comparing Policies, Governance, and State Capacity Along Levels of Horizontal Legitimacy in Africa

Variable	States with horizontal legitimacy < 0.75 (n)	States with horizontal legitimacy ≥ 0.75 (n)	P Value
Developmental policy index*	-1.69 (24)	–0.94 (13)	0.0165
Good governance index**	–2.23 (23)	–0.77 (13)	0.0002
Developmental capacity index**	–0.99 (21)	–0.44 (13)	0.0012

Notes: The first two columns compare the average performance on all three indices of countries with horizontal legitimacy below 0.75 and countries with horizontal legitimacy equal to or greater than 0.75. In the third column, P value (one-tailed) refers to the probability that the difference is due to chance. The variables are respectively POLICY, GOVNANCE, and CAPACITY.

See Appendix 1 for definitions, sources, and methodology.

Significance levels: ** = 1%; * = 5%.

state capacity. The differences are in the expected direction and statistically significant for each of the three indicators. With respect to policies, the difference represents 17 percent of the total range of the policy index in Africa. Although it is still significant, it is a weaker effect than that of vertical legitimacy (see Table 7.1). Looking closer at the component elements of the policy index, one sees that the variables for which horizontal legitimacy made the greater difference were investments in education and infrastructure, openness to trade, financial depth, and foreign indebtedness. To some extent, the same explanations prevail with respect to vertical legitimacy. Governments that preside over arbitrary countries are more likely to allocate resources toward placating centrifugal tendencies and competing sources of allegiance than toward the accumulation of human and physical (infrastructure) capital. The fact that the governments of nonlegitimate countries systematically sacrifice economic accumulation to political survival is one of the most consistent empirical findings of my work.

There is still more to the data in the present case. Specifically, the findings with respect to trade openness and financial depth call for an additional level of interpretation. It is probably not so much that horizontally illegitimate states stifle foreign trade and repress their financial systems. What is more likely is that countries with a high percentage of partitioned citizens suffer from greater levels of smuggling and illegal trade and greater exit by their citizens into the

Figure 7.1   Horizontal Legitimacy and Institutional Quality in Africa

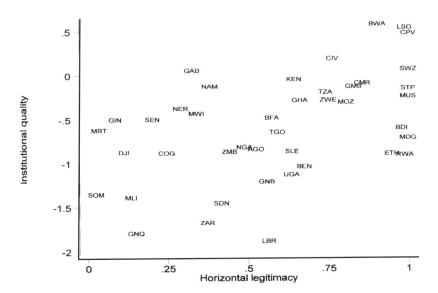

Notes: Institutional quality refers to the principal component of contract enforceabili-ty, risk of expropriation, extent of corruption, quality of institutions and citizens' trust in them, and quality of the bureaucracy. These are the five variables from Political Risk Service, also known as the IRIS variables (after the Institutional Reform and Informal Sector Center of the University of Maryland, which first used them in growth regressions). Country codes are as follows: AGO Angola, BEN Benin, BWA Botswana, BFA Burkina, BDI Burundi, CMR Cameroon, CPV Cape Verde, COG Congo, CIV Côte d'Ivoire, DJI Djibouti, GNQ Equatorial Guinea, ETH Ethiopia, GAB Gabon, GMB Gambia, GHA Ghana, GIN Guinea, GNB Guinea-Bissau, KEN Kenya, LSO Lesotho, LBR Liberia, MDG Madagascar, MWI Malawi, MLI Mali, MRT Mauritania, MUS Mauritius, MOZ Mozambique, NAM Namibia, NER Niger, NGA Nigeria, RWA Rwanda, STP São Tomé and Principe, SEN Senegal, SLE Sierra Leone, SOM Somalia, SDN Sudan, SWZ Swaziland, TZA Tanzania, TGO Togo, UGA Uganda, ZAR Democratic Republic of Congo (formerly Zaire), ZMB Zambia, ZWE Zimbabwe.

informal economy. Indeed, the social connections between similar peoples across borders are likely to favor the economic integration of both sides of the border at the expense of the formal economies of the states on each side. This situation then results in weaker official trade flows and formal financial sectors.

Horizontal legitimacy is, however, a stronger predictor of good governance than of good policy and accounts for 27 percent of the variation in governance quality across Africa. Government behavior vis-à-vis markets and economic agents in states with low horizontal legitimacy is either unpredictable or predictably hostile, because markets and investments represent useful resources in building up power foundations that substitute for national cohesion. As a result, contractual commitments by these governments are unreliable, and they are more likely to expropriate foreign investors when it suits their domestic political needs. Compare the "Zaireanization" of 1974 by President Mobutu, when assets of foreigners were simply given by the president to domestic elites, with the unilateral cancellation by President Kabila in 1997 of foreign investment contracts in mining ventures worth up to $1 billion (Economist Intelligence Unit 1998). Governments of nonlegitimate states, whatever their political orientation, cannot help but violate private property and renege on their contractual engagements in their scramble for a stable political hegemony.

The loyalty of their bureaucrats is also weak, which encourages corruption,[9] and citizens do not trust their underperforming and superficial institutions, a distrust magnified by the fact that the state usually does not even speak their language (85 percent of the households of states with low horizontal legitimacy do not speak the official language at home). Meanwhile, faced with societies that refuse to fit into their states, political elites answer with repression, leading to further alienation and disengagement by their citizens. Figure 7.1 illustrates the remarkable consistency of the relationship between horizontal legitimacy and institutional quality across Africa.

Again, however, with Table 7.3 as with Table 7.1, the performance of legitimate states remains below the world average for each index.[10] Thus there is more than a deficit of state legitimacy to Africa's capacity crisis. What else matters and how does it compare with the effects of legitimacy? To answer this question, I performed a multivariate regression analysis with the good governance index as the dependent variable. This statistical technique allows us to estimate the actual impact of horizontal legitimacy on governance, even when other potential relevant variables are accounted for, and to compare this impact with that of these other factors.[11]

But what other variables were likely to have an impact on African governance? I hypothesized that in addition to state legitimacy, three sets of variables can be conceived of as determinants of good governance. First, it seems that a country's colonial background would affect postcolonial traditions of public service, accountability, and rule of law.[12] Colonial powers had not only different domestic traditions of governance (e.g., more centralized in France and possibly more accountable in England) but also different colonial systems, favoring more or less direct administration and greater or smaller involvement of indigenous peoples in the administration of colonies. Compare, for example, France to Belgium: The former sent African representatives to its metropolitan parliament from 1948 onward (some of whom actually served as ministers in French governments); Belgium, however, did not authorize political parties until the late 1950s, had but a handful of university-trained Congolese, and kept them in clerical positions in its colonial administration and army. Colonial powers also differ in the ways they granted independence to their colonies. The French and the British presided over usually well-ordered transitions, with a few exceptions. The Belgians decolonized in haste and panic in the face of growing unrest. The Portuguese hung on to their colonies by force well into the 1970s. Whether a country had to lead a protracted struggle for its independence or received it literally against the will of its elites[13] may well affect how "empirical"[14] the successor state became.

The social characteristics of a country are also likely to affect the quality of its governance. Because a small homogeneous state should arguably be easier to administer than a large heterogeneous one, I investigate the effects on governance of the multiplicity of precolonial political cultures within each country. In order to gauge this precolonial political heterogeneity, I use the standard deviation of a variable created by Donald Morrison et al. (1989) that measures for each African country the average precolonial political system, with stateless societies scoring 1, petty chiefdoms 2, and larger tribal chiefdoms and kingdoms 3 (see Table 7.4). What is measured here is the spread of precolonial systems encompassed by the modern state, the dispersion of institutional experiences. I also look at whether linguistic heterogeneity plays a role. Benedict Anderson (1983) has argued that linguistic unification is a crucial element in the formation of political communities. I model this dimension with a variable measuring the number of languages spoken per million inhabitants, also derived from Morrison et al. (1989).[15] Finally, I consider the effects of civil war. One would expect that states that engage in civil wars have weakened bureaucracies, are less capable of guaranteeing private property, and are less likely to be accountable or to encourage development of the rule of law.

Third, I consider the prevailing traditions of political culture. To what extent do precolonial traditions of statehood affect the quality of governance in the postcolonial state? Does the experience of statehood lead to more efficient states, or do stateless societies assimilate

Table 7.4   **Statelike Nature and Heterogeneity of Precolonial Systems**

	Statelike nature	Heterogeneity		Statelike nature	Heterogeneity
Angola	1.00	0.00	Liberia	2.40	0.80
Benin	2.67	0.47	Madagascar	2.00	1.00
Botswana	2.00	0.00	Malawi	1.80	0.40
Burkina Faso	1.25	0.97	Mali	2.00	0.58
Burundi	3.00	0.00	Mauritania	1.67	0.47
Cameroon	1.50	0.76	Mozambique	1.00	0.00
Central African of Republic	1.33	0.47	Niger	2.20	0.75
Chad	2.00	0.82	Nigeria	2.25	0.66
Congo	1.40	1.49	Rwanda	3.00	0.00
Côte d'Ivoire	1.71	0.45	Senegal	1.67	0.47
Equatorial Guinea	1.00	0.00	Sierra Leone	2.25	1.09
Ethiopia	1.86	0.83	Somalia	2.00	0.00
Gabon	1.00	0.00	Sudan	2.00	0.58
Gambia	1.60	0.49	Swaziland	3.00	0.00
Ghana	2.00	0.71	Tanzania	1.67	0.82
Guinea	2.00	0.00	Togo	1.33	0.47
Guinea-Bissau	1.67	0.47	Uganda	1.83	0.90
Kenya	1.83	0.69	Zaire	1.71	0.93
Lesotho	3.00	0.00	Zambia	2.00	0.58

Source: Morrison et al. (1989:53).

Notes: The first column refers to the arithmetic mean of each country's pre-colonial political systems, with greater values representing increasingly state-like features of political organization (1=stateless or segmentary societies, 2=petty and paramount chiefdoms, and 3=tribal chiefdoms). The second column is the standard deviation of the distribution of each country's precolonial political systems. These variables are respectively labeled HIEAFVM and HIEAFVS in Appendix 1.

postcolonial institutions better? I return to the variable created by Morrison et al. (1989) to assess the statelike nature of precolonial culture, but this time I use the simple mean for each country instead of its standard deviation (see Table 7.4). What is measured now is no longer the heterogeneity of precolonial political cultures but how much on average these cultures favored the idea of organized and centralized political authority. The greater the value of this variable, the more statelike the precolonial system. According to my hypothesis, one would expect this variable to provide an inverse measure of postcolonial state legitimacy. The more statelike the precolonial system, the more opportunities there are for clashing institutions in the postcolonial state and, therefore, the lower the capacity of the postcolonial state. In other words, following Peter Ekeh's (1975) terminology, the more statelike the precolonial system, the more compelling the "second public." An alternative hypothesis would stress, however, that precolonial traditions of statehood and civic culture would favor contemporary attachment to the state and increase the

quality of governance and state capacity. This would fit Robert
Putnam's model of civic culture (1993a) and would support Mancur
Olson's little-known argument that Africa's developmental weakness
comes in part from its historical lack of large-scale institutions
(Olson 1987). In the end, this measure of precolonial political culture
may provide an interesting test of the state legitimacy hypothesis
versus alternative theories.

Table 7.5 summarizes the regression results, with and without
state legitimacy. The most striking result is no doubt the massive
effect of horizontal state legitimacy, which by itself improves the
explanatory power of the regression (as measured by the adjusted R^2)
from 50 percent to 76 percent of Africa's cross-national variation in
governance performance. It has the strongest effect of all variables in

**Table 7.5 A Closer Look at the Effects of Horizontal Legitimacy on Good
Governance in Sub-Saharan Africa (dependent variable: good
governance index, average 1985–1995)**

Variable	(1)	(2)
Income level	0.0002	0.0002
	(0.802)	(1.052)
French colony	0.8796	1.0139*
	(1.076)	(2.496)
British colony	1.3371	1.1594**
	(1.865)	(4.946)
Belgian colony	–0.2238	–0.5295*
	(0.271)	(2.134)
Portuguese colony	–0.4828	–1.4413*
	(0.415)	(2.541)
Heterogeneity of precolonial systems	–1.8340**	–1.9117**
	(3.960)	(5.475)
Linguistic heterogeneity	–0.0537*	–0.0640**
	(2.640)	(7.098)
Civil wars	–0.0411**	–0.0216*
	(3.588)	(2.158)
Statelike nature of precolonial systems	–0.3333	–0.8811*
	(0.737)	(2.222)
Horizontal legitimacy	—	2.2765**
		(5.860)
Adj. R^2	0.50	0.76
N	34	34

Notes: OLS regressions with White (1980) heteroskedasticity-consistent t statistics in
parentheses. Intercept not reported. The explanatory variables are respectively INCLEV-
EL, PARIS, LONDON, BRUSSELS, LISBON, HIEAFVS, LANGUAGES, WARCIV,
HIEAFVM, and HLEGIT. For data definitions, sources, and units of measurement, see
Appendix 1.
Significance levels: ** = 1%; * = 5%.

the model, with a 1 standard-deviation increase in horizontal legitimacy leading to a 0.59 standard-deviation improvement in governance, and also the greatest statistical significance. This result provides compelling evidence that the developmental capacity of the state in Africa is an inverse function of its historical arbitrariness. The greater the misfit between people's historical sense of political community and the contemporary state, the less legitimate the latter, the more likely the leadership to resort then to neopatrimonial policies to foster its power, and therefore the weaker the quality of its governance.

Colonization by France or England also has significantly positive effects on the quality of governance, distinct from those of horizontal legitimacy. Note that the magnitude (but not the significance) of the positive effect of British colonization falls somewhat after controlling for horizontal legitimacy, which is consistent with the earlier remark that the British were typically more sensitive to local social realities when drawing their borders. Thus, the positive impact of British colonization in the first regression captured some of this horizontal legitimacy effect. There is no meaningful difference in the effects of France versus Britain in this respect, however, suggesting that at least with respect to postcolonial governance, Fashoda turned out to be irrelevant. Former Belgian and Portuguese colonies start therefore with a handicap over the French and British counterparts. It appears that the long liberation struggles of the Portuguese colonies did not improve their state capacity, even after controlling for the civil wars that plagued two of them (Angola and Mozambique) for the longest part of their independent life.

As expected, all measures of social heterogeneity hurt the quality of governance, and all of them are robust to the inclusion of horizontal legitimacy. The heterogeneity of the precolonial systems has the most powerful negative effect on governance of all indicators of social heterogeneity. This suggests that leaders of states containing a wide range of precolonial political systems have to use more state resources to co-opt these multiple groups into contemporary power structures, further weakening the capacity of their state to be developmental. Linguistic heterogeneity also puts additional demands on state capacity. Multilingual states are more costly to administer than homogeneous ones. To name but a few of their handicaps, communication is more difficult between the state and citizens in heterogeneous societies, especially those who speak minority indigenous languages; the size of the civil service is likely to be greater than optimal, as functions must be duplicated for different linguistic groups; and translations either take a toll on human resources or, if neglected, lower the capacity of the state to reach some groups and increase their likelihood of defection. Note, however, that a similar regression with the ethnolinguistic fractionalization variable (Easterly and Levine 1997) showed no significant effect of this variable, reinforcing the earlier findings (Chapter 4) on the lack of relevance of the ethnic heterogeneity theory to variations in performance within Africa. What seems to matter instead are the intensity of precolonial institutional affiliations and the administrative costs of linguistic diversity.

Precolonial traditions of statehood do not affect governance in the first regression but do have a significantly negative effect after controlling for horizontal legitimacy. This is an interesting result. In fact, by simply looking at traditions of statehood, we have no information about the contemporary nature of the state. Quite obviously, the traditions of statehood of the Bakongo, split as they are between Angola, Congo, and former Zaire, will affect the governance of these states differently from those of the Tswana in Botswana, where the contemporary state is in many ways a continuation of their precolonial system. Hence, if we fail to control for horizontal legitimacy, as in the first column, these diverse experiences cancel each other out. Once we control for the closeness of fit between the postcolonial state and precolonial institutions, the impact of traditions of statehood surfaces quite powerfully. And this impact is negative, further reinforcing the state legitimacy hypothesis: the more statelike the precolonial systems, the greater the social challenge to contemporary statehood and the weaker the postcolonial state. This finding brings an element of refutation to Olson's (1987) hypothesis that some developing states fail to perform because of their lack of historical experience with large-scale organizations such as the state. Stereotypes about the political adaptability of the Igbo of Nigeria (Ottenberg 1960), the baLuba of former Zaire, and the Kikuyu of Kenya—all three lineage societies—reinforce this interpretation.

In conclusion, the horizontal legitimacy of the state may not be the only determinant of state capacity in Africa, but it appears to be the most important, significant, and robust one.[16]

ESTIMATING THE EFFECTS OF STATE LEGITIMACY ON GROWTH IN AFRICA

In Africa as elsewhere, deficits of state legitimacy reduce political allegiance and weaken the power of the ruling elites, therefore raising the political returns of neopatrimonial over developmental leadership. On the one hand, neopatrimonial leadership involves a set of economic policies that is generally inimical to growth because it neglects the foundations of capital accumulation and introduces excessive distortions. In addition, its use of state institutions as instruments of clientelism and prebendalism weakens the quality of governance provided by the state. On the other hand, faced with arbitrary policies and crumbling institutions, citizens of low-legitimacy states are also more likely to disengage from the state and the formal economy and to escape into illegal, informal, or subsistence activities. Leaving the realm of formality entails, however, additional transaction costs for these African citizens and reduces their overall welfare and their potential contribution to national output. In summary, the absence of state legitimacy results in a double source of economic losses: a reduction in state capacity and a reaction of societal disengagement.

Table 7.6 captures both these dimensions and provides estimations of the total effects of state legitimacy on economic growth in Africa. It uses the same estimation technique as in Chapter 6, which involves first regressing the developmental capacity index on state legitimacy. From this first regression, one can estimate the portion of state capacity that is not a function of state legitimacy (the regression's "residual"). Both this residual and the state legitimacy variables are then put back together into multivariate growth regressions. The coefficient of state legitimacy in these regressions captures both the effects of state legitimacy that are mediated through developmental capacity and any additional effects legitimacy may have on growth, such as those suggested by the disengagement hypothesis. The coefficient of the capacity index expresses the remaining influence on growth of that portion of state capacity that is independent of state legitimacy.

The results of Table 7.6 confirm the considerable explanatory power of state legitimacy for differentiating economic performance within the African continent. Controlling for the influence on growth of different levels of initial development, different climatic conditions, and different access to the oceans, vertical legitimacy alone accounts on average for between 4 percent and 5 percent annual per capita GDP growth, or about eight times Africa's average rate of growth since 1960. These results represent between 43 percent and 54 percent of the total range of economic performance across the continent. Their magnitude is unexpected, even to the faithful, and are probably overestimations based on other elements missing in the model. Indeed, these regressions account for about 60 percent of the

Table 7.6 Estimating the Effects of State Legitimacy on Growth in Africa (dependent variable: average annual per capita GDP growth, 1960–1992)

Variable	(1)	(2)	(3)	(4)
Initial income level	-0.0129**	-0.0140**	-0.0137**	-0.0147**
	(3.267)	(3.442)	(2.696)	(2.944)
Tropical climate	0.0063	0.0104	-0.0024	0.0029
	(0.898)	(1.415)	(0.234)	(0.222)
Landlocked country	-0.0042	-0.0052	-0.0025	-0.0025
	(1.266)	(1.911)	(0.661)	(0.655)
Developmental capacity index[a]	0.0279**	0.0243**	0.0321**	0.0248**
	(5.147)	(4.332)	(4.704)	(3.653)
Developmental capacity index[a] for legitimate states only[b]	—	0.0165	—	0.0160
		(1.947)		(1.227)
Vertical state legitimacy	0.0409**	0.0533**	—	—
	(5.572)	(5.850)		
Horizontal state legitimacy	—	—	0.0176*	0.0169*
			(2.232)	(2.180)
Adjusted R^2	0.59	0.62	0.56	0.57
N	35	35	34	34

Notes: OLS estimation with White (1980) heteroskedasticity-consistent *t* statistics in parentheses. The dependent variable is RGDPCH. The explanatory variables are, respectively, INC60, TROPICS, LANDLOCK, CAPACITY, CAPACITY*LEGIT, LEGIT, and HLEGIT. See Appendix 1 for additional data definitions, sources, and methodology.

Significance levels: ** = 1%; * = 5%.

a. Orthogonal to legitimacy, meaning the portion of the variable that is *not* a function of state legitimacy.

b. Interaction term of the index and the legitimacy dummy (this coefficient refers to the additional growth impact of the index in legitimate states over the nonlegitimate ones).

growth variance in Africa (as measured by their adjusted R^2), leaving some 40 percent unexplained. Yet controls for changes in terms of trade, commodity dependence, rates of population growth, ethnic heterogeneity, and occurrences of civil war raised the adjusted R^2 to 70 percent but did not reduce the magnitude of the legitimacy effect (sometimes even further increasing it), and the controls usually had no significant impact on their own. It is hard to conceive of additional potential influences on growth, short of the entrepreneurial nature of local cultures, the idiosyncrasies of each country's economic history, and the skills of their leaders, all of which could hardly be measured. Even if the "true" legitimacy effect is weaker than suggested by Table 7.6, the sheer magnitude of its results virtually guarantees that such true effect will still be substantial and significantly positive.

State legitimacy also has a small but not quite statistically significant effect on the productive effects of state capacity. Indeed, the effects of legitimacy on capacity can be conceived in two different ways. On the one hand, legitimacy affects the *level* of state capacity. On the other, it also affects the *impact* of state capacity on growth. Not only do low-legitimacy states have poorer records of developmental capacity, but in such states a given level of state capacity may also have fewer developmental effects than in a legitimate one. This is the meaning of the positive coefficients associated with the variable labeled "developmental capacity index for legitimate states only" in Table 7.6.

How are we to make sense of this potential additional effect? We need to keep in mind some of the components of the state capacity index. For example, part of the policy index is accounted for by public investments in infrastructure. Nonlegitimate states are not only likely to have fewer such investments but also to choose less productive ones as they privilege projects that boost their sense of sovereignty and allow for theatrical displays of statehood (e.g., national airlines, monuments), or those based on regional patronage rather than expected returns. As a result, the usually robust relationship between accumulation policies and growth is weaker among nonlegitimate states in Africa. With regard to the other variables, it is possible that the economic context of nonlegitimate states is so poor that some policies, although "right," fail to have the expected effects on growth. For example, an improvement in policies or institutional quality brought about by a reform program such as those sponsored by structural adjustment or public sector reform credits may not result in improved economic performance if a large proportion of the population has already escaped into informal social and economic relations, depriving the government of a "supply" response to its policies.

The overall effects of horizontal legitimacy on growth are weaker, yet remain positive and statistically significant. Although the effects of horizontal legitimacy on governance are quite robust, it has a weaker impact on policies, and its overall influence on growth is therefore less forcefully captured by these regressions.[17] Nevertheless, horizontal legitimacy still accounts for about 1.7 percent average annual per capita GDP growth after controlling for differences in initial income level, climate, and access to the oceans, or about 18 percent of the range of economic performance in Africa.

Note also that within Africa, differences in climate and access to the oceans are no longer significant determinants of growth upon controlling for differences in state capacity and legitimacy. This suggests that David Bloom and Jeffrey Sachs's (1998) hypothesis on the impact of geography on development also fails the test of accounting for intra-African variations in economic performance, although it should be borne in mind that climatic variations are smaller among African countries than in the world as a whole.

In these regressions, as with the other empirical evidence discussed earlier, one can argue, however, that most of the African legitimate countries are rather small, which may facilitate governance and policymaking. Is legitimacy capturing, therefore, a size effect? This is unlikely. Setting aside the fact that on a worldwide scale, vertically legitimate states include some of the largest ones on earth, in Africa the average population of these states is 7.9 million with Ethiopia and 3.2 million without. In comparison, no fewer than nine countries scoring 0 on the legitimacy variable actually have populations smaller than 3 million, and the average population size of sub-Saharan states (excluding Nigeria and South Africa) is 8.8 million.[18] At any rate, the regression estimations were controlled for land and population size, and both failed to have an effect either on growth or on the growth impact of state legitimacy. Nevertheless, it is clear that the colonial process, by arbitrarily bringing several groups together, increased the size of African polities compared to precolonial standards. This is what leads to legitimate states being on average smaller than the others. But it is a consequence of the historical determinants of legitimacy or lack thereof, not an alternative issue accidentally captured by the variable.

And finally, is the legitimacy effect in Africa an island effect? Because a large proportion of both the vertically and horizontally legitimate states are islands, could one argue that island economies may be more open, yielding faster rates of growth, or that they are not really "African," with significant cultural or human capital differences or other special circumstances unwittingly captured by state legitimacy? Again, the answer is no. For every Mauritius, there is a Madagascar, and for every Cape Verde, there are Comoro Islands. Controlling for island status in the regressions did not alter the effects of state legitimacy. In fact, it led to a positive effect on growth of being a continental country, suggesting that if there is an island miracle, it is entirely accounted for by the propensity of islands to have greater state legitimacy.

NOTES

1. Translation mine, and with the exception of Madagascar (see Chapter 5).

2. Bear in mind that the indicator of corruption used here (CORRUPT from the ICRG data set) measures the *perception* of corruption by foreign consulting firms.

3. For a somewhat germane point in the distinction of corruption between Africa and East Asia, see Sindzingre (1997).

4. This variable is referred to as HLEGIT in Appendix 1.

5. See Connor (1973) for a classic statement of this dominant view in ethnic studies. O'Sullivan (1998) discusses the evolution of the field from a "primordial" to an "instrumental" view of ethnicity.

6. See Appendix 1 for methodological details and additional sources on this variable (HLEGIT).

7. To some extent, the partition of people from Somali culture hardly matters for this argument since the different Somali clans displayed little if any political integration before colonization. Yet many of the different Somali subgroups were themselves partitioned by colonial borders, giving the argument institutional rather than ethnic substance (see Figure 5.1).

8. See Sanders (1975) and Brownlie (1979).

9. Unlike with vertical legitimacy, there is a significant difference in corruption levels (at the 10 percent level) between horizontally legitimate and nonlegitimate states.

10. The average for the whole world on each index is 0.

11. I chose to use a regression on governance with horizontal legitimacy as an explanatory variable because of its superior goodness of fit. With similar control variables, the effects of horizontal legitimacy on the policy index were also positive but not significant. Vertical legitimacy had, however, a statistically significant impact (the largest of all explanatory variables) on the policy index with the same control variables. In general, vertical legitimacy is a better predictor of policy choices and horizontal legitimacy a better predictor of good governance.

12. One cannot stress enough, however, how colonial powers applied a different set of principles in their colonies than in their own polities, with even the most democratic powers substituting authoritarian policies for their domestic traditions of accountability. Young (1994) makes this amply clear.

13. Here is what the African prime minister of Upper Volta, Maurice Yaméogo, had to say in 1959 about France's plans to grant his country independence a year later: "There are lunatics who dare ask for independence. We cannot even build matchboxes and they want us to be independent . . . We do not care for independence" (quoted in Bassolet 1968:73).

14. In the sense Jackson and Rosberg (1982a) use the term.

15. This is the LANGUAGE variable in Appendix 1. I chose this variable based on the findings of Chapter 4 that the ethnolinguistic fractionalization (ELF) index had no explanatory power on state capacity within Africa. I nevertheless controlled for ELF in these regressions and discuss my findings in the following pages.

16. The results of Table 7.5 were also robust to controls for the rate of economic growth, mainland status, and country and population sizes.

17. In addition, horizontal legitimacy was not a significant determinant of African growth when controlled for the residual of governance alone, instead of state capacity, even though it is itself the most robust determinant of governance in Africa. Statistically, this finding suggests that the variance in horizontal legitimacy affects a portion of the variance in governance that is only weakly associated with the variance in growth.

18. All population data here are mid-1992 estimates from World Bank (1995).

8

Conclusion:
The African State in Transition

> Illegitimacy is something we should talk about in terms of not hav-
> ing it.
>
> —Dan Quayle, 1992

The historical endogeneity of the state, its congruence with underlying political institutions and norms of political authority—in a word,
its legitimacy—is a crucial variable in understanding the choice of
policies that rulers of developing countries adopt and the quality of
the overall governance they provide. Both, in turn, are important factors contributing to economic development. Deficits of state legitimacy are therefore at the core of the developmental failure of many
African states.

Leaders of nonlegitimate states not only are faced with a peculiar
challenge but also are limited in the options available to them to
address it. Their challenge arises from the lack of hegemonic control
of their state over society. Nonlegitimate states, having originated
outside domestic social relations and having failed to be endogenized
into domestic power relations, do not represent the established
instruments of hegemonic control of their ruling classes, nor do they
fit patterns of political relations in society. Because no agreement
among the constitutive groups of the state preceded its creation, con-
testations of policies are more likely to turn into challenges to the
state itself. This propensity for crises weakens the actual power of
political leaders and ties their hands as policymakers.

For these elites, fostering political support by providing efficient
government is rarely an option. Indeed, such developmental policies
are less likely to be successful than elsewhere because they require
the active involvement of the state apparatus to be implemented and

assume some level of supply response on the part of private agents. Both of these expectations are less likely to be fulfilled the more the state is perceived as illegitimate. Hence, the lack of initial state legitimacy reduces the relative payoffs of developmental policies for rulers. They are more likely to adopt what is commonly referred to as neopatrimonial policies, meaning a propensity to resort to corruption, clientelism, nepotism, regionalism, and other forms of factionalism. The point of these policies is to create the foundations of some instrumental legitimacy, to substitute patron-client links for the lack of moral legitimacy of the state and thereby to provide the regime with a semblance of social foundations. Thus, neopatrimonial policies can be perceived as the equilibrium outcome of a set of historical conditions, which I have characterized as state illegitimacy.

Although neopatrimonialism occasionally does provide the state with some level of stability and imposes some accountability onto the government, it does so at the expense of the state's capacity to design and implement policies that favor growth. Weakened capacity arises from the fact that neopatrimonial policies either hijack the proper use of state agencies or use its resources to finance parallel networks of support. As Michael Bratton and Nicolas van de Walle put it, in neopatrimonial regimes,

> relationships of loyalty and dependence pervade a formal political and administrative system, and officials occupy bureaucratic positions less to perform public service, their ostensible purpose, than to acquire personal wealth and status. Although state functionaries receive an official salary, they also enjoy access to various forms of illicit rents, prebends, and petty corruption, which constitute a sometimes important entitlement of office. The chief executive and his inner circle undermine the effectiveness of the nominally modern state administration by using it for systematic patronage and clientelist practices in order to maintain political order. Moreover, parallel and unofficial structures may well hold more power and authority than the formal administration. (1997:62)

State legitimacy is a crucial initial variable in determining the odds of such a course of events unfolding in any given country. The absence of state legitimacy compels leaders to maximize their power ahead of their country's development and constrains the choices available to them to do so, heavily skewing the odds toward adopting neopatrimonial policies. State legitimacy derives from the endogeneity of the state in society, from the degree to which its institutions reflect local relations of power, historical agreements, and domestic norms of political culture. State legitimacy addresses both the legitimacy of the right to rule (i.e., the foundations of political authority) and the agreement as to what constitutes the political society, the polity, the community of participants in the social contract (Holsti 1996).

I have categorized here most states in the world according to criteria designed to capture their level of historical legitimacy, ranging from whether a country was colonized to whether the institutions of a country created by colonialism reflect preexisting relations of power. In addition, in the specific case of Africa, I have measured the extent to which borders inherited from colonialism were artificial and therefore the degree to which the postcolonial state is arbitrary.

My empirical results, based on these two measures of legitimacy, seem to agree with my hypothesis. Other things being equal, legitimate states grow 2 percent faster, year in, year out, than their nonlegitimate counterparts. The most important vectors of this effect are the propensity of nonlegitimate states to prefer short-term policies over long-term investments and their failure to make credible commitments to other economic agents and to provide guarantees to local markets. With regard to policies, nonlegitimate states systematically underperform legitimate ones with respect to educational expenses and attainment, as well as investments in infrastructure. They neglect such investments in human and physical capital because returns from them are distributed over the long run, and the immediate payoffs in terms of power are minimal. Instead, they privilege current spending, especially on wages and salaries of civil servants, as instruments of their neopatrimonial strategies of state formation. When they do invest, it is more often based on a perception of political interests than on economic considerations, and the productivity of these investments is typically low.

With regard to governance, nonlegitimate states' greatest weakness lies in their incapability to make credible commitments to other economic agents and in their erratic behavior as providers and enforcers of property rights. Their use of the state apparatus and its resources to finance and support networks of patronage leads to a weakening of the rule of law, which discourages private economic agents. Their need for access to economic resources makes them more likely to expropriate investors and renege on their contractual engagements, which further discourages domestic and foreign investors, leads to a shortage of investments and a tendency to avoid the formal financial system, and results in an underprovision of public goods by the state.

The evidence here suggests, therefore, that state legitimacy is an important element of what differentiates sub-Saharan Africa from the rest of the world in terms of economic performance—aside from "real" supply shocks such as climatic conditions, geographical situation, and even changes in the terms of trade. Africa does have the greatest concentration of nonlegitimate states of all regions of the world. The results also reveal the explanatory power of state legitimacy in differentiating development fortunes within Africa, for despite a shared colonial experience, there remains some significant variation in levels of state legitimacy. This variation also correlates with differences in economic performance across the continent, accounting in large part for Africa's success stories.

There are also indications that the theory may be relevant to other regions of the world. If no intrinsic quality differentiates Africa from other regions in terms of economic performance apart from its greater concentration of nonlegitimate states, one would expect to see variations in state capacity and economic performance within other regions also affected by differences in state legitimacy. With the caveat that most other regions do not have the sample size and the degree of variance in legitimacy that Africa displays, Table 8.1 nevertheless suggests legitimacy's global relevance. Comparing average levels of state capacity for legitimate and nonlegitimate states within the main regions of the developing world, it suggests that on average legitimate states display greater capacity everywhere than their nonlegitimate counterparts. These results are not statistically significant outside of Africa, however, but the diminutive size of the other regions' samples may account for this lack of robustness.

Table 8.1   The Relevance of State Legitimacy Across the World

	Average scores on the developmental capacity index		
	Nonlegitimate states (n)	Legitimate states (n)	P>|t|
Africa*	−0.86 (28)	−0.34 (7)	0.0347
Asia	−0.14 (5)	0.35 (11)	0.1111
Middle East and North Africa	−0.33 (3)	0.17 (4)	0.2781
Latin America and the Caribbean	−0.21 (3)	−0.00 (18)	0.2125

Notes: The first two columns show the average score on the developmental capacity index (CAPACITY) for countries scoring 0 on the legitimacy variable and those scoring 1, respectively, in each of the four regions. The third column shows the probability that the difference between these averages is due to chance (one-tailed t test). See Appendix 1 for variable definitions, sources and technical notes.

Significance levels: * = 5%.

On the other hand, the difference is always in the expected direction
and hints at the potential analytical returns of expanding state legitimacy theory to other regions.[1]

Altogether, my findings highlight the contribution that political
science can make to the understanding of economic development.
Economic theory has certainly come a long way over the last decade
toward the inclusion of political variables among the determinants of
economic performance. Yet these advances have been constrained by
a relative lack of theoretical borrowing from the field of political science. Polarization, externalities, and credible commitment remain
essentially economic ways to analyze the effects of political factors.
They are modeled as median-voter effects, prisoner-dilemma solutions, or some other dimension of collective action. What I have tried
to show here instead is that a consideration of the mechanisms by
which power is established and maintained, a field to which political
science has much to contribute, provides crucial additional insight
into the roots of economic performance.

A comprehensive approach to development calls for a consideration of political questions, including issues of power and of the historical origins of institutions. The state is better understood not as a
uniform variable across the world but as the outcome of differing
local circumstances. Ignoring that the "state" category actually
encompasses different realities may reduce the scope of any theory.
Some economists are aware of the need to further incorporate the
insights of political science in the study of political economy. Dani
Rodrik, for example, acknowledges that "a political scientist or his-
torian may well find much of the economics literature on the political
economy of reform naive or simplistic" (1996:38). Looking at the
relative theoretical simplicity of models of policy choices, he also
concedes that "the habit of attributing myopia or irrationality to
political actors . . . persists."[2] I hope this book offers an example of
the potential rewards of merging political and economic analysis and
of the further benefits to be reaped from such methodology in development studies.

My findings have potentially far-reaching policy implications for
Africa, which are discussed below. First, they challenge the accepted
wisdom of structural adjustment policies and public sector reform
programs by highlighting the extent to which economic policies and
institutional quality are themselves a function of some deeper structural conditions. Second, they question the very existence of the
African state as we know it. The African state is undergoing a
process of restructuring before our eyes, and it is often a violent one.

Understanding the roots of this process and offering avenues to channel it through more peaceful mechanisms may well be all the West can do at present to truly help long-term development and stability in Africa.

THE TROUBLE WITH STRUCTURAL ADJUSTMENT
AND PUBLIC SECTOR REFORM PROGRAMS IN AFRICA

Since the early 1980s, many African countries have adopted, at one time or another and with different levels of commitment and resilience, so-called structural adjustment programs usually supported by the World Bank. These programs involve the commitment by governments to follow specific macroeconomic and trade policies in exchange for hard-currency loans, which they are more or less free to use as they please and which they typically auction to their domestic importers. The policy reforms that adjustment programs call for usually involve devaluing currency, harnessing monetary supply, reducing fiscal deficits, encouraging trade by reducing levels of effective protection against imports and taxes on exports, liberalizing domestic price systems to let them reflect actual resource scarcities, privatizing parastatals, and so on.

Most of the policies in these reform packages are those known to be conducive to long-run growth, even when they have short-term recessionary effects such as monetary and fiscal restraints. They make good economic sense. Yet the rate of success of adjustment programs in Africa is appallingly low. The World Bank itself, in its 1994 assessment of *Adjustment in Africa,* was hard put to claim success for any more than four states out of a total of about thirty that have embarked at one time or another on such programs. Moreover, one of these states was Burkina Faso, which had not adopted a structural adjustment program during the time period the Bank was studying, and another was Tanzania, whose subsequent economic convulsions raised some doubts over the Bank's endorsement of its performance.

To those who question the usefulness of adjustment programs, the Bank has often answered with the claim that few countries actually implement the reforms they subscribe to at the time of the loan agreement. The Bank's point is well taken, and the failure of adjustment in Africa is indeed, to a large extent, a failure of implementation. One cannot, however, simply argue that African leaders should be more consistent in their implementation of policy reforms (Sachs 1996). The systematic weakness of implementation of adjustment packages suggests that understanding the roots of policy choices in Africa is more important than recommending the adoption of specific policies without an understanding of their context.

What I hope has been shown here is that economic policies in poorly performing African states follow the noneconomic logic of their leaders' quest for political hegemony. This quest, in turn, is partly brought about by the legitimacy deficits of the states they inherited from the colonial period. In the end, no matter how appetizing the carrot of adjustment lending or how large the stick of suspended flows of foreign capital, African leaders cannot lastingly escape the constraints of illegitimate statehood. Even though the policy distortions they adopt eventually ruin their economies and deprive them of the resources needed to sustain their neopatrimonial systems, feeding the cycle of political instability and state failure, African elites can rarely afford to consistently and sustainably choose policies for growth. Difficult economic policies, which imply losses for some segments of the population, generate unmanageable levels of challenge to the state. Policies in place have a purpose of political survival and cannot easily be disposed of or reformed by the government. Demanding the end of some subsidy, public employment policy, transfer, or public enterprise ignores the political nature of these policies and threatens the survival of the regime (see Whitaker 1991). Hence, governments are likely to try to bypass these demands. Indeed, conditionality can never be exhaustive enough that alternative methods of transfer cannot be implemented. In fact, Stephen Morris and Stephen Coate (1995) have shown that conditionality may be costly in terms of economic development if the government actually substitutes an alternative transfer with greater transaction costs. In the end, it may therefore be a blessing, or at least the lesser of two evils, that African states fail to implement adjustment reforms. Such economic recommendations are meaningful but out of sequence in Africa.

The failure of adjustment has progressively led the World Bank to recognize that something was amiss upstream of economic policy-making.[3] While not abandoning adjustment programs, it has first broadly redefined their content. Recent adjustment programs and similar "multisector" loans to Africa have, for example, included reforms to "correct public sector institutional weaknesses" in Burkina Faso, "establish a more favorable environment for private sector growth" in Chad, "help the government improve governance" in Madagascar, and "build . . . capacity" in Tanzania, all of which were not typically part of such programs in the 1980s (World Bank 1999a:169–171). In addition, the Bank has allocated increasing resources over the last few years to what it labels "public sector management reform" programs. Whereas adjustment lending represented about 13.2 percent of the Bank's portfolio between 1990 and 1995, as against 3.3 percent for public sector reform programs, the ratios respectively became 8.5 percent and 6.8 percent over the next three years. On two occasions the Bank actually spent more on public sector reform than on structural adjustment.[4] Instead of making loans conditional upon macroeconomic policies, public sector reform programs actually finance improvements in bureaucratic services, the judicial system, or the overall provision of the rule of law. They typically consist in training bureaucrats or other civil servants and shielding agencies from specific redistributive pressures, as was done with the adoption of performance-based pay in the customs authority of Ghana (see Dia 1996). Based on an understanding that states fail to properly implement developmental policies and provide good governance to their economies, they attempt to better the African state, to increase the effectiveness and efficiency of its institutions. Recent public sector management loans have included support to Ghana's "government efforts to improve the efficiency, effectiveness, and quality of public services" and financing improvements in "capacity-building" in Mauritania and in the "efficiency of the public sector" in Niger (World Bank 1999a:172–174). Similar loans in previous years had covered the creation of "a more secure legal and judicial environment for new investors and existing businesses" in Côte d'Ivoire and a "performance-based capacity-building program" in Guinea (World Bank 1998c:130), as well as sponsoring the "reform of public administration and the judiciary" in Madagascar, "thereby increasing effectiveness, efficiency, and transparency in the public sector" (World Bank 1997c:106).

Yet not unlike structural adjustment policies, these programs are also somewhat misguided. They emphasize training, incentives, downsizing, and institutional innovations. It is doubtful, however, whether African bureaucrats need additional training and more imported institutions. They are neither less competent nor less moral than civil servants elsewhere. Patterns of bureaucratic inefficiency, corruption, delinquent rule of law, and the like answer to a political logic and are the consequences of the dichotomization between statehood and power in African nonlegitimate states. It is hard to see how public sector management programs address these deeper issues.

They may provide temporary Band-Aids, but they are unlikely to bring about lasting improvements. In fact, as Alice Sindzingre (1998) has argued, the sheltering of specific agencies from social pressure, which many of these programs entail, may well accelerate the deliquescence of the other branches of the state and is unlikely to contribute to the accumulation of developmental capacity. Alternatively, these policies are liable to trigger increased polarization among branches of the state, as in Ghana where the reform of the customs authority was followed in 1992 by demands from all civil servants for wage parity, resulting in salary increases equivalent to no less than 3 percent of GDP (World Bank 1995b).

The logic of my argument calls instead for policy reform in Africa to confront the state in a more radical manner and to sponsor the recovery or the development of legitimate institutions of collective action. In some cases, this agenda may conceivably lead to a process of territorial redefinition of African political structures. In others, redefining institutions and their connection to societies within given territorial structures may provide the necessary impetus for recovery. I discuss below the details and implications of each approach.

"THESE BORDERS ARE NOT SACRED": RESTRUCTURING THE AFRICAN STATE[5]

The question of the territorial redefinition of the African state is a complex one. As Richard Joseph has acknowledged, most Africanists have avoided this "treacherous area of analysis, where few serious scholars are prepared to tread" (1997:181). According to the most common argument against it, the Pandora's box of territorial restructuring is better left unopened, lest Africa embark on a path of total anarchy, war, and disintegration. This is by no means a far-fetched conclusion, and the potential dangers of reshuffling boundaries cannot be ignored. Yet two increasingly pressing empirical trends suggest that at least for some countries, it may be time to take the plunge. First, as shown earlier, Africa has paid a high price in terms of foregone growth by failing in the early 1960s to question the state structures inherited from colonialism. Every year, arbitrary African states sacrifice about 2 percent per capita GDP growth on the altar of nation-building and neopatrimonial policies. There should be little doubt left that the stability of arbitrary African states—brought about by international recognition and enforcement (Jackson and Rosberg 1982a) and by the need of African leaders to guarantee their sovereignty despite their lack of actual territorial control (Herbst 1989)—has in fact hindered the development of African economies and continues to do so.

Second, although the potential costs of anarchy and chaos that a territorial restructuring of Africa could bring about are legitimate concerns, they need to be weighted against the current ongoing decay that prevails in several parts of Africa. In many ways, the process of African state formation, by relying on neopatrimonial instruments of power, has led to the decay of the formal institutions of statehood, which have increasingly assumed a ghostlike nature. As William Reno (1998) has argued in the cases of Sierra Leone, Liberia, the Democratic Republic of Congo, and even Nigeria, a "shadow state" exists parallel to formal state structures, and it uses the latter's resources for its own advancement. Shadow states and warlord politics are spreading with alarming speed across the continent. In addition to Reno's cases, one can also think of at least Somalia, Sudan, and Congo-Brazzaville, where the state has become little else than one faction of armed bandits. And more stable states whose diplomacy has brought them in close contact with warlord politics are increasingly paying a price for it in terms of restructuring of their own power away from democratic forms. This includes Côte d'Ivoire, a neighbor of Liberia, where the army finally turned praetorian in 1999 after forty years of constitutional restraint, and Burkina Faso, an ally to Liberia's Charles Taylor, where criminality and shadow relations of power now appear to supersede formal politics.

In addition, several countries have already de facto split or begun a process of boundary change. It took decades of civil war for Eritrea to break free of Ethiopia in 1993, but the seeming partition of the Democratic Republic of Congo is processing at a faster, although no less violent pace. As of the end of 1999, Uganda and Rwanda had all but seized control of the Kivu and Haut-Congo provinces, setting up a puppet local government, and their control also seems to extend deeply into the Equateur province. In Kinshasa, the maintenance of peace and order owed much to the presence of Angolan and Zimbabwean troops. Meanwhile, the province of Eastern Kasai had all but unofficially seceded, as would neighboring Katanga if the president did not hail from there.[6] Southern Sudan is beyond the control of the Karthoum government, as are substantial parts of northern Mali and Niger. Even Senegal, one of the most empirically effective African states, cannot exert full control over its Casamance province.

And since 1991, Somaliland has progressively set up its own government away from the rest of Somalia.

Yet it is true that few of these de facto partitions—Somaliland aside—have so far resulted in the creation of alternative state formations. In fact, few of the rebel leaders in these countries are officially fighting for secessions. In the Democratic Republic of Congo, for example, the different rebel leaders all claim their intention to march onto Kinshasa and take over the country as a whole, as did Kabila in 1997. The lack of subnational ambitions of African guerrilla movements and warlords may in fact be due to their treatment of the state as an economic resource and their understanding of the limited likelihood of obtaining international recognition for seceded entities (see Clapham 1996; Reno 1998). Capturing the national state entitles them to the resources of international aid and patronage that sovereignty and international recognition bring about. If prevailing international norms looked favorably upon partitioned states and granted them sovereignty, these rebel leaders might confine their claims to more localized ambitions. Yet the enduring international isolation of Somaliland sends a strong message against territorial breakups.

At any rate, the reshuffling of African boundaries has begun in many parts of Africa, either through the incapacity of the state to wrestle territorial control away from local warlords and guerrillas or because of foreign occupation. It has taken on a violent nature in part because of the resistance to change that the sanctity of postcolonial borders has brought about. Compounded with the other deleterious consequences of African territorial stability, it has become difficult to argue that it was "in renouncing to revise the borders inherited from colonization and [in] the signing of the OAU Charter that African leaders managed at least to spare their continent a general deflagration in the wake of independences" (Bayart 1996:13).[7] Michael Schatzberg may be right when stating that "those old rules [of territorial integrity] had their drawbacks, but they were effective in keeping the genie of interstate conflict in the bottle," but he neglects all the other negative consequences they imposed and continue to impose on Africans.[8] Clearly, the principle of *uti possidetis,* by which African independent states committed to honor the borders they had inherited from colonization, has led, some forty years down the road, to collapsed states, generalized predation, and the political and economic alienation of grassroot Africans. It is hard to argue that African leaders have spared their continent anything.

As time goes by, therefore, the costs of African state restructuring decrease relative to the costs of territorial stability. As warlordism, secessions, regional wars, and failed states generalize, the alleged threat that "trying to redraw [African borders] could plunge the continent into chaos" seems less and less credible (*The Economist* 1997). If keeping Zaire together required the making of a Mobutu, the repression of Katanga's wishes for self-determination, the crushing of political liberties, the regression of the economy toward mere subsistence, the abuse of the human rights of minorities and the displacement of thousands of Congolese, then it is hard to find any redeeming value in further keeping it together. As Jeffrey Herbst puts it, "At some point, the reality of disintegrating, dysfunctional African states stands in such contrast to the legal fiction of sovereign states that experimentation with regards to new states is in order" (1996:137).

Furthermore, the principle of territorial integrity of Africa's borders has been so repeatedly violated by African governments themselves over the last few years that it makes little sense still to claim any peace dividend from it. African governments who so strongly cling to their own borders no longer hesitate to violate those of their neighbors. Not only did Uganda and Rwanda intervene in former Zaire, but so have Angola, Chad, Zimbabwe, and Namibia. Since then, Angola has also intervened in Congo-Brazzaville to facilitate the overthrow of an existing government. Nigeria has massively intervened in both Liberia and Sierra Leone, at the head of a consortium of West African countries, and Senegal has ventured militarily in both Gambia and Guinea-Bissau.

My findings support Francis Deng's argument, made in the context of the Great Lakes region and the plight of local populations, that "Africans must modify state borders, widen the scope of participation, and make creative arrangements that would diffuse the tensions and foster economic and political cooperation" (1996:A27). Whether African states need a redefinition of their boundaries or a restructuring of their institutions within existing boundaries is likely to be a function of the extent of their horizontal legitimacy. States with dramatically ill-defined polities, such as the Democratic Republic of Congo, may find no other shortcut to sustainable development. Other countries may need "only" a process of institutional rebirth, a new social contract among the segments of their societies.

Uti Possidetis?

Should the reconfiguration of African polities involve territorial dimensions, how could these best be worked out? The eventual answer belongs, of course, to Africans themselves. Yet just as the international community has encouraged the status quo over the last forty years and contributed thereby to constraining African development, so too now is there room for international leverage to facilitate institutional dynamics on the continent.

A common fallacy needs to be disposed of first: Africa will not return to precolonial forms of government and political organization. There is some naive romanticism to the occasionally heard claims for a revival of precolonial entities since most either lost their effectiveness during the colonial period, were transformed to become little more than an idea, or were "perverted" by their role as indirect colonial administrators (Mamdani 1996). In addition, what would be done with the many "anarchical" lineage-societies? My findings do not militate for such a return, nor should they provide fodder for ethnic cleansing arguments. My analytical use of precolonial institutions is meant to highlight the arbitrariness of postcolonial political arrangements, not to fetishize the precolonial state. As for the lack of ethnic homogeneity of African states, I have argued and shown empirically that it is not a factor affecting Africa's development prospects. Many precolonial African states were actually also multiethnic. In fact, M. Fortes and E. E. Evans-Pritchard (1940) made clear in their classical analysis of African political systems that all precolonial statelike African societies actually were amalgams of different peoples.

What are the remaining options? Herbst (1996) has suggested that secessions of viable parts of existing countries be encouraged if the new entities can demonstrate their capacity to provide services and effective governance to their populations.[9] From this perspective, extending recognition to breakaway areas would send the signal to governments that their territorial integrity will no longer be guaranteed at any costs. Despite the allegedly sacred nature of territorial integrity, this would hardly be a novel diplomatic stance. The West's resistance to territorial change in Africa stands in contrast to its tolerance of the breakup of the Soviet Union after 1989. Ideas of self-determination won the day then, as opposed to the arbitrary outcome of tsarist and Soviet imperialism. Some would argue that now is the time to recognize also the arbitrariness of African states created by Western imperialism and encourage the emancipation of Africans from these oppressive structures. Joseph (1996) contends that Africans do not need secessions but better rule of law. But African states are unlikely to display better rule of law until they have more legitimate structures.

Because the power of most African elites is predicated upon the fallacy of national states, secessions or irredenta are anathema to many of them. Former president Pasteur Bizimungu of Rwanda seemed to be an exception, however. At the November 1998 France-Afrique summit in Paris, he uttered the forbidden words, asking that "the debate be centered around the question of artificial borders inherited from colonialism" and claiming that "Africa needs a new Berlin conference."[10] The reaction of other heads of state was predictable, with presidents Rawlings of Ghana and Nujoma of Namibia "showing their irritation" and president Kabila of Congo, who is at war with Rwanda, allegedly laughing and whispering to the person sitting next to him, "And you want me to negotiate with this gentleman?"[11]

Bizimungu's statement was truly unique for an African head of state, although it made sense for Rwanda, where population pressure is intense. The reaction of his peers, on the other hand, was to be expected. A restructuring of their states would probably cost them their power. The fact that Rawlings rebuffed Bizimungu's proposal of such a reform of state borders suggests the lasting significance of Ewé irredentism in Ghana. More than forty years after the end of colonialism, the president of Ghana is still not confident enough in the loyalty of his citizens to accept discussions of boundary reform.

According to this territorial reconfiguration approach, countries and agencies in search of a strategy toward African development assistance may want to focus on devising instruments that would alleviate the reticence of African elites toward boundary changes and reduce their potential for violence. Such a quest should focus on providing an environment in which these changes are possible without degenerating into all-out wars. So far, foreign intervention has privileged maintaining the status quo. Troops have been sent, for example, to prevent the collapse of Somalia. Setting up of an African rapid-intervention military force has also been discussed as a possible OAU mechanism for conflict prevention and has received support from the United States government.[12] Supporting territorial reconfiguration would involve a switch from conflict prevention to mechanisms of peaceful conflict resolution instead. One option could involve the creation of a multinational military force whose presence in contested areas would facilitate negotiated rather than military settlements of intra- and interstate territorial disputes. There is much experience, both at the United Nations and within the African community, for the logistics of such intervention. The newness would pertain to their purpose. Instead of preventing change, they would supervise its peaceful implementation.

A less dramatic option could substitute financial incentives for military might. Existing structural adjustment programs exchange inflows of foreign capital for the adoption of policy packages that promote better allocations of resources and macroeconomic stabilization. Some countries, such as the United States, also impose democratic conditionalities. Such conditional lending could be extended to cover programs to adjust *political* structures. Governments would receive loans if they agreed to surrender their claims of territorial sovereignty over some areas of their country or at least if they accepted the principle of such territorial reshuffling and committed to negotiations with groups having separatist claims. As with current *economic* structural adjustment programs, they would be largely free to use these funds as they please. To some extent, they could be thought of as compensation for territorial losses. Governments may not be the only recipients. In fact, the government's political clients, such as regional elites, could be in even greater need of incentives to let go of the system that has provided them the benefits of patronage for so long and to face the uncertainty of new political orders.

Finally, one may want to consider President Bizimungu's suggestion of convening a new Berlin conference, as far-fetched as it may appear. Such a conference would have to invite representatives of both the governments and societies of African countries and allow for widespread discussions about state reform. It would have the advantage over the national conferences many Francophone African states held in the early 1990s of not presupposing who the participants to the new social contract should be. The national conferences often succeeded in bringing together a wide cross-section of African societies, yet never went back as far as to define whom these societies should comprise. At a new Berlin conference, groups from within a given country or from different countries could come together to negotiate their claims toward the governments of existing states. If the Western world committed to enforce the principles and the outcomes of this conference, as it enforced the decisions of the 1884–1885 Berlin Conference, African governments would have few options but to "play the game." Holding such a conference in Berlin might also have a strong symbolic value, marking the end of the colonial rupture in African history, the end of Africans' alienation, and their repossession of history.

It is not my intention to endorse any of these policy recommendations. I raise them here in the hope of opening up the African policy debate to the consideration of territorial issues that have been taboo for a long time but with little to show for it. Nor do I presume to know how any such reconfiguration would actually look. Should the Democratic Republic of Congo, for example, be split into three or 150 countries? And according to what criteria? Of course, the answers to these questions would belong to the Congolese. The West can only provide the framework and the incentives for peaceful discussion of these issues.

In fact, a more realistic perspective may wish to further explore Deng's (1996) concept of *elasticity* of borders. Deng's idea is to keep borders as they are but essentially empty them of much of their stifling nature:

> What the current situation calls for first is a radically different view of borders. In the past, neighbors and farmers and herders moved across borders in search of pastures and sources of water. Colonial state borders interfered with that relative freedom of movement. From being a constraint to population mobility, these otherwise artificial borders should be modified to allow freedom of movement and regional cooperation among the neighboring states. (1996:A27)

By allowing for free movement of persons across borders and making residence—rather than a hypothetical nationality—the condition for membership in a political community, the constraining nature of African boundaries could be alleviated.[13] The changes implied by this policy recommendation are twofold. At the domestic level, a more inclusive principle of citizenship must be defined that allows for the multiplicity of African identities. The Banyamulenge who have lived all their lives in Congo's Kivu provinces should no longer be denied citizenship because their parents were not born in the Congo, as was the case under the Mobutu regime. Opposition politicians should no longer be prevented from running for office because they were not born in the current territory of the postcolony, a stratagem that then Ivorian president Konan Bédié used in his 1999 attempt to neutralize former prime minister Allasane Ouattara, who comes from a northern region that was once part of the colony of Upper Volta. Making borders more elastic could also improve the accountability of governments, as citizens would be able to vote with their feet. Governments hoping to collect tax revenues from their citizens would have to be responsive to their demands or risk losing them.

At the international level, this strategy calls for greater integration of African countries, greater supranational federalism. The idea of larger political structures is not a new concept. The legitimacy deficits of the states they were about to inherit had already struck several preindependence African leaders, who tried in vain to bypass the fallacy of African nation-states by setting up and lobbying for interterritorial structures. This idea led to the creation of the cross-border party Rassemblement Démocratique Africain (RDA) in French West Africa in 1946 (later badly betrayed by founder Félix Houphouët-Boigny himself) and the Pan-African Freedom Movement in British East and Central Africa in 1958. It was also the vision that led Julius Nyerere to recommend in the 1950s that the British take steps toward creating an East African federation of Uganda, Kenya, and Tanganyika and was the will underlying the attempt at merging Senegal and French Soudan in 1960 into the Fédération du Mali. Finally, the same perception provided the rationale behind constitutional clauses in Ghana and Guinea that allowed for "reductions of national sovereignty in favor of federal union" (Davidson 1992:184). That Houphouët sold out and that Nyerere, Senghor, Keita, Sékou Touré, and Nkrumah failed or changed their mind once in power does not invalidate the accuracy of their original perception. It only serves to show the formidable obstacles to integration laid down by the colonial creation of states in Africa.[14]

Terrence Lyons (1998) has argued, however, that weak states typically make up weak international organizations. Regional construction based on institutional foundations different from the postcolonial states could bypass this problem. But what would be the component units of a new African federalism? Answering this question leads me to one last level of possible policy recommendations: institutional restructuring. Whereas some African states are falling into obsolescence, substitute institutions of collective action have risen throughout Africa. Whether contemporary states are here to stay or will eventually move toward supranational regional construction, new public institutions will certainly lie at the core of Africa's next generation of political arrangements.

Institutional Reform

Locally embedded institutions of collective action have the potential to provide the ferment for the creation of state legitimacy in Africa. Although one cannot presuppose what these institutions might be, an impressionistic overview of the social and political experiments currently ongoing in Africa suggests that traditional indigenous groups (and their contemporary extensions), trade organizations, church associations, regions, and even warlords may be called upon by history to play a role in the rebirth of the African state.

With an eye toward democratization and the resolution of political conflicts, Deng has argued that Africans must

> broaden the basis of participation to include not only the wide array of organizations within the now popular idea of civil society, but also, and primarily, Africa's indigenous, territorially defined, local communities, with their organizational structures, value systems, institutional arrangements, and ways of using their human and material resources. (1998:140)

This inclusive strategy may have economic payoffs too. There is increasing evidence that states that incorporate preexisting sources of political authority into their systems, without denying their validity, do better than those that repress them. Botswana, Swaziland, and Lesotho are compelling cases in point. But even among Africa's less legitimate states, the restoration of precolonial institutions seems to be associated with greater levels of capacity. Both Ghana and Uganda, whose economic performances have dominated those of most other African countries over the last decade after long periods of decline, adopted constitutional revisions, respectively in 1992 and 1993, which rehabilitated previously abolished chieftaincy systems. Although their roles have so far remained largely cultural, they illustrate the fact that states recognizing "traditional" sources of authority may well manage to ride on the coattails of their legitimacy. As Richard Sklar nicely put it, denying recognition to traditional authority will not make it disappear:

> traditional authorities do not exist as a consequence of their recognition and appointment by the governments of sovereign states. On the contrary, they are recognized and appointed to traditional offices, in accordance to customary laws, because those offices are legitimated by the beliefs of the people, who expect them to exist in practice. (1999:169)

But if the national state builds upon the historical authority of these traditional power structures and the loyalty from which they benefit among the population, they can in turn derive legitimacy from them. The policy recommendation therefore is to integrate preexisting authorities or their remnants in ways that build upon their legitimacy rather than as clients in a neopatrimonial system. The point, as Sklar makes clear, is for traditional rulers to be "incorporated into the constitutional system of the nation" (1999:168). Many countries do this at the consultative level, but this bears little weight on national politics and allows the state to derive few legitimacy benefits. In Nigeria, for example, traditional leaders and their councils, although formally recognized, do not have executive, legislative, or judicial powers. Furthermore, like colonial powers previously, the Nigerian government does not hesitate to dismiss and replace popular traditional rulers who threaten its authority. In 1996, the government deposed the traditional sultan of Sokoto in favor of a less threatening rival (Sklar 1999).

What is called for is recognition of the legitimacy and relative autonomy of these traditional systems and their integration into the management of contemporary countries (a criterion that both Ghana and Uganda still fall short of). If the postcolonial state is to be legitimated, it cannot afford to destroy, repress, or even ignore these repositories of political legitimacy.

Indigenous institutions are a crucial building block for the legitimation of postcolonial African states, but they need not be the only possible option. Deborah Brautigam (1997) has shown, for example, that industrialists in Eastern Nigeria, a region long neglected by the central government, used culturally based local networks to reduce their transaction costs, thus substituting for the state in providing a public good. In the province of Eastern Kasai in former Zaire, other local institutions have successfully developed. As Zaire's national economy broke down in the early 1990s, Eastern Kasai progressively increased its autonomy from Kinshasa, refusing to recognize the monetary reform of 1993 and sticking instead to old banknotes, thereby avoiding inflation altogether, increasing the production of diamonds several years in a row, harnessing public investments, and even creating a university a couple of years ago.[15] It appears in fact that Kasai's provincial authorities, embedded in segments of civil society such as the local Catholic clergy and other associations, may have substituted themselves for the Zairean state structure, providing an instrument of collective action and reduction of transaction costs for the local population. Kasai may therefore be an example of the birth or rebirth of legitimate institutions in an instance of state decay. The fact that Kasai is the institutional heir of the precolonial Lunda empire may not be irrelevant to its success.

Warlords themselves, for all the hardship they currently drag in their wake, also represent an institutional rebirth across the continent. They are at the center of Mafia-like protostates that, hardened now by violence, may eventually be tamed into more contractual institutions.[16] They may represent what Mancur Olson (1993) called the transition from "roving" to "stationary" bandits, setting themselves up as heads of state, turning theft into taxes, and progressively offering an escape from the state of nature in collapsed institutional environments.

All these possibilities and many more are part of the ongoing "reconfiguration" of state power in Africa (Boone 1998; Joseph 1999). Western donors should no longer hamper these changes but be open instead to sponsoring original institutional solutions. The legacies of colonialism have constrained the lives of Africans for too long. But they need no longer constrain their and our imaginations.

NOTES

1. Another reason for the lack of statistical significance of the t tests in the other regions is that they include more legitimate than nonlegitimate countries. For the reasons already discussed here, nonlegitimate countries tend to systematically develop weak state capacity. Among legitimate states, however, there is some measure of variation. Legitimacy is a necessary condition for capacity but not a sufficient one. Other factors intervene that make some states more capable than others. Therefore, although legitimate states display greater average capacity than nonlegitimate ones in all regions of the world, the remaining variation in capacity among them reduces the statistical significance of the t tests.

2. An exception is provided by Robinson (1997b), who looks at the redistributive effects of development on power and hypothesizes that leaders whose stability is likely to be threatened by the development process will be more likely to turn predatory, that is, to choose "bad policies" for growth.

3. The same realization is actually prevailing at the IMF too, where the talk is now about "second-generation reforms" that address social, political, and institutional constraints to macroeconomic policies (see International Monetary Fund 1999).

4. Data computed by the author, based on World Bank annual reports, miscellaneous years. The figures quoted for adjustment actually cover all multisector loans, a somewhat more inclusive category. This trend was interrupted by the Bank's response to the East Asian crisis of 1997–1998, for which loans were typically categorized as multisector credits before becoming financial sector credits in 1999.

5. The quote in the title of this section is from the title of a *Washington Post* op-ed by Francis Deng (1996).

6. For thorough coverage of the evolution of Central Africa, see the NCN web page at http://www.marekinc.com/NCN.html.

7. Translation mine.

8. Interview of Michael Schatzberg in *New York Times,* 12 January 1999.

9. Fortes and Evans-Pritchard (1940) remind us that secessions were a

frequent pattern of institutional dynamics in precolonial Africa. In fact, the whole system of segmentary lineage, which provided the foundations for both state and nonstate political formations in precolonial Africa, relied on the concept of political separation.

10. Translation mine. Quoted in *Jeune Afrique*, 8–14 December 1998.

11. Translation mine. Quoted in *Jeune Afrique*, 8–14 December 1998.

12. See the Final Communique issued at the end of the Entebbe Summit for Peace and Prosperity, 25 March 1998, on the occasion of President Clinton's trip to Africa.

13. See also Francis Deng, "Managing Diversity in Africa: A Challenge to State Borders" (paper presented at the annual meeting of the African Studies Association, Chicago, October 1998).

14. There is little doubt that former colonial powers, France foremost, used considerable leverage to prevent regional integration in Africa and to keep African states in their position of dependency.

15. See *The Economist*, 27 April 1996, and *The New York Times*, 18 September 1996.

16. See Reno (1998) on warlord politics in Africa and Herbst (1996) for an earlier suggestion to build new institutions upon them.

APPENDIX I

Notes on Methodology, Definitions, and Data Sources

The data set used in this book is available in Stata format at the author's web page at www.politics.pomona.edu/englebert.html. The data on economic growth are compiled from the Penn World Table, Mark 5.6 (Heston and Summers 1991), covering the period from independence or 1960, whichever comes later, to 1992 (or most recent available estimate). Growth rates are calculated from the Penn World Table's variable labeled RGDPCH, real purchasing-power-parity per capita GDP based on the chain index method. The label RGDPCH is retained for the growth rate of GDP in this data set. All growth rates are calculated according to the formula:

$$[\ln(X_{t2}) - \ln(X_{t1})]/n$$

where X_{t2} is the value of the variable whose growth rate is calculated at the end of the period, X_{t1} is its value in the year preceding the beginning of the period (if not available, the first year of the period is used instead, and n is adjusted accordingly) and n is the number of years in the period.

The Penn World Table's RGDPCH variable is also used to estimate the initial level of income at the time of independence or in 1960, whichever comes later, expressed in logarithmic form and referred to as INC60 and INC60SQ in the data set. The AFRICA and HPAE dummies are based on World Bank regional identifications and on World Bank (1993). The tropical climate variable (TROPICS) comes from Jeffrey Sachs and Andrew Warner (1997b) but is expanded to cover a larger sample (see variable definitions and sources below). Data for countries missing in their sample are personal estimations based on inference from available data. LAND-LOCK is derived from standard political maps.

The variables comprised in the policy index (POLICY), a first principal component, are SCHOOL (average educational attainment in terms of years of attendance, expressed in log form), TELPW (the log of the number of telephones per thousand workers), G (government spending as a percentage of GDP), BLCK (the log of the black market premium in foreign exchange), OPEN (the ratio of trade imports and exports to GDP), and LLY (the ratio of liquid liabilities to GDP). The first three of these variables cover accumulation policies and the last three, distortion policies. The index of good governance is mainly derived from data sold by Political Risk Service (PRS), a Syracuse-based consulting firm that provides country risk analyses for its clients. These data were first used in growth regressions by Paolo Mauro (1995) and Philip Keefer and Stephen Knack (1995a) and are usually referred to as ICRG data, from the name of the PRS publication *Inter-Country Risk Guide*, or as the IRIS data set for the name of the University of Maryland's Institutional Reform and the Informal Sector (IRIS) Center, which sponsored Keefer and Knack's research. Because both papers by Mauro and Keefer and Knack present the data in aggregated form as averages of several variables over several years, I purchased the original data set from PRS in order to get more detailed information. The data set comes in panel format for 148 countries and covers at most the years 1982 to 1995, although many countries have no data before 1984. I entered for each observation the average of each variable over the available years. Although the growth regressions cover the period 1960–1992, the relative stability of the indicators over the available years suggest that using the 1984–1995 value of the ICRG indicators was an acceptable solution (see Appendix Table 1).

Appendix Table 1   Time Correlation Matrix of the ICRG Indicators

	1984–1987	1988–1991	1992–1995
1984–1987	1		
1988–1991	0.9671	1	
1992–1995	0.8233	0.8813	1

Notes: The table measures the partial correlations between the averages of the five ICRG variables in three different time periods. The five ICRG variables are COMMIT, EXPROP, CORRUPT, INSTQUAL, and BUROQUAL. All correlations are significant at the 1 percent level.

Still, it could be argued that the ICRG indicators are poor predictors of growth to the extent that they are measured at the end of the period over which growth is measured (1984–1995 versus 1960–1992). However, additional regressions performed over the 1985–1995 period, including some with lagged ICRG variables, confirmed their predictive power on growth, as have other studies before (Mauro 1995; Keefer and Knack 1995a; Barro 1997; and Easterly and Levine 1997), all of whom used some form of control for endogeneity. Furthermore, this has little effect on the regressions where governance indicators are used as dependent variables since they are measured ex post facto to the explanatory variables.

The five ICRG variables are the extent of government's respect for contractual obligations (COMMIT); the risk of expropriation of foreign assets (EXPROP); the extent of corruption (CORRUPT); the quality of public institutions, including the court system, and the degree of citizens' trust in them (INSTQUAL); and the quality of the bureaucracy (BUROQUAL). Each ICRG variable is measured on a scale of 0-10, with larger numbers indicating better performance. This involved rescaling some ICRG variables originally measured on a 0-6 scale. The specific questions that underlie each of the five measures are spelled out below in the section on variable definitions and sources.

There were, however, fifteen African countries with missing ICRG data, including eight that scored 1 on the LEGIT variable (out of a total of ten African countries scoring 1). To compensate for this shortcoming of the data, I sent a questionnaire replicating the same questions as those underlying the ICRG variables to forty-three Africa authors for the Economist Intelligence Unit, a country-risk consultancy based in London that publishes quarterly analyses of the economies of most countries in the world. PRS follows the same approach of questioning country specialists. I received twenty-one responses, eleven of which were for missing countries, including seven for countries scoring 1 on the LEGIT variable. The questionnaire called for answers on the five variables over three periods of time: 1984–1987, 1988–1991, and 1992–1995, in order to allow for some variation over time without requiring annual data, which would have been too much to ask respondents ex post facto. The eleven answers for missing observations were added to the ICRG data in this data set. For the ten countries for which both ICRG and EIU data were available, the averages of the five variables correlated at 0.67, which suggests only limited measurement errors. At any rate, ICRG variables are mostly used as dependent variables for which measurement error is not a serious problem (Greene 1993).

To the five ICRG variables, I added the Gastil index of civil liberties (CIVL) and an indicator of the percentage of households that speak the national language (HOMELANG). I generated the first principal component of these seven indicators to capture a summary measure of good governance (GOVNANCE).

Other data sources included George T. Kurian (1997) for religious affiliation and ethnic homogeneity; Charles L. Taylor and Michael Hudson (1974) for ethnic heterogeneity; Kalevi Holsti (1996) for the prevalence of wars and civil wars; Ronald Inglehart (1997) for measures of social capital; and Donald Morrison et al. (1989) for several Africa-specific variables such as the heterogeneity of precolonial political systems (HIEAFVS) and their statelike qualities (HIEAFVM).

DEFINITIONS AND SOURCES FOR THE VARIABLES IN THE DATA SET

AFRICA	Dummy for sub-Saharan Africa.
BLCK	Log of 1 + foreign exchange black market premium. (Easterly and Levine 1997). Average of their decade averages.
BRUSSELS	Dummy for colonization by Belgium.
BUROQUAL	Measures the quality of the bureaucracy. Answers the following question on a 0-10 scale: "Assess the extent to which the bureaucracy had the strength and expertise to govern without drastic changes in policy or interruptions in government services over the following periods. Was the bureaucracy autonomous from political pressure and did it have established mechanisms for recruitment and training? Give a high rating for good bureaucratic performance and a low rating for poor performance." (ICRG data set and author's questionnaire)
CAPACITY	First principal component of POLICY (the policy index) and GOVNANCE (the governance index).
CAPSQ	Square of CAPACITY.
CIVL	Gastil index of civil liberties for the 1960–1989

period. Takes any value between 1 (very free) and 7 (no liberties). (Levine and Renelt 1992)

COMMIT Measures the state's capacity to commit to economic agents. Answers the following question on a 0-10 scale: "Assess the possibility that foreign businesses, contractors, and consultants faced the risk of a modification in a contract in the form of repudiation, postponement or scaling down (low points signify a greater likelihood of repudiation) over the given period." (ICRG data set and author's questionnaire)

CORRUPT Measures the extent of corruption in government. Answers the following question on a 0-10 scale: "Assess the extent of financial corruption in the form of demands for special payments and bribes connected with import and export licences, exchange controls, tax assessments, police protection or loans, over the given period. Include excessive patronage, nepotism, job reservations and 'favor-for-favors.'" Give a low rating for high incidence of corruption and a high rating for a country with little corruption." (ICRG data set and author's questionnaire)

COUNTRY List of countries from Table 1.1 of World Bank (1997b). Russia was treated as Soviet Union. Taiwan was added. Czech and Slovak Republics were replaced with Czechoslovakia. Germany was replaced with East and West Germany. Regional groupings as defined by the World Bank (see www.worldbank.org).

DRELIEF Sum of the episodes of debt rescheduling from 1980 to 1994. (Bruno and Easterly 1996)

ELF Index of ethnolinguistic fractionalization. Measures the probability that two randomly selected individuals belong to different ethnic groups. (Taylor and Hudson (1972), based on 1963 Soviet *Atlas Norodov Mirna;* Easterly and Levine (1997) use the same source but omit reporting about a dozen countries in their data set.)

EXPROP Measures the risk of expropriation by the government. Answers the following question on a 0-10 scale: "Assess the risk of expropriation of private foreign investments, including outright confiscation and forced nationalization (0 = highest risk, 10 = no risk at all) over the given period." (ICRG data set and author's questionnaire)

G   Average real government share of GDP (percent), 1985 international prices, starting in the year of independence to 1992. (Heston and Summers 1991)

GOVNANCE   First principal component of COMMIT, EXPROP, CORRUPT, INSTQUAL, BUROQUAL, CIVL, and HOMELANG.

GOVSQ   Square of GOVNANCE.

HIEAFVM   Mean hierarchy above the family. Refers to the number of levels of community structure above the family, ranging from stateless groupings (=1), to petty chiefdoms (=2), and up to tribal chiefdoms (=3). See entry for HIEAFVS for further discussion of relevance to this variable. (Morrison et al. 1989)

HIEAFVS   This variable is equal to the standard deviation of Morrison et al.'s (1989:53) "hierarchy above family" variable (HIEAFVM). The variable is defined as the number of levels of community structure above the family with ordinal scaling from stateless or segmentary societies (1) to petty and paramount chiefdoms (2) and tribal chiefdoms (3). According to the authors, "the greater the standard deviation, the greater the cultural pluralism" (1989:53). There are two potential problems with this approach. First, the standard deviation (or the mean) of an ordinal variable is not quite meaningful by itself since there can be no agreement as to whether the difference between 1 and 2 is equal to a difference between 2 and 3. Yet, as the authors acknowledge, this is an "approximation of an ideal measure of pluralism" (1989:40). Second, the authors equate variation in the data with pluralism in society. They use the term cultural pluralism to refer to "the extent to which national populations are divided into mutually exclusive and culturally distinctive groups" (1989:25). More specifically, they refer to ethnic pluralism as "the degree of variation in the cultural characteristics of ethnic groups in a nation"

(1989:34). Hence, whereas a country with one stateless group, one tribal group, and one kingdom would have the most heterogeneous distribution, a country with one stateless group and one kingdom would be culturally more plural in the sense that the mutual exclusion between the groups would be greater, and ethnically more plural in the sense that the variation in the data would be greater. My use of the concept of heterogeneity is similar to this idea of pluralism. What the variable really captures is the dispersion of the data, not necessarily the heterogeneity of its distribution stricto sensu.

HLEGIT   Horizontal legitimacy (as per Holsti 1996). The variable is calculated by subtracting from 1 the percentage of a country's population (expressed in decimals) that belongs to an ethnic group that was split between at least two countries by colonization (but not by migration). This variable captures the arbitrariness of colonial borders with respect to precolonial political institutions (proxied for by ethnic groups) and applies only to sub-Saharan Africa. The list of partitioned groups comes from Asiwaju (1985). The detailed table for the generation of this variable is available online at www.politics.pomona.edu/englebert.htm. A few groups were added to the list in Asiwaju (1985) when other sources provided evidence for it, in which cases the other sources are indicated. Some groups were not counted when the only connection across borders was a matter of shared language rather than shared political institutions or cultural identity (see Morrison et al. 1989, for a discussion of identity groups). This was the case, for example, of the Mossi of Burkina Faso and Ghana or the Hutu and Tutsi of Rwanda and Burundi, who lived in separate political systems before colonization and were thus not split by the colonial episode. In such cases, the sources underlying the decision not to count a group as split are indicated. In the case of the Tswana of Botswana and South Africa, only the specific kingdom of Kgatla was taken into account because it comprises the only Tswana whose state institution is split across borders (see Morton 1985). In some cases, not enough information was available to differentiate mere language from identity groups. Such instances, however, account for extremely small percentages of populations since it is the small obscure groups for which little data is available, whereas large groups are well documented. The same observations apply to a few groups for which no data was found and that can therefore be assumed to be of very small size. In case of unresolved conflict between Asiwaju (1985) and another source, Asiwaju (1985) was chosen to prevail, as it stresses "partitioned culture areas" rather than merely common languages. Ethnic population data comes from Morrison et al. (1989), Reddy (1994), Grimes (1996), CIA (1996), the Library of Congress's *Country Study Handbooks,* and other sources as indicated. The Comoro Islands, which have a heterogeneous population spread over all four of them, were split upon independence as the French retained Mayotte (Mahore), and thus they score 0 on HLE-GIT. However, it was entered as 0.0001 in the data set to allow for some specifications that take the natural log of the variable (log of 0 is impossible).

HOMELANG   Percentage of a country's population that speaks a different language at home from the national language, expressed as the midpoint of the following ranges: 0-10%, 10-25%, 25-50%, 50-75%, 75-90%, 90-100%. (Kidron and Segal 1995; Easterly and Levine 1997 for the midrange method)

HPAE   Dummy for "High-Performing Asian Economies." (World Bank 1993)

I   Average real investment share of GDP (percent), 1985 international prices, starting in the year of independence to 1992. (Heston and Summers 1991)

INC60   Natural log of the level of per capita GDP in 1960 or year of independence, whichever comes latest. Source: Heston and Summers (1991).

INC60SQ   Square of INC60.

INCLEVEL   Average per capita real GDP from 1960 or date of independence to 1992. (Heston and Summers 1991)

INDEP   Year of independence. Dates of independence are

from *Africa South of the Sahara 1995* (1994) and CIA (1996).

INSTQUAL   Measures the quality of institutions and the extent of the rule of law. Answers the following question on a 0-10 scale: "Assess the extent to which the country had sound institutions, a strong court system, and provisions for an orderly succession of power, and the extent to which citizens were willing to accept the established institutions to make and implement laws and adjudicate disputes, over the given period. This is essentially a measure of the extent of the 'rule of law.' Give a high rating for good performance and a low rating for poor performance." (ICRG data set and author's questionnaire)

JESUS   Percentage of a country's population that is Christian (Catholic and Protestant). (Taylor and Hudson 1972)

LANDLOCK   Dummy variable taking on the value 1 for a land-locked country, 0 otherwise, following Kurian's (1997) list of landlocked countries. Ethiopia, which Kurian (1997) lists as landlocked, is considered instead as having access to the sea because it still comprised Eritrea in the time frame of this study.

LANGUAGE   Estimated number of languages per million population, 1972. (Morrison et al. 1989:43)

LEGIT   Dummy variable capturing the idea of vertical legitimacy (as per Holsti 1996). The variable is built through a series of five dichotomous outcomes (see Table 6.1 and Figure 6.1). First, it takes the value 1 if a country was not colonized in modern times. If a country was colonized, it takes the value 1 if the country recovered its previous sovereignty upon independence. If the country was instead created by colonialism, but there was no human settlement before colonization, then it scores 1. Fourth, if a civilization predated colonization but it was physically eliminated or marginalized in the process of colonization, LEGIT takes on the value of 1. Finally, if the country was created by colonization and large segments of precolonial populations persist, the variable takes on the value 1 if the new state does not do severe violence to the preexisting political institutions, 0 otherwise. (Emerson 1960; Bayart 1993, 1996; Holsti 1996; Young 1988, 1994; Kurian 1997; CIA 1996; *Merriam-Webster Geographical Dictionary,* 3rd ed. 1996, *Encyclopedia Britannica;* and Geertz 1973b)

LISBON   Dummy for colonization by Portugal.

LLY   Financial depth: Ratio of liquid liabilities of the financial system to GDP. Liquid liabilities consist of currency held outside the banking system, demand and interest-bearing liabilities of banks, and non-bank financial intermediaries. Average of their decade averages. (King and Levine 1996)

LONDON   Dummy for colonization by Great Britain.

MAINLAND   Dummy variable for a country being continental or an island or group of islands (if island is shared by two or more countries, then MAINLAND = 1). (*National Geographic* Political Map of the World)

MARY   Percentage of a country's population that is Catholic. (Kurian 1997, from the Vatican's *Annuario Statistico;* Morrison et al. 1989)

MOHAMMED   Percentage of a country's population that is Muslim. (Taylor and Hudson 1972)

OECD   Dummy for OECD countries. Countries scoring 1 do not include South Korea and Mexico, which became OECD members after the period under consideration.

OPEN   Average degree of economic openness, equal to the sum of exports and imports over nominal GDP, starting with the year of independence to 1992. (Heston and Summers 1991)

PARIS   Dummy for colonization by France.

POLICY   First principal component of SCHOOL, TELPW, G, BLCK, OPEN, and LLY.

POPGROW   Average population growth rate from 1960 or date of independence to 1992. (Heston and Summers 1991)

POPSIZE   Size of total population in 1978, that is, at midperiod. (World Bank 1997b)

PRIMED   Gross primary school enrollment ratio in 1960 or at the time of independence. (Easterly et al. 1993)

RGDPCH   Growth rate of the real GDP per capita in constant dollars (Chain Index) expressed in international prices, base 1985, measured form the year of independence onward. (Heston and Summers 1991)

SECED   Gross secondary school enrollment ratio in 1960 or year of independence. (Easterly et al. 1993)

SCHOOL   Log of 1 + average year of schooling attainment (average of quinquennial values 1960–1965, 1970–1975, and 1980–1985). In order to expand sample size, I regressed Barro and Lee's variable on gross primary school enrollments (PRIMED) in 1960 and used the corresponding predicted values of their LSCHOOL variable to create SCHOOL. (Barro and Lee 1993, 1996)

SIZE   A country's total land area in square miles. (Kurian 1997)

TELPW   Log of telephones per one thousand workers. Average of their decade averages. In order to expand sample size, I regressed Easterly and Levine's variable on the average investment share of GDP (I) and used the corresponding predicted values of LTELPW. (Easterly and Levine's 1997 LTELPW)

TOTCH   Change in the natural log of terms of trade over years of available data. (Bruno and Easterly 1996)

TOTS   Standard deviation of TOTCH.

TROPICS   Approximate fraction of a country's land area that is subject to tropical climate. (Sachs and Warner 1997b, with coverage deductively expanded by author)

TRUST   Percentage of respondents who answered that most people can be trusted when asked: "Generally speaking, would you say that most people can be trusted or that you can't be too careful in dealing with people?" (Inglehart 1997)

WARCIV   Number of years between independence and 1995 during which a country experienced episode(s) of civil war, including irredenta, secession, and resistance. (calculated from appendix in Holsti 1996)

WBCODE   World Bank country codes. Codes were added for East Germany (EGE), Taiwan (TAI), and South Yemen (YES).

APPENDIX 2

Descriptive Statistics

ENTIRE SAMPLE

Variable	Observation	Mean	Standard Deviation	Minimum	Maximum
africa	212	.2358491	.4255331	0	1
blck	124	.2626639	.3370831	−.0053725	1.47433
brussels	212	.0141509	.1183926	0	1
buroqual	142	5.329836	2.43656	.6666667	10
capacity	100	−1.86e-09	.9052061	−1.644034	1.853258
capsq	100	.8112041	.8152651	.0040489	3.434563
civl	118	3.991525	1.852722	1	6.9
commit	142	6.186948	2.006105	1.59	10
corrupt	142	5.494225	2.293013	0	10
drelief	133	2.142857	3.012959	0	12
elf	135	.3881481	.2944187	0	.93
exprop	142	6.979601	1.881251	1.64	10
g	133	19.01604	7.761917	4.596667	44.21818
govnance	107	−2.70e-09	2.274603	−4.099721	4.253657
govsq	107	5.125465	5.617841	.0004287	18.0936
hieafvm	38	1.857895	.5839759	.67	3
hieafvs	38	.5031579	.3880102	0	1.49
hlegit	46	.5724804	.3212765	.0001	1
homelang	146	38.61301	38.86319	5	95
hpae	212	.0377358	.1910077	0	1
i	133	16.83214	8.821682	1.4	39.25385
inc60	133	7.390491	.8874097	5.529429	9.225327
inc60sq	133	55.40093	13.33987	30.57458	85.10667
inclevel	133	3747.523	3550.291	299.3333	14340.76
indep	189	1854.286	336.8201	−660	1993
instqual	142	5.483662	2.47145	.8333333	10
jesus	135	47.07778	39.40977	0	100
landlock	212	.1792453	.3844654	0	1
language	41	6.534146	6.984218	.1	27.7
legit	180	.6444444	.4800166	0	1
lisbon	212	.0377358	.1910077	0	1
lly	109	.3456335	.2440076	.0338825	1.502162

london |	212	.2830189	.4515317	0	1
mainland |	212	.7358491	.4419236	0	1
mary |	122	46.37541	35.66509	0	100
mohammed |	134	20.62687	33.02054	0	100
oecd |	212	.1132075	.3175963	0	1
open |	133	64.87572	41.29835	10.41067	314.4314
paris |	212	.1603774	.3678242	0	1
policy |	114	−7.45e-09	1.532695	−3.696014	4.099576
popgrow |	133	.0205745	.0105159	−.0034265	.0454424
popsize |	194	2.19e+07	8.62e+07	31400	9.56e+08
primed |	135	74.61926	35.87445	3	155
rgdpch |	133	.0177664	.0203456	−.037919	.0697063
seced |	132	22.18939	21.71085	1	86
school |	135	1.358644	.5722862	.2161401	2.640916
size |	187	275479.2	751270.6	.75	6592800
telpw |	133	3.513817	1.617221	.6847447	7.624241
totch |	53	−.0069346	.0165383	−.0751062	.0239895
tots |	53	.1017274	.0675704	.0175484	.3645823
tropics |	147	.5401361	.4765256	0	1
trust |	41	35.17073	14.82043	7	66
warciv |	212	4.915094	10.01337	0	40

AFRICAN SUBSAMPLE

Variable |	Observation	Mean	Standard Deviation	Minimum	Maximum
africa |	50	1	0	1	1
blck |	40	.3028455	.3417315	0	1.410676
brussels |	50	.06	.2398979	0	1
buroqual |	43	4.239457	1.910449	.6666667	10
capacity |	35	−.7560882	.4906742	−1.644034	.3462951
capsq |	35	.8055516	.6472525	.0040489	2.702847
civl |	39	5.423077	1.083722	2.5	6.8
commit |	43	4.943876	1.456648	1.68	8
corrupt |	43	4.384419	1.947803	0	8.71
drelief |	38	3.342105	3.078051	0	11
elf |	38	.6513158	.2470712	.04	.93
exprop |	43	5.897752	1.637699	2	9.333333
g |	44	23.85714	7.201183	11.11111	44.21818
govnance |	37	−1.640861	1.236567	−4.099721	1.300899
govsq |	37	4.180196	4.279259	.001826	16.80772
hieafvm |	38	1.857895	.5839759	.67	3
hieafvs |	38	.5031707	.3880102	0	1.49
hlegit |	46	.5724804	.3212765	.0001	1
homelang |	46	72.77174	35.90585	5	95
hpae |	50	0	0	0	0
i |	44	10.24759	6.203372	1.4	25.61667
inc60 |	44	6.668753	.5299619	5.529429	8.03722
inc60sq |	44	44.74674	7.18562	30.57458	64.59691
inclevel |	44	1123.313	877.7771	299.3333	4103.84
indep |	48	1921.083	284.512	−4	1993
instqual |	43	4.153953	1.768927	.8333333	8.33
jesus |	38	26.60526	21.72001	0	75

landlock		50	.28	.4535574	0	1
language		41	6.534146	6.984218	.1	27.7
legit		47	.212766	.4136881	0	1
lisbon		50	.1	.3030458	0	1
lly		36	.1937038	.1104143	.0338825	.5445734
london		50	.34	.4785181	0	1
mainland		50	.84	.370328	0	1
mary		45	25.51111	24.19018	0	94
mohammed		38	24.36842	28.5017	0	96
oecd		50	0	0	0	0
open		44	65.22953	31.08971	22.28576	140.0318
paris		50	.38	.4903144	0	1
policy		38	−1.37326	.9345076	−3.696014	.6667639
popgrow		44	.0270059	.0057972	.0094647	.0380539
popsize		47	7640783	1.17e+07	61710	6.69e+07
primed		40	39.475	26.14554	5	98
rgdpch		44	.0040155	.0200543	−.037919	.055944
seced		37	3.351351	4.237506	1	24
school		40	.7980066	.417086	.2480451	1.731625
size		48	195861.2	226460.2	176	966757
telpw		44	2.306716	1.137223	.6847447	5.124227
totch		10	−.0114611	.0279124	−.0751062	.0188107
tots		10	.1388389	.0618012	.043174	.2566063
tropics		49	.9142857	.2565801	0	1
trust		2	25.5	3.535534	23	28
warciv		50	6.2	10.33322	0	38

Bibliography

Achebe, Chinua. 1960. *No Longer at Ease*. New York: Fawcett Premier.

————. 1966. *A Man of the People*. London: Heinemann.

————. 1983. *The Trouble with Nigeria*. Enugu, Nigeria: Fourth Dimension.

Africa South of the Sahara 1995. 1994. London: Europa Publications Ltd.

African Development: Lessons from Asia. 1991. Proceedings of a seminar on Strategies for the Future of Africa sponsored by the U.S. Agency for International Development and Winrock International, Baltimore, Maryland, 5–7 June. Arlington, Va.: Winrock International Institute for Agricultural Development.

Alesina, Alberto. 1994. "Political Models of Macroeconomic Policy and Fiscal Reform." In Stephan Haggard and Steven Webb, eds., *Voting for Reform: Democracy, Political Liberalization, and Economic Adjustment*. New York: Oxford University Press.

Alesina, Alberto, and Roberto Perotti. 1993. "Income Distribution, Political Instability, and Investment." Working paper no. 4486 (October), National Bureau of Economic Research (NBER), Washington, D.C.

————. 1994. "The Political Economy of Growth: A Critical Survey of the Recent Literature," *The World Bank Economic Review* 8(3):351–371.

Alesina, Alberto, and Dani Rodrik. 1994. "Distributive Politics and Economic Growth," *Quarterly Journal of Economics* 109:465–490.

Alexandre, P. 1981. *Les Africains*. Paris: Lidis.

Alexandrowicz, Charles H. 1969. "New and Original States: The Issue of Reversion to Sovereignty," *International Affairs* 47 (July):465–480.

————. 1974. "The Partition of Africa by Treaty." In K. Ingham, ed., *Foreign Relations of African States*. London: Butterworths, 129–157.

Allen, Philip M. 1995. *Madagascar: Conflicts of Authority in the Great Island*. Boulder, Colo.: Westview Press.

Almond, Gabriel A., and Sidney Verba. 1963. *Civic Culture*. Princeton: Princeton University Press.

————. 1980. *The Civic Culture Revisited*. Boston: Little, Brown.

Amin, Samir. 1974. *Accumulation on a World Scale*. New York: Monthly Review Press.

Amsden, Alice. 1979. "Taiwan's Economic History: A Case of Etatisme and a Challenge to Dependency Theory," *Modern China* 5(3):341–380.

———. 1985. "The State and Taiwan's Economic Development." In P. B. Evans, D. Rueschmeyer, and T. Skocpol, eds., *Bringing the State Back In.* Cambridge: Cambridge University Press, 78–106.

Anderson, Benedict. 1983. *Imagined Communities: Reflections on the Origins and Spread of Nationalism.* London: Verso.

Apter, David. 1968. *Ghana in Transition.* New York: Atheneum.

Aron, Janine. 1997. "Political, Economic and Social Institutions: A Review of Growth Evidence (with an Africa Focus)." CSAE White paper no. 97:02, Oxford University, Centre for the Study of African Economies, Oxford.

Asiwaju, A. I., ed. 1985. *Partitioned Africans: Ethnic Relations across Africa's International Boundaries 1884–1984.* New York: St Martin's Press.

Ayittey, George B. N. 1998. *Africa in Chaos.* New York: St. Martin's Press.

Badie, Bertrand. 1992. *L'Etat importé: L'occidentalisation de l'ordre politique.* Paris: Fayard.

Badie, Bertrand, and Pierre Birnbaum. 1979. *Sociologie de l'Etat.* Paris: Grasset.

Banfield, Edward C. 1958. *The Moral Basis of a Backward Society.* Chicago: The Free Press.

Banks, Arthur S. [1979] 1994. "Cross-National Time-Series Data Archive." SUNY Binghampton (data set rereleased in 1994).

Barbour, K. M. 1961. "A Geographical Analysis of Boundaries in Inter-Tropical Africa." In K. M. Barbour and R. M. Prothero, eds., *Essays on African Population.* London: Routledge and Kegan Paul, 303–323.

Barker, Rodney. 1991. *Political Legitimacy and the State.* Oxford: Oxford University Press.

Barkindo, Bawuro M. 1985. "The Mandara Astride the Nigeria-Cameroon Boundary." In A. I. Asiwaju, ed., *Partitioned Africans . . . 1884–1984.* New York: St. Martin's Press, 29–50.

Barr, Abigail M. 1997. "Enterprise Performance and the Functional Diversity of Social Capital." CSAE White paper no. 97:24, Oxford University, Centre for the Study of African Economies, London.

Barro, Robert J. 1990. "Government Spending in a Simple Model of Endogenous Growth," *Journal of Political Economy* 98(5):S103–S125.

———. 1991. "Economic Growth in a Cross-Section of Countries," *Quarterly Journal of Economics* 106(2): 407–444.

———. 1997. *Determinants of Economic Growth: A Cross-Country Empirical Study.* Cambridge, Mass.: MIT Press.

Barro, Robert J., and Jong-Wha Lee. 1993. "International Comparisons of Educational Attainment," *Journal of Monetary Economics* 32(3):363–394.

———. 1996. "International Measures of Schooling Years and Schooling Quality," *American Economic Review Papers and Proceedings* 86(2):218–223.

Barro, Robert J., and Xavier Sala-i-Martin. 1995. *Economic Growth.* New York: McGraw-Hill.

Barth, Fredrik, ed. 1969. *Ethnic Groups and Boundaries*. Boston: Little, Brown.

Bassolet, François. 1968. *Evolution de la Haute-Volta*. Ouagadougou, Burkina Faso: Imprimerie Nationale.

Bates, Robert, ed. 1981. *Markets and States in Tropical Africa: The Political Basis of Agricultural Policies*. Berkeley: University of California Press.

———. 1983. "Modernization, Ethnic Competition, and the Rationality of Politics in Contemporary Africa." In D. Rothchild and V. A. Olorunsola, eds., *State versus Ethnic Claims: African Policy Dilemmas*. Boulder, Colo.: Westview, 152–171.

———. 1988. *Toward a Political Economy of Development: A Rational Choice Perspective*. Berkeley: University of California Press.

Bayart, Jean-François. 1993. *The State in Africa: The Politics of the Belly*. London and New York: Longman.

———. 1996. "L'Historicité de l'Etat Importé." In Jean-François Bayart, ed., *La Greffe de l'Etat*. Paris: Karthala, 11–39.

———. 1999. "The 'Social Capital' of the Felonious State or the Ruses of Political Intelligence." In J. F. Bayart, S. Ellis, and B. Hibou, eds., *The Criminalization of the State in Africa*. London: James Currey, 32–48.

Bayart, Jean-François, Stephen Ellis, and Béatrice Hibou, eds. 1999. *The Criminalization of the State in Africa*. London: James Currey.

Berman, Bruce. 1992. "Structure and Process in the Bureaucratic States of Colonial Africa." In B. Berman and J. Lonsdale, eds., *Unhappy Valley: Conflict in Kenya and Africa*. Athens: University of Ohio Press, 1:140–176.

Berman, Bruce, and John Lonsdale. 1992. *Unhappy Valley: Conflict in Kenya and Africa*. Vol. 1, *State and Class;* Vol. 2, *Violence and Ethnicity*. Athens, Ohio: University of Ohio Press.

Bertrand, Joel. 1997. "Ouganda: Des rois en République," *Afrique Contemporaine* 182 (2nd semester):16–31.

Bienen, Henry S., and Nicolas van de Walle. 1991. *Of Time and Power: Leadership Duration in the Modern World*. Stanford, Calif.: Stanford University Press.

Binet, Jacques. 1970. *Psychologie Economique Africaine: Eléments d'une Recherche Interdisciplinaire*. Paris: Payot.

Bloom, David E., and Jeffrey Sachs. 1998. "Geography, Demography, and Economic Growth in Africa." Harvard Institute for International Development. Mimeographed.

Boix, Carles, and Daniel N. Posner. 1998. "Social Capital: Explaining Its Origins and Effects on Government Performance," *British Journal of Political Science* 28(4):686–693.

Boone, Catherine. 1992. *Merchant Capital and the Roots of State Power in Senegal, 1930–1985*. Cambridge: Cambridge University Press.

———. 1994. "States and Ruling Classes in Postcolonial Africa: The Enduring Contradictions of Power." In J. Migdal, A. Kohli and V. Shue, eds., *State Power and Social Forces*. Cambridge: Cambridge University Press, 108–139.

———. 1996. "Social Structure, Rules, Discourse: Theoretical Competitions in Comparative Politics." Paper prepared for the 1996 annual meeting of the American Political Science Association, 29 August–1 September, San Francisco.

———. 1998. "'Empirical Statehood' and Reconfiguration of Political Order." In L. Villalón and P. Huxtable, eds., *The African State at a Critical Juncture*. Boulder, Colo.: Lynne Rienner, 129–142.

Booth, Alan R. 1983. *Swaziland: Tradition and Change in a Southern African Kingdom*. Boulder, Colo.: Westview Press.

Bourges, Hervé, and Claude Wauthier. 1979. *Les 50 Afriques*. 2 vols. Paris: Seuil.

Bratton, Michael. 1994. "Civil Society and Political Transitions in Africa." In J. Harbeson, D. Rothchild, and N. Chazan, eds., *Civil Society and the State in Africa*. Boulder, Colo.: Lynne Rienner, 51–81.

Bratton, Michael, and Nicolas van de Walle. 1994. "Neopatrimonial Regimes and Political Transitions in Africa," *World Politics* 46(July):453–489.

———. 1997. *Democratic Experiments in Africa: Regime Transitions in Comparative Perspective*. Cambridge: Cambridge University Press.

Brautigam, Deborah. 1991. "Governance and Economy: A Review." Working paper WPS 815 (December), The World Bank, Policy and Review Department, Washington, D.C.

———. 1996. "State Capacity and Effective Governance." In B. Ndulu and N. van de Walle, eds., *Agenda for Africa's Economic Renewal*. Washington, D.C.: Overseas Development Council, 81–108.

———. 1997. "Substituting for the State: Institutions and Industrial Development in Eastern Nigeria," *World Development* 25(7):1063–1080.

———. 1999. "The 'Mauritius Miracle': Democracy, Institutions and Economic Policy." In Richard Joseph, ed., *State, Conflict and Democracy in Africa*. Boulder, Colo.: Lynne Rienner, 137–162.

Breuilly, John. 1982. *Nationalism and the State*. New York: St. Martin's Press.

Brown, Mervyn. 1995. "Madagascar: Recent History." In *Africa South of the Sahara 1995*. London: Europa Publications, 546–550.

Brownlie, Ian. 1979. *African Boundaries: A Legal and Diplomatic Encyclopaedia*. London: C. Hurst & Company; Berkeley and Los Angeles: University of California Press.

Bruno, Michael, and William Easterly. 1996. "Inflation's Children: Tales of Crises That Beget Reforms," *American Economic Review Papers and Proceedings* 86(2):213–217.

Callaghy, Thomas. 1984. *The State-Society Struggle: Zaire in Comparative Perspective*. New York: Columbia University Press.

Callaghy, Thomas, and John Ravenhill, eds. 1993. *Hemmed In: Responses to Africa's Economic Decline*. New York: Columbia University Press.

Campos, Jose E., and Hilton L. Root. 1996. *The Key to the Asian Miracle: Making Shared Growth Credible*. Washington, D.C.: Brookings Institution.

Campos, Nauro F., and Jeffrey B. Nugent. 1997. "In Instability's Eye." Paper prepared for the 72nd Annual Western Economic Association International Conference, 9–13 July, Seattle. Mimeographed draft.

Central Intelligence Agency (CIA). 1996. *World Factbook 1996.* Washington, D.C.: CIA. Available online http://www.odci.gov/cia/ publications/nsolo/wfb-all.htm).

Chabal, Patrick, ed. 1986. *Political Domination in Africa.* Cambridge: Cambridge University Press.

Chilcote, Ronald. 1994. *Theories of Comparative Politics: The Search for a Paradigm Reconsidered.* Boulder, Colo.: Westview Press.

Claessen, Henri J. M. 1998. "Lawgiving and the Administration of Justice in Some African and Other Early States," *African Studies Quarterly* 2(3). Available online http://web.africa.ufl.edu/asq/v2/v2i3a4.htm.

Clague, Christopher, ed. 1997. *Institutions and Economic Development: Growth and Governance in Less-Developed and Post-Socialist Countries.* Baltimore: Johns Hopkins University Press.

Clague, Christopher, Philip Keefer, Steve Knack, and Mancur Olson. 1996. "Property and Contract Rights in Autocracies and Democracies," *Journal of Economic Growth* 1 (June):243–276.

Clapham, Christopher. 1982. "Clientelism and the State." In C. Clapham, ed., *Private Patronage and Public Power: Political Clientelism in the Modern State.* New York: St Martin's Press, 1–35.

———. 1996. *Africa and the International System: The Politics of State Survival.* Cambridge: Cambridge University Press.

Coleman, James S. 1990. *Foundations of Social Theory.* Cambridge: Harvard University Press, Belknap Press.

Coleman, James Smoot, and Carl Rosberg, eds. 1964. *Political Parties and National Integration in Tropical Africa.* Berkeley and Los Angeles: University of California Press.

Collier, Paul. 1996. "The Role of the State in Economic Development: Cross Regional Experiences." Oxford University, Centre for the Study of African Economies. Paper presented at the plenary sessions of the African Economic Research Consortium, December, Nairobi.

———. 1998a. "The Political Economy of Ethnicity." Paper presented at the Annual Bank Conference on Development Economics, 20–21 April, Washington, D.C.: The World Bank. Mimeographed.

———. 1998b. "The Economics of Civil War." Paper presented at the CREDIT Tenth Anniversary Conference, University of Nottingham, 17 September, Nottingham, England.

———. 1998c. "Social Capital and Poverty." Social Capital Initiative (SCI) working paper no. 4 (December). Washington, D.C.: World Bank.

Collier, Paul, and Jan Willem Gunning. 1997. "Explaining African Economic Performance." Working paper WPS/97-2.1, Oxford University, Centre for the Study of African Economies.

Collier, Paul, and Anke Hoeffler. 1998. "The Coming Anarchy? The Global and Regional Incidence of Civil War." Working paper 98:01, Oxford University, Centre for the Study of African Economies.

Connor, Walker. 1973. "The Politics of Ethnonationalism," *Journal of International Affairs* 27(January):1–21.

Coquery-Vidrovitch, Catherine. 1992. *L'Afrique Occidentale au temps des Français: colonisateurs et colonisés, c. 1860–1960.* Paris: La Découverte.

Cornell, Stephen, and Joseph P. Kalt. 1995. "Where Does Economic Development Really Come From? Constitutional Rule among the Contemporary Sioux and Apache," *Economic Inquiry* 33(3):402–426.

Craig, Gordon A. 1972. *Europe, 1815–1914.* Hinsdale, Ill.: Dryden Press.

Dale, Richard. 1995. *Botswana's Search for Autonomy in Southern Africa.* Westport, Conn.: Greenwood Press.

Davidson, Basil. 1992. *The Black Man's Burden. Africa and the Curse of the Nation-State.* New York: Times Books.

Decalo, Samuel. 1991. *Coups and Army Rule in Africa.* New Haven: Yale University Press.

Deng, Francis. 1996. "These Borders Are Not Sacred," *Washington Post*, 20 December.

———. 1998. "African Policy Agenda: A Framework for Global Partnership." In F. Deng and T. Lyons, eds., *African Reckoning.* Washington, D.C.: Brookings Institution Press, 136–175.

Deng, Francis, and Terrence Lyons. 1998. *African Reckoning: A Quest for Good Governance.* Washington, D.C.: Brookings Institution Press.

Deng, Francis, Sadikiel Kimaro, Terrence Lyons, Donald Rothchild, and I. William Zartman, eds. 1996. *Sovereignty as Responsibility: Conflict Management in Africa.* Washington, D.C.: Brookings Institution Press.

De Soto, Hernando. 1989. *The Other Path: The Invisible Revolution in the Third World.* New York: Perennial Library.

Dia, Mamadou. 1993. *A Governance Approach to Civil Service Reform in Sub-Saharan Africa.* World Bank Technical paper 225. Washington, D.C.: The World Bank.

———. 1996. *Africa's Management in the 1990s and Beyond: Reconciling Indigenous and Transplanted Institutions.* Washington, D.C.: The World Bank.

Du Toit, Pierre. 1995. *State Building and Democracy in Southern Africa: Botswana, Zimbabwe, and South Africa.* Washington, D.C.: United States Institute of Peace Press.

Easterly, William. 1994. "Economic Stagnation, Fixed Factors, and Policy Thresholds," *Journal of Monetary Economics* 33(3):525–557.

Easterly, William, and Ross Levine. 1997. "Africa's Growth Tragedy: Policies and Ethnic Divisions," *Quarterly Journal of Economics* 112(4) (November):1203–1250.

Easterly, William, and Sergio Rebelo. 1993. "Fiscal Policy and Growth: An Empirical Investigation," *Journal of Monetary Economics* 32(2):417–458.

Easterly, William, Michael Kremer, Lant Pritchett, and Lawrence H. Summers. 1993. "Good Policy or Good Luck? Country Growth Performance and Temporary Shocks," *Journal of Monetary Economics* 32(2):459–483.

Easton, David. 1957. "An Approach to the Analysis of Political Systems," *World Politics* 9(3):383–400.

Eckstein, Harry. 1961. "A Theory of Stable Democracy." Research monograph no. 10, Center of International Studies, Princeton University.

———. 1966. *Division and Cohesion in Democracy: A Study of Norway.* Princeton: Princeton University Press.

———. 1979. "Support for Regimes: Theories and Tests." Research monograph no. 44, Center of International Studies, Princeton University.

———. 1980. *The Natural History of Congruence Theory.* Monograph Series in World Affairs, vol. 18. Denver, Colo.: Graduate School of International Studies, University of Denver.

Economist, The. 1996. "A Provincial Gem," 27 April, 46–47.

———. 1997. "Africa's Bizarre Borders," 25 January, 17.

Economist Intelligence Unit. 1994. *Zaire: Country Profile.* London: Economist Intelligence Unit.

———. 1995. *Country Report: Zambia, Zaire.* 2nd quarter. London: Economist Intelligence Unit.

———. 1998. *Country Report: Zambia, Zaire.* 1st quarter. London: Economist Intelligence Unit.

Eggertsson, Thráinn. 1990. *Economic Behavior and Institutions.* Cambridge: Cambridge University Press.

Ekeh, Peter. 1975. "Colonialism and the Two Publics in Africa: A Theoretical Statement," *Comparative Studies in Society and History* 17(1):91–112.

Emerson, Rupert. 1960. *From Empire to Nation: The Rise and Self-Assertion of Asian and African Peoples.* Cambridge: Harvard University Press.

———. 1963. "Nation-Building in Africa." In Karl W. Deutsch and William J. Foltz, eds., *Nation-Building.* New York: Atherton Press, 95–116.

Englebert, Pierre. 1996. *Burkina Faso: Unsteady Statehood in West Africa.* Boulder, Colo.: Westview Press.

———. 1997. "The Contemporary African State: Neither African, Nor State," *Third World Quarterly* 18(4): 767–775.

Etounga-Manguellé, Daniel. 1990. *L'Afrique a-t-elle besoin d'un programme d'ajustement culturel?* Ivry-sur-Seine, France: Editions Nouvelles du Sud.

Evans, Peter. 1989. "Predatory, Developmental, and Other Apparatuses: A Comparative Political Economy Perspective on the Third World State," *Sociological Forum* 4(4):561–587.

———. 1995. *Embedded Autonomy: States and Industrial Transformation.* Princeton: Princeton University Press.

———. 1996a. "Introduction: Development Strategies across the Public-Private Divide," *World Development* 24(6):1033–1037.

———. 1996b. "Government Action, Social Capital and Development: Reviewing the Evidence on Synergy," *World Development* 24(6):1119–1132.

Evans, Peter, Dietrich Rueschmeyer, and Theda Skocpol, eds. 1985. *Bringing the State Back In.* Cambridge: Cambridge University Press.

Fafchamps, Marcel. 1992. "Solidarity Networks in Preindustrial Societies: Rational Peasants with a Moral Economy," *Economic Development and Cultural Change* 41(1):147–174.

Fanon, Frantz. 1967. *Black Skin, White Masks.* New York: Grove Press.

Fearon, James D., and David D. Laitin. 1996. "Explaining Interethnic Cooperation," *American Political Science Review* 90(4):715–735.

Fedderke, Johannes, and Robert Klitgaard. 1998. "Economic Growth and

Social Indicators: An Exploratory Analysis," *Economic Development and Cultural Change* 46(3):455–489.

Findlay, Ronald, and John D. Wilson. 1984. "The Political Economy of the Leviathan." Seminar paper no. 285, Institute for International Studies, Stockholm.

Fischer, Stanley. 1993. "The Role of Macroeconomic Factors in Growth," *Journal of Monetary Economics* 32 (December):485–512.

Fiske, Alan P. 1991. *Structures of Social Life. The Four Elementary Forms of Human Relations: Communal Sharing, Authority Ranking, Equality Matching, Market Pricing.* New York: Free Press.

Foltz, William J. 1973. "Political Boundaries and Political Competition in Tropical Africa." In S. N. Eisenstadt and Stein Rokkan, eds., *Building States and Nations: Analyses by Region.* Vol. 2. Beverly Hills, Calif.: Sage Publications, 357–383.

Fortes, M., and E. E. Evans-Pritchard. 1940. *African Political Systems.* Oxford: Oxford University Press.

Foy, Colm. 1988. *Cape Verde: Politics, Economics and Society.* London and New York: Pinter Publishers.

French, Howard. 1996. "A Neglected Region Loosens Ties to Zaire." *New York Times,* 18 September, A1–A4.

Fukuyama, Francis. 1995. *Trust: The Social Virtues and the Creation of Prosperity.* New York: Free Press.

———. 1997. "Social Capital: The 1997 Tanner Lectures." Brasence College, Oxford University. Mimeographed.

Gambetta, Diego, ed. 1988. *Trust: Making and Breaking Cooperative Relations.* London: Blackwell.

Geertz, Clifford. 1973a. "After the Revolution: The Fate of Nationalism in the New States." In *The Interpretation of Cultures.* New York: Basic Books, 234–254.

———. 1973b. "The Integrative Revolution: Primordial Sentiments and Civil Politics in the New States." In Clifford Geertz, *The Interpretation of Cultures.* New York: Basic Books, 255–310.

———. 1973c. "The Politics of Meaning." In Clifford Geertz, *The Interpretation of Cultures.* New York: Basic Books, 311–326.

———. 1983. *Local Knowledge: Further Essays in Interpretive Anthropology.* New York: Basic Books.

Gellar, Sheldon. 1973. "State-Building and Nation-Building in West Africa." In S. N. Eisenstadt and Stein Rokkan, eds., *Building States and Nations: Analyses by Region.* Vol. 2. Beverly Hills, Calif.: Sage Publications, 384–426.

Grabowski, Richard. 1994. "The Successful Developmental State: Where Does It Come From?" *World Development* 22(3):413–422.

Granovetter, Mark. 1985. "Economic Action and Social Structure: The Problem of Embeddedness," *American Journal of Sociology* 91(3):481–510.

Gray, Christopher. 1995. "Territoriality, Ethnicity and Colonial Rule in Southern Gabon 1850–1960." Ph.D. diss., Indiana University.

Greene, William, H. 1993. *Econometric Analysis.* New York: Macmillan.

Grimes, Barbara F., ed. 1996. *Ethnologue.* 13th ed. Dallas, Tex: Summer Institute of Linguistics. Available online www.sil.org/ethnologue.

Grootaert, Christiaan. 1998. "Social Capital: The Missing Link?" SCI working paper no. 3 (April). Washington, D.C.: World Bank.

Haggard, Stephan. 1990. *Pathways from the Periphery: The Politics of Growth in the Newly Industrializing Countries.* Ithaca and London: Cornell University Press.

Hall, John A., ed. 1986. *States in History.* New York: Basil Blackwell.

Hall, Robert, and Charles Jones. 1997. "Levels of Economic Activity across Countries," *American Economic Review Papers and Proceedings* 87(2):173–177.

Harbeson, John W., Donald Rothchild, and Naomi Chazan, eds. 1994. *Civil Society and the State in Africa.* Boulder, Colo.: Lynne Rienner Publishers.

Harrison, S. 1956. "The Challenge to Indian Nationalism." *Foreign Affairs* 34 (April). Cited in Clifford Geertz, *The Interpretation of Cultures* (New York: Basic Books, 1973), 256.

Harvey, Charles. 1992. "Botswana: Is the Economic Miracle Over?" *Journal of African Economies* 1(3):335–368.

Helliwell, John F. 1994. "Empirical Linkages Between Democracy and Economic Growth," *British Journal of Political Science* 24 (April):225–248.

———. 1996. "Economic Growth and Social Capital in Asia." Working paper no. 5470, National Bureau of Economic Research.

Helliwell, John F., and Robert Putnam. 1995. "Social Capital and Economic Growth in Italy," *Eastern Economic Journal* 21(3):295–307.

Herbst, Jeffrey. 1989. "The Creation and Maintenance of National Boundaries in Africa," *International Organization* 43(4):673–692.

———. 1990. "War and the State in Africa," *International Security* 14(4):117–139.

———. 1996. "Responding to State Failure in Africa," *International Security* 21(3) (Winter):120–144.

Heston, Alan, and Robert Summers. 1991. "The Penn World Table (Mark 5): An Expanded Set of International Comparisons, 1950–1988," *Quarterly Journal of Economics* 106(2):327–368.

Hirschman, Albert O. 1958. *The Strategy of Economic Development.* New Haven: Yale University Press.

———. 1970. *Exit, Voice and Loyalty: Responses to Decline in Firms, Organizations, and States.* Cambridge: Harvard University Press.

Hodges, Tony, and Malyn Newitt. 1988. *São Tomé and Principe: From Plantation Colony to Microstate.* Boulder, Colo.: Westview Press.

Holm, John. 1993. "Political Culture and Democracy: A Study of Mass Participation in Botswana." In Stephen Stedman, ed., *Botswana: the Political Economy of Democratic Development.* Boulder, Colo.: Lynne Rienner, 91-112.

Holsti, Kalevi J. 1996. *The State, War, and the State of War.* Cambridge: Cambridge University Press.

Horowitz, Donald L. 1985. *Ethnic Groups in Conflict.* Berkeley: University of California Press.

Humphrey, John, and Hubert Schmitz. 1996. "Trust and Economic Development," Institute for Development Studies discussion paper 355 (August), Sussex, UK.

Hyden, Goran. 1980. *Beyond Ujamaa in Tanzania: Underdevelopment and an Uncaptured Peasantry.* London: Heinemann Educational.
———. 1983a. "Problems and Prospects of State Coherence." In D. Rothchild and V. A. Olorunsola, *State versus Ethnic Claims: African Policy Dilemmas.* Boulder, Colo.: Westview Press, 67–84.
———. 1983b. *No Shortcuts to Progress.* London: Heinemann.
———. 1990. "The Changing Context of Institutional Development in Sub-Saharan Africa." In World Bank 1990a, 43–59.
Hyden, Goran, and Michael Bratton, eds. 1992. *Governance and Politics in Africa.* Boulder, Colo.: Lynne Rienner.
Inglehart, Ronald. 1997. *Modernization and Postmodernization: Cultural, Economic and Political Change in 43 Societies.* Princeton: Princeton University Press.
International Monetary Fund. 1999. "Second-Generation Reforms Call for Varied Approaches to Institution Building and Growth," *IMF Survey* 28(22) 22 November 375–37.
Isaksen, Jan. 1981. *Macroeconomic Management and Bureaucracy: The Case of Botswana.* Research report no. 59. Uppsala, Sweden: Scandinavian Institute of African Studies.
Jackman, Robert W. 1993. *Power without Force: The Political Capacity of Nation-States.* Ann Arbor: University of Michigan Press.
Jackson, Robert H. 1990. *Quasi-States: Sovereignty, International Relations and the Third World.* Cambridge: Cambridge University Press.
Jackson, Robert H., and Carl G. Rosberg. 1982a. "Why Africa's Weak States Persist: The Empirical and the Juridical in Statehood," *World Politics* 35(1):1–24.
———. 1982b. *Personal Rule in Black Africa: Prince, Autocrat, Prophet, Tyrant.* Berkeley: University of California Press.
———. 1985. "The Marginality of African States." In Gwendolin M. Carter and Patrick O'Meara, eds., *African Independence. The First Twenty-Five Years.* Bloomington: Indiana University Press, 45–70.
———. 1986. "Sovereignty and Underdevelopment: Juridical Statehood in the African Crisis," *Journal of Modern African Studies* 24(1):1–31.
Jeune Afrique (Paris). 1998. 8–14 December.
Johnson, Chalmers. 1982. *MITI and the Japanese Miracle.* Stanford: Stanford University Press.
Jones, Charles. 1998. *Introduction to Economic Growth.* New York: W. W. Norton and Company.
Jones, Eric L. 1981. *The European Miracle: Environments, Economies and Geopolitics in the History of Europe and Asia.* Cambridge: Cambridge University Press.
Joseph, Richard. 1987. *Democracy and Prebendal Politics in Nigeria: The Rise and Fall of the Second Republic.* Cambridge: Cambridge University Press.
———. 1997. "Correspondence: Responding to State Failure in Africa," *International Security* 22(2):175–181.
———, ed. 1999. *State, Conflict and Democracy in Africa.* Boulder, Colo.: Lynne Rienner Publishers.
Kaplan, Robert. 1994. "The Coming Anarchy," *Atlantic Monthly* 273(2):44–76.

Keefer, Philip, and Stephen Knack. 1995a. "Institutions and Economic Performance: Cross-Country Tests Using Alternative Institutional Measures," *Economics and Politics* 7(3):207–227.

———. 1995b. "Polarization, Property Rights and the Links between Inequality and Growth." Working paper no. 153, Center for Institutional Reform and the Informal Sector, University of Maryland at College Park.

———. 1997. "Does Social Capital Have an Economic Payoff? A Cross-Country Investigation," *Quarterly Journal of Economics* 112(4):1251–1288.

Kennedy, Peter. 1992. *A Guide to Econometrics.* Cambridge, Mass.: MIT Press.

Kevane, Michael, and Pierre Englebert. 1999. "A Developmental State without Growth: Explaining the Paradox of Burkina Faso in a Comparative Perspective." In Karl Wolmuth, Hans H. Bass, Frank Messner, eds., *Good Governance and Economic Development.* Hamburg: Lit Verlag; New Brunswick, N.J.: Transaction Publishers, 259–285.

Keynes, John Maynard. 1953. *The General Theory of Employment, Interest and Money.* San Diego, Calif.: Harvest/HBJ Books.

Kidron, Michael, and Ronald Segal. 1995. *The State of the World Atlas.* London: Penguin Books.

King, Gary, Robert O. Keohane, and Sidney Verba. 1994. *Designing Social Inquiry: Scientific Inference in Qualitative Research.* Princeton: Princeton University Press.

King, Robert, and Ross Levine. 1993. "Finance, Entrepreneurship and Growth: Theory and Evidence," *Journal of Monetary Economics* 32:513–542.

Krueger, Anne. 1974. "The Political Economy of the Rent-Seeking Society," *American Economic Review* 64(2):291–303.

Kurian, George Thomas. 1991. *The New Book of World Rankings.* 3rd ed., updated by James Marti. New York and Oxford: Facts on File.

———. 1997. *The Illustrated Book of World Rankings.* Armonk, N.Y.: M. E. Sharpe.

Lancaster, Carol. 1993. "Governance and Development: The Views from Washington," *IDS Bulletin* 24(1):9–15.

La Porta, Raphael, Florencio Lopez-de-Silanes, Andrei Shleifer, and Robert Vishny. 1997. "Trust in Large Organizations," *American Economic Review Papers and Proceedings* 87(2):333–338.

Leftwich, Adrian. 1994. "Governance, the State and the Politics of Development," *Development and Change* 25(2):363–386.

Lemarchand, René. 1964a. *Political Awakening in the Belgian Congo.* Berkeley: University of California Press.

———. 1964b. "Congo (Léopoldville)." In J. Coleman and C. Rosberg, eds., *Political Parties and National Integration in Tropical Africa.* Berkeley and Los Angeles: University of California Press, 560–596.

———. 1970. *Rwanda and Burundi.* New York: Praeger Publishers.

———. 1983. "The State and Society in Africa: Ethnic Stratification and Restratification in Historical and Comparative Perspective." In D. Rothchild and V. A. Olorunsola, eds., *State versus Ethnic Claims: African Policy Dilemmas.* Boulder, Colo.: Westview Press, 44–66.

———. 1994. *Burundi: Ethnocide as Discourse and Practice*. Cambridge: Cambridge University Press.

Leslie, Winsome J. 1993. *Zaire: Continuity and Political Change in an Oppressive State*. Boulder, Colo.: Westview Press.

Levine, Ross, and David Renelt. 1992. "A Sensitivity Analysis of Cross-Country Growth Regressions," *American Economic Review* 82(4):942–963.

Le Vine, Victor. 1980. "African Patrimonial Regimes in Comparative Perspective," *Journal of Modern African Studies* 18(4):657–673.

Lewis, Peter M. 1996. "Economic Reform and Political Transition in Africa: The Quest for a Politics of Development," *World Politics* 49(1):92–129.

Lewis, Stephen R. 1993. "Policymaking and Economic Performance: Botswana in Comparative Perspective." In Stephen Stedman, ed., *Botswana: The Political Economy of Democratic Development*. Boulder, Colo.: Lynne Rienner, 11–25.

Lian, Brad, and John R. Oneal. 1997. "Cultural Diversity and Economic Development: A Cross-National Study of 98 Countries, 1960–1985," *Economic Development and Cultural Change* 46(1):61–77.

Library of Congress. Various years. *Country Studies*. Area Handbook Series. Washington, D.C.: Library of Congress.

———. 1983. *Zimbabwe: A Country Study*. Area Handbook Series. Washington, D.C.: Library of Congress.

Liebenow, J. Gus. 1987. *Liberia: The Quest for Democracy*. Bloomington: Indiana University Press.

Lin, Justin Yifu, and Jeffrey B. Nugent. 1994. "Institutions and Economic Development." In *Handbook of Development Economics*. Vol. 3. Amsterdam: Elsevier, 230–237.

Lipset, Seymour Martin. 1981. *Political Man: The Social Bases of Politics*. Baltimore: Johns Hopkins University Press.

Lipton, Michael. 1977. *Why Poor People Stay Poor: Urban Bias in World Development*. Cambridge: Harvard University Press.

Lofchie, Michael F. 1975. "Political and Economic Origins of African Hunger," *Journal of Modern African Studies* 13(4): 551–567.

Lonsdale, John. 1981. "States and Social Processes in Africa: A Historiographical Survey," *African Studies Review* 24(2/3):139–225.

Loury, Glenn. 1977. "A Dynamic Theory of Racial Income Differences." In P. A. Wallace and A. Le Mund, eds., *Women, Minorities and Employment Discrimination*. Lexington, Mass.: Lexington Books.

Lucas, Robert. 1988. "On the Mechanics of Economic Development," *Journal of Monetary Economics* 22(1):3–42.

Lyons, Terrence. 1998. "Can Neighbors Help? Regional Actors and African Conflict Management." In F. Deng and T. Lyons, eds., *African Reckoning: A Quest for Good Governance*. Washington, D.C.: Brookings Institution Press, 67–99.

Lyons, Terrence, and Ahmed I. Samatar. 1995. *Somalia: State Collapse, Multilateral Intervention, and Strategies for Political Reconstruction*. Washington, D.C.: The Brookings Institution.

McGaffey, Janet. 1987. *Entrepreneurs and Parasites: The Struggle for Indigenous Capitalism in Zaire*. Cambridge: Cambridge University Press.

_____. 1994. "Civil Society in Zaire: Hidden Resistance and the Use of Personal Ties in Class Struggle." In J. W. Harbeson, D. Rothchild, and N. Chazan, eds., *Civil Society and the State in Africa*. Boulder, Colo.: Lynne Rienner, 169–189.

Maddala, G. S. 1983. *Limited-Dependent and Qualitative Variables in Econometrics*. Cambridge: Cambridge University Press.

Mamdani, Mahmood. 1996. *Citizens and Subjects. Contemporary Africa and the Legacy of Late Colonialism*. Princeton: Princeton University Press.

Mann, Michael. 1986. "The Autonomous Power of the State: Its Origins, Mechanisms and Results." In John A. Hall, ed., *States in History*. New York: Basil Blackwell, 109–136.

Matthews, Graham. 1995. "Swaziland: Economy." In *Africa: South of the Sahara 1995*. London: Europa Publications Ltd.

Mauro, Paolo. 1995. "Corruption and Growth," *Quarterly Journal of Economics* 110(3):681–712.

Maylam, Paul. 1980. *Rhodes, the Tswana, and the British: Colonialism, Collaboration, and Conflict in the Bechuanaland Protectorate, 1885–1899*. Westport, Conn.: Greenwood Press.

Mazrui, Ali A. 1983. "Francophone Nations and English-Speaking States: Imperial Ethnicity and African Political Formations." In D. Rothchild and V. A. Olorunsola, eds., *State versus Ethnic Claims: African Policy Dilemmas*. Boulder, Colo.: Westview Press, 25–43.

Mazrui, Ali A., and Michael Tidy. 1984. *Nationalism and New States in Africa*. London: Heinemann.

Mbembe, Achille. 1990. "Pouvoir, violence et accumulation," *Politique Africaine* 39(24):7–24.

Médard, Jean-François. 1982. "L'Etat sous-développé en Afrique noire: clientélisme politique ou néo-patrimonialisme?" Travaux et documents no. 1, Centre d'Etudes d'Afrique Noire, Institut d'Etudes Politiques, Bordeaux, France.

_____, ed. 1991. *Etats d'Afrique noire: formations, mécanismes et crise*. Paris: Karthala.

Meisenhelder, Thomas. 1997. "The Developmental State in Mauritius," *Journal of Modern African Studies* 35(2):279–297.

Migdal, Joel. 1988. *Strong Societies and Weak States: State-Society Relations and State Capabilities in the Third World*. Princeton: Princeton University Press.

Migdal, Joel, Atul Kohli, and Vivien Shue, eds. 1994. *State Power and Social Forces*. Cambridge: Cambridge University Press.

Monga, Célestin. 1998. *The Anthropology of Anger: Civil Society and Democracy in Africa*. Boulder, Colo.: Lynne Rienner Publishers.

Moore, Mick. 1993. "Declining to Learn from the East? The World Bank on 'Governance and Development,'" *IDS Bulletin* 24(1):39–50.

Morris, Stephen, and Stephen Coate. 1995. "On the Form of Transfers to Special Interests," *Journal of Political Economy* 103(6):1210–1235.

Morrison, Donald, Robert Mitchell, and John Paden. 1989. *Black Africa: A Comparative Handbook*. New York: Paragon House.

Morrison, D., R. Mitchell, J. Paden, and H. Stevenson. 1972. *Black Africa: A Comparative Handbook*. New York: The Free Press.

Morrison, J. Stephen. 1987. "Developmental Optimism and State Failure in Africa: How to Understand Botswana's Relative Success?" Ph.D. diss., University of Wisconsin, Madison.

———. 1993. "Botswana's Formative Late Colonial Experiences." In S. Stedman, ed., *Botswana: The Political Economy of Democratic Development.* Boulder, Colo.: Lynne Rienner, 27–49.

Morton, R. F. 1985. "Chiefs and Ethnic Unity in Two Colonial Worlds: The Bakgatla Baga Kgalefa of the Bechuanaland Protectorate and the Transvaal, 1872–1966." In A. I. Asiwaju, ed., *Partitioned Africans . . 1884–1984.* New York: St. Martin's Press, 127–153.

Mukyala-Makiika, Rebecca. 1998. "Traditional Leaders and Decentralisation." In Apolo Nsibambi, ed., *Decentralisation and Civil Society in Uganda: The Quest for Good Governance.* Kampala: Fountain Publishers, 96–109.

Munro, William A. 1967. *Ethnographic Atlas.* Pittsburgh, Pa.: University of Pittsburgh Press.

———. 1995. "Building the Post-Colonial State: Villagization and Resource Management in Zimbabwe," *Politics and Society* 23(1):107–140.

Murdock, George P. 1959. *Africa: Its People and Their Culture History.* New York: McGraw-Hill Book Company.

Naipaul, V. S. *A Bend in the River.* New York: Knopf.

Narayan, Deepa, and Lant Pritchett. 1997. "Cents and Sociability: Household Income and Social Capital in Rural Tanzania." World Bank, 6 February. Mimeographed.

National Bureau of Economic Research (NBER). 1994. *Penn World Tables 5.6.* Washington, D.C.: NBER. Available online www.nber.org.

Ndulu, Benno J., and Stephen A. O'Connell. 1999. "Governance and Growth in Sub-Saharan Africa," *Journal of Economic Perspectives* 13(3):41–66.

Ndulu, Benno J., and Nicolas van de Walle. 1996. "Africa's Economic Renewal: From Consensus to Strategy." In Benno Ndulu and Nicolas van de Walle, eds., *Agenda for Africa's Economic Renewal.* Washington, D.C.: Overseas Development Council, 3–31.

Newitt, Malyn. 1984. *The Comoro Islands: Struggle against Dependency in the Indian Ocean.* Boulder, Colo.: Westview Press; London: Gower.

North, Douglass C. 1981. *Structure and Change in Economic History.* New York: W. W. Norton and Company.

Nsibambi, Apolo R. 1994. "The Restoration of Traditional Rulers." In Holger Bernt Hansen and Michael Twaddle, eds., *From Chaos to Order: The Politics of Constitution-Making in Uganda.* Kampala: Fountain Publishers; London: James Currey.

Nugent, Jeffrey B. 1997. "Institutions, Markets and Developmental Outcomes." Paper presented at the World Bank Conference on Evaluation and Development: The Institutional Dimension, 1–2 April, Washington, D.C.

Nugent, Paul. 1996. "Arbitrary Lines and the People's Minds: A Dissenting View on Colonial Boundaries in West Africa." In P. Nugent and A. I. Asiwaju, eds., *African Boundaries: Barriors, Conduits and Opportunities.* London: Pinter, 35–67.

Nugent, Paul, and A. I. Asiwaju, eds. 1996. *African Boundaries: Barriers, Conduits and Opportunities*. London: Pinter.

Ofcansky, Thomas. 1996. *Uganda: Tarnished Pearl of Africa*. Boulder, Colo.: Westview Press.

Ojo, Oladeji, and Temitope Oshikoya. 1995. "Determinants of Long-Term Growth: Some African Results," *Journal of African Economies* 4(2):163–191.

Olson, Mancur. 1970. *The Logic of Collective Action: Public Goods and the Theory of Groups*. Cambridge: Harvard University Press.

———. 1982. *The Rise and Decline of Nations: Economic Growth, Stagflation, and Social Rigidities*. New Haven and London: Yale University Press.

———. 1987. "Diseconomies of Scale and Development," *Cato Journal* 7(1):77–98.

———. 1993. "Dictatorship, Democracy, and Development," *American Political Science Review* 87(3):567–576.

Organization of African Unity. 1980. *Lagos Plan of Action for the Economic Development of Africa 1980–2000*. Geneva: International Institute for Labour Studies.

O'Sullivan, Meghan. 1998. "Identity and Institutions in Ethnic Conflict: The Muslim Minority of Sri Lanka." Ph.D. diss., Oxford University, England.

Ottenberg, Simon, ed. 1960. *Cultures and Societies of Africa*. New York: Random House.

Ouédraogo, Bernard L. 1990. *Entraide villageoise et développement: groupements paysans au Burkina Faso*. Paris: L'Harmattan.

Pabanel, Jean-Pierre. 1991. "Le Burundi: un Etat d'origine traditionelle." In Jean-François Médard, ed., *Etats d'Afrique noire*. Paris: Karthala, 277–290.

Packenham, Thomas. 1991. *The Scramble for Africa*. New York: Random House.

Picard, Louis. 1987. *The Politics of Development in Botswana: A Model for Success?* Boulder, Colo.: Lynne Rienner.

Poirson, Hélène. 1998. "Economic Security, Private Investment, and Growth in Developing Countries." Working paper WP/98/4 (January), International Monetary Fund, Washington, D.C.

Prescott, J. R. V. 1987. *Political Frontiers and Boundaries*. London: Allen and Unwin.

Przeworski, Adam, and Fernando Limongi. 1993. "Political Regimes and Economic Growth," *Journal of Economic Perspectives* 7(3):51–69.

Putnam, Robert D. 1993a. *Making Democracy Work: Civic Traditions in Modern Italy*. Princeton: Princeton University Press.

———. 1993b. "The Prosperous Community: Social Capital and Public Life," *American Prospect* 4 (13):35–42.

Ragin, Charles C. 1987. *The Comparative Method: Moving beyond Qualitative and Quantitative Strategies*. Berkeley: University of California Press.

Ramsay, Jeff, Barry Morton, and Fred Morton. 1996. *Historical Dictionary of Botswana*. Lanham, Md.: Scarecrow Press.

Reddy, Marlita A., ed. 1994. *Statistical Abstract of the World.* New York: Gale Research Inc.

Reno, William S. K. 1995. *Corruption and State Politics in Sierra Leone.* New York and Cambridge: Cambridge University Press.

———. 1998. *Warlord Politics and African States.* Boulder, Colo.: Lynne Rienner Publishers.

Richard, Dale. 1995. *Botswana's Search for Autonomy in Southern Africa.* Westport, Conn.: Greenwood Press.

Robinson, James. 1996. "Theories of 'Bad Policy.'" Working paper, Department of Economics, University of Southern California. Mimeographed.

———. 1997a. "When Is a State Predatory?" Working paper, Department of Economics, University of Southern California. Mimeographed.

———. 1997b. "A Political Theory of Underdevelopment." Working paper, Department of Economics, University of Southern California. Mimeographed.

Rodney, Walter. 1972. *How Europe Underdeveloped Africa.* Washington, D.C.: Howard University Press.

Rodrik, Dani. 1994. "King Kong Meets Godzilla: The World Bank and the East Asian Miracle." Discussion paper no. 994 (April), Center for Economic Policy Research (CEPR), Cambridge, Mass.

———. 1996. "Understanding Economic Policy Reform," *Journal of Economic Literature* 34 (March):9–41.

———. 1998. "Where Did All the Growth Go? External Shocks, Social Conflict, and Growth Collapses." Working paper no. W6350 (January), National Bureau of Economic Research (NBER).

Romer, Paul M. 1986. "Increasing Returns and Long-Run Growth," *Journal of Political Economy* 94(5):1002–1037.

Rothchild, Donald. 1997. *Managing Ethnic Conflict in Africa: Pressures and Incentives for Cooperation.* Washington, D.C.: Brookings Institution Press.

Rothchild, Donald, and Victor A. Olorunsola, eds. 1983. *State versus Ethnic Claims: African Policy Dilemmas.* Boulder, Colo.: Westview Press.

Russet, Bruce, Hayward Alker, Karl Deutsch, and Harold Lasswell. 1972. *World Handbook of Political and Social Indicators.* Revised and edited by Charles Lewis Taylor and Michael C. Hudson. New Haven: Yale University Press.

Sachs, Jeffrey. 1996. "Growth in Africa: It Can Be Done," *The Economist,* 26 June 23–25.

Sachs, Jeffrey, and Andrew Warner. 1997a. "Fundamental Sources of Long-Run Growth," *American Economic Review Papers and Proceedings* 87(2):184–188.

———. 1997b. "Sources of Slow Growth in African Economies," *Journal of African Economies* 6(3):335–376.

Sala-i-Martin, Xavier. 1997. "I Just Ran Two Million Regressions," *American Economic Review Papers and Proceedings* 87(2):178–183.

Samatar, Abdi Ismail. 1997. "Leadership and Ethnicity in the Making of African State Models: Botswana versus Somalia," *Third World Quarterly* 18(4):687–707.

———. 1999. *An African Miracle: State and Class Leadership and Colonial Legacy in Botswana Development.* Portsmouth, N.H.: Heinemann.

Samatar, Abdi Ismail, and Sophie Oldfield. 1995. "Class and Effective State Institutions: The Botswana Meat Commission," *Journal of Modern African Studies* 33(4):651–668.

Samatar, Said S. 1985. "The Somali Dilemma: Nation in Search of a State." In A. I. Asiwaju, ed., *Partitioned Africans . . . 1884–1984.* New York: St. Martin's Press, 155–193.

Sandbrook, Richard. 1985. *The Politics of Africa's Economic Stagnation.* Cambridge: Cambridge University Press.

———. 1986. "The State and Economic Stagnation in Tropical Africa," *World Development* 14(3):319–332.

Sanders, Peter B. 1975. *Moshoeshoe, Chief of the Sotho.* London: Heinemann and Philip.

Sautter, Gilles. 1982. "Quelques réflexions sur les frontières africaines." In Catherine Coquery-Vidrovitch, ed. *Problèmes frontières dans le Tiers-Monde.* Paris: Université de Paris.

Schatzberg, Michael. 1989. *The Dialectics of Oppression in Zaire.* Bloomington: Indiana University Press.

———. 1991. *Mobutu or Chaos? The United States and Zaire, 1960–1990.* Lanham, Md.: University Press of America.

Schumpeter, Joseph. [1934] 1983. *The Theory of Economic Development.* New Brunswick, N.J.: Transactions Publisher.

Serageldin, Ismail, and Christiaan Grootaert. 1997. "Defining Social Capital: An Integrating View." Paper presented at the World Bank Operations Evaluation Department Conference on Evaluation and Development: The Institutional Dimension, Washington, D.C.

Serageldin, Ismail, and June Taboroff, eds. 1994. *Culture and Development in Africa: Proceedings of an International Conference Held at the World Bank, Washington, D.C., April 2 and 3, 1992.* Washington, D.C.: The World Bank.

Servén, Luis. 1997. "Irreversibility, Uncertainty and Private Investment: Analytical Issues and Some Lessons for Africa," *Journal of African Economies* 6(3) (AERC Special Supplement):229–268.

Sillery, Anthony. 1952. *The Bechuanaland Protectorate.* Cape Town and New York: Oxford University Press.

Sindzingre, Alice. 1994. "Etat, développement et rationalité en Afrique: contribution à une analyse de la corruption." Travaux et documents no. 43, Centre d'Etudes d'Afrique Noire, Bordeaux, France.

———. 1995. "Conditionnalités démocratiques, gouvernementalité et dispositif du développement en Afrique." In Sophia Mappa, ed., *Développer par la démocratie?* Paris: Karthala, 429–458.

———. 1996. "Institutions, incertitude et ajustement structurel: L'exemple du Bénin." Mimeographed.

———. 1997. "Corruptions africaines: éléments d'analyse comparative avec l'Asie de l'Est," *Revue Internationale de Politique Comparée* 4(2):377–412.

———. 1998. "Crédibilité des Etats et économie politique des réformes en Afrique," *Economies et Sociétés* Série P (4):117–147.

Skinner, Elliott P. 1989. *The Mossi of Burkina Faso: Chiefs, Politicians and Soldiers.* Prospect Heights, Ill.: Waveland Press, 1989.

Sklar, Richard. 1983. "Democracy in Africa," *African Studies Review* 26(3/4):11–24.

———. 1987. "Developmental Democracy," *Comparative Studies in Society and History* 29(4):686–714.

———. 1999. "African Polities: The Next Generation." In Richard Joseph, ed., *State, Conflict and Democracy in Africa.* Boulder, Colo.: Lynne Rienner, 165–177.

Skocpol, Theda. 1985. "Bringing the State Back In: Strategies of Analysis in Current Research." In P. B. Evans, D. Rueschmeyer, and T. Skocpol, eds., *Bringing the State Back In.* Cambridge: Cambridge University Press, 3–37.

Smith, Adam. [1776] 1976. *An Inquiry into the Nature and Causes of the Wealth of Nations.* Chicago: University of Chicago Press.

Smith, Anthony D. 1986. "State-Making and Nation-Building." In John A. Hill, ed., *States in History.* London: Basil Blackwell, 228–263.

Solow, Robert. 1956. "A Contribution to the Theory of Economic Growth," *Quarterly Journal of Economics* 70(1):65–94.

Spruyt, Hendrik. 1994. *The Sovereign State and Its Competitors: An Analysis of Systems Change.* Princeton: Princeton University Press.

Stedman, Stephen John, ed. 1993. *Botswana: The Political Economy of Democratic Development.* Boulder, Colo.: Lynne Rienner.

Stolle, Dietlind, and Thomas R. Rochon. 1997. "Associations and the Creation of Social Capital." Paper prepared for the Conference on the Political Economy of Growth, 25–26 April, Claremont Graduate School, Claremont, Calif.

Tarr, Byron. 1990. "Political Developments and Environment in Africa." In World Bank, 1990a, 32–42.

Tarrow, Sidney. 1995. "Bridging the Quantitative-Qualitative Divide in Political Science," *American Political Science Review* 89(2):471–474.

Taylor, Charles Lewis, and Michael C. Hudson. 1972. *World Handbook of Political and Social Indicators.* 2nd ed. New Haven and London: Yale University Press.

Taylor, Charles L., and David A. Jodice. 1983. *World Handbook of Political and Social Indicators.* Vol. 1, *Cross-National Attributes and Rates of Change.* New Haven and London: Yale University Press.

Temple, Jonathan, and Paul A. Johnson. 1998. "Social Capability and Economic Growth," *Quarterly Journal of Economics* 113(3):965–990.

Thomas, J. J. 1992. *Informal Economic Activity.* Ann Arbor: University of Michigan Press.

Tilly, Charles. 1975. *The Formation of National States in Western Europe.* Princeton: Princeton University Press.

———. 1985. "War Making and State Making as Organized Crime." In P. Evans, D. Rueschmeyer, and T. Skocpol, eds., *Bringing the State Back In.* Cambridge: Cambridge University Press, 169–191.

———. 1990. *Coercion, Capital and European States, A.D. 990–1990.* Cambridge, Mass.: Basil Blackwell.

Touval, Saadia. 1966. "Treaties, Borders, and the Partition of Africa," *Journal of African History* 7(2):279–292.

Valenzuela, J. Samuel, and Arturo Valenzuela. 1978. "Modernization and Dependency: Alternative Perspectives in the Study of Latin American Underdevelopment," *Comparative Politics* 10 (July):543–557. Reprinted in Mitchell A. Seligson and John T. Passé-Smith. 1998. *Development and Underdevelopment: The Political Economy of Global Inequality.* Boulder, Colo.: Lynne Rienner.

van de Walle, Nicolas. 1994a. "Neopatrimonialism and Democracy in Africa, with an Illustration from Cameroon." In Jennifer Widner, ed., *Economic Change and Political Liberalization in Sub-Saharan Africa.* Baltimore: Johns Hopkins University Press, 129–157.

———. 1994b. "Review Essay: Adjustment Alternatives and Alternatives to Adjustment," *African Studies Review* 37(3):103–117.

———. 1998. "Africa's Economic Prospects: Is the Current Optimism Warranted?" *Jobs and Capital* 7(1):9–13.

Vansina, Jan. 1966. *Introduction à l'ethnographie du Congo.* Kinshasa: Editions Universitaires du Congo.

———. 1982. "Mwasi's Trials," *Daedalus* 111(2):49–70.

Verhaegen, Benoît. 1966. *Rébellions au Congo.* 2 vols. Brussels: Centre de Recherches et d'Informations Socio-Politiques (CRISP).

Villalón, Leonardo A., and Phillip Huxtable, eds. 1998. *The African State at a Critical Juncture: Between Disintegration and Reconfiguration.* Boulder, Colo.: Lynne Rienner.

Wade, Robert. 1990. *Governing the Market: Economic Theory and the Role of Government in East Asian Industrialization.* Princeton: Princeton University Press.

Weber, Max. 1947. *The Theory of Social and Economic Organization.* New York: Free Press.

———. 1958. "Politics as a Vocation." In H. H. Gerth and C. Wright Mills, eds., *From Max Weber: Essays in Sociology.* New York: Oxford University Press.

Wedeman, Andrew. 1997. "Looters, Rent-Scrapers, and Dividend-Collectors: Corruption and Growth in Zaire, South Korea, and the Philippines," *Journal of Developing Areas* 31(4):457–478.

Wheeler, David. 1984. "Sources of Stagnation in Sub-Saharan Africa," *World Development* 12(1):1–23.

Whitaker, C. S. 1991. "Doctrines of Development and Precepts of the State: The World Bank and the Fifth Iteration of the African Case." In Richard Sklar and C. S. Whitaker, eds., *African Politics and Problems in Development.* Boulder, Colo.: Lynne Rienner, 333–353.

White, H. 1980. "A Heteroskedasticity-consistent Covariance Matrix Estimator and a Direct Test for Heteroskedasticity," *Econometrica* 48:817–838.

Widner, Jennifer, and Alexander Mundt. 1998. "Researching Social Capital in Africa," *Africa* 68(1):1–23

Wilentz, Sean, ed. 1985. *Rites of Power: Symbolism, Ritual, and Politics since the Middle Ages.* Philadelphia: University of Pennsylvania Press.

230 Bibliography

Williams, David, and Tom Young. 1994. "Governance, the World Bank and Liberal Theory," *Political Studies* 42(1):84–100.

Wiseman, John A. 1992. *Botswana*. Oxford, Engl., and Santa Barbara, Calif.: Clio Press.

World Bank. 1981. *Accelerated Development in Sub-Saharan Africa: An Agenda for Action ["Berg Report"]*. Washington, D.C.: The World Bank.

———. 1984. *Toward Sustained Development in Sub-Saharan Africa: A Joint Program of Action*. Washington, D.C.: The World Bank.

———. 1986. *Financing Adjustment with Growth in Sub-Saharan Africa: 1986–1990*. Washington, D.C.: The World Bank.

———. 1989. *Sub-Saharan Africa: From Crisis to Sustainable Growth. A Long-term Perspective Study*. Washington, D.C.: The World Bank.

———. 1990a. *The Long-Term Perspective Study of Sub-Saharan Africa*. Vol. 3, *Institutional and Political Issues*. Washington, D.C.: The World Bank.

———. 1990b. *World Development Report*. Washington, D.C.: The World Bank.

———. 1992. *Governance and Development*. Washington, D.C.: The World Bank.

———. 1993. *The East-Asian Miracle*. Washington, D.C.: The World Bank.

———. 1994a. *Adjustment in Africa: Reforms, Results and the Road Ahead*. A World Bank Policy Research Report. Oxford: Oxford University Press.

———. 1994b. *Development in Practice: Governance. The World Bank's Experience*. Washington, D.C.: The World Bank.

———. 1995a. *African Development Indicators 1994–1995*. Washington, D.C.: The World Bank.

———. 1995b. *A Continent in Transition: Sub-Saharan Africa in the Mid–1990s*. Washington, D.C.: The World Bank.

———. 1997a. *World Development Report 1997: The State in a Changing World*. New York: Oxford University Press.

———. 1997b. *World Development Indicators*. New York: Oxford University Press.

———. 1997c. *The World Bank Annual Report 1997*. Washington, D.C.: The World Bank.

———. 1998a. "The Initiative on Defining, Monitoring and Measuring Social Capital: Overview and Program Description." World Bank, Social Capital Initiative Working paper no. 1 (April). Washington, D.C.

———. 1998b. *World Development Indicators*. Washington, D.C.: The World Bank.

———. 1998c. *The World Bank Annual Report 1998*. Washington, D.C.: The World Bank.

———. 1999a. *The World Bank Annual Report 1999*. Washington, D.C.: The World Bank.

———. 1999b. *World Development Indicators on CD-ROM*. Washington, D.C.: The World Bank.

Young, Crawford. 1965. *Politics in the Congo: Decolonization and Independence*. Princeton: Princeton University Press.

———. 1976. *The Politics of Cultural Pluralism.* Madison, Wisc.: University of Wisconsin Press.

———. 1983. "Comparative Claims to Political Sovereignty: Biafra, Katanga, Eritrea." In D. Rothchild and V. A. Olorunsola, eds., *State versus Ethnic Claims: African Policy Dilemmas.* Boulder, Colo.: Westview, 199–232.

———. 1988. "The African Colonial State and Its Political Legacy." In Donald Rothchild and Naomi Chazan, eds., *The Precarious Balance: State and Society in Africa.* Boulder, Colo.: Westview Press, 25–66.

———. 1994. *The African Colonial State in Comparative Perspective.* New Haven and London: Yale University Press.

———. 1996. "Zaire: Anatomy of a Failed State." Mimeographed draft.

Young, Crawford, and Thomas Turner. 1985. *Rise and Decline of the Zairean State.* Madison, Wisc.: University of Wisconsin Press.

Zartman, I. William. 1965. "The Politics of Boundaries in North and West Africa," *The Journal of Modern African Studies* 3(2):155–173.

———, ed. 1995. *Collapsed States: The Disintegration and Restoration of Legitimate Authority.* Boulder, Colo.: Lynne Rienner Publishers.

Zolberg, Aristide R. 1966. *Creating Political Order: The Party-States of West Africa.* Chicago: Rand McNally.

Index

State developmental capacity;
Vertical legitimacy
Stevens, Siaka, 95
Structural adjustment programs, 5,
105, 177, 178–179; and political
structural change, 187
Sudan, 10, 67, 68, 95, 131(table),
182; measuring development in,
3(fig.), 27(table), 29(table),
31(table), 158(table), 160(fig.);
precolonial systems in, 163(table)
Swazi, 82, 89, 157
Swaziland, 50, 82–83, 89, 100,
127(table), 129, 130, 152, 157;
measuring development in,
3(fig.), 27(table), 29(table),
31(table), 49(table), 158(table),
160(fig.); precolonial systems in,
163(table)

Tanzania, 62, 63, 67, 97, 98, 100,
102, 121(n36), 131(table), 152,
178, 180; measuring development in, 3(fig.), 27(table),
29(table), 31(table), 158(table),
160(fig.); precolonial systems in,
163(table)
Tariffs, 46
Taxation, 20, 22
Temple, Jonathan, 62
Territorial restructuring, 9–11,
181–186, 187
Thomas, J. J., 103
Tiv, 95
Togo, 94, 95, 131(table); measuring
development in, 3(fig.), 27(table),
29(table), 31(table), 158(table),
160(fig.); partitioning in, 88; precolonial systems in, 163(table)
Tombalbaye, Chadian government
of, 94
Touré, Sékou, 97, 98, 100, 136,
189
Trade openness, 21–22, 26, 38(n5),
44, 46, 134(table), 135, 153,
159–160, 204
Traditional authority, 1, 63, 107,
113, 162, 190–191. See also
State, endogenous roots of postcolonial
Tropical climatic conditions. See

Climatic conditions
Trust, 1, 26, 47(table), 70(n13), 197,
205; and legitimacy, 113, 116,
144, 145, 149(nn 17, 19), 154,
161, 197; and social capital,
56–58, 61–64
Tshisekedi, Etienne, 100
Tshombé, Moïse, 108, 109,
121(n43)
Tswana, 82, 112, 113, 166, 201
Tuaregs, 10, 88
Tutsi, 68, 83, 201

Uganda, 10, 13(n7), 64, 78, 94,
131(table), 182, 190, 191; and
border action, 182, 184; measuring development in, 3(fig.),
27(table), 29(table), 31(table),
158(table), 160(fig.); precolonial
systems in, 163(table)
Ujamaa, 97, 98
Unions, 93
United States, 38(n7), 80
Upper Volta, 77, 91, 94, 97, 162,
171(n13)
Urban bias, 11, 69(n3), 153

Valenzuela, Arturo, 7
Van de Walle, Nicolas, 174
Vansina, Jan, 106
Vertical legitimacy, 7–9, 76–84,
171(n11), 203; and capacity,
152–155, 168(table); and hori-
zontal legitimacy, 89–90, 158;
and size, 170
Villagization, 102
Violence, 73, 94, 95

Wade, Abdoulaye, 100
Warlords, 47, 182, 183, 191–192
Warner, Andrew, 24, 28
Wars, civil, 47, 134(table), 137, 198,
205. See also Secession
Weber, Max, 13(n8), 73
Widner, Jennifer, 64, 106
World Bank, 73, 105, 178–179; and
social capital, 59–60, 61; and
state governance, 23–24, 38(n6),
143, 179–180, 192(n4)
World Value Surveys (Inglehart), 62,
64, 144

About the Book

Although it typically is taken for granted that African economies perform poorly, it is less well-known that there are a small but significant number of success stories on the continent. What accounts for Africa's average stagnation and for the wide regional variations in developmental fortunes? Englebert argues with compelling statistics and the liberal use of examples that differences in economic performance both in Africa and across the developing world can be linked to differences in historical state legitimacy.

Showing how the arbitrary nature of postcolonial African states conditions the type of policies that African elites adopt, Englebert establishes the impact of imported government institutions on government performance. His analysis calls into question the relevance of both structural adjustment and public-sector reform programs, pointing to institutional and territorial restructuring as prerequisites for sustainable African development.

Pierre Englebert is assistant professor of politics at Pomona College.